Table of Contents

D0223633

5   Banking and Currency Related Crimes   131

6   Racketeer and Organized Crime   145

10   Control and Prevention of White-Collar Crimes   227

Preface

From the time when sociologist Edwin H. Sutherland first used the phrase "white-collar crime" during the 1939 meeting of the American Sociological Society, the concept of white-collar crime has grown to encompass almost every crime motivated by profit. *An Introduction to Corporate and White-Collar Crime* is designed to provide the reader with an understanding of what constitutes white-collar crime, how the crime works, and the extent of it. In the following chapters, the authors will also analyze the opportunity structures for committing white-collar crime and explore new ways of thinking about controlling white-collar crime. One of our purposes in this text is to bring together under a single book the numerous theories and concepts that here before have been differently categorized.

In teaching white-collar crime issues and concepts for many years, the authors were surprised at the number of students and professionals in the field who have never read Sutherland's famous article on white-collar crime. The said article was actually the Thirty-Fourth Annual Presidential Address for the American Sociological Association, and it was delivered in Philadelphia, PA, on December 27, 1939. It is attached as Appendix A. Read it before you start reading the study of white-collar crime.

Acknowledgments

While we are listed as the authors, there are numerous individuals who have provided us guidance, encouragement, and assistance. Those individuals include editor Carolyn Spence, project editor Jennifer Stair, and project manager Amor Nanas. We would also like to thank Professors Ronald Rufo, Cloud Miller, Lauren Barrow, John Eterno, Eli Silverman, Gary Bayens, Robert Winters, and Harrison Watts for their advice and encouragement.

Author

Cliff Roberson LLM, Ph.D., is an emeritus professor of criminal justice at Washburn University, Topeka, Kansas, and an adjunct professor in the School of Legal Studies, Kaplan University. Cliff is also the former Managing Editor of the international journal *Police Practices and Research (PPR)*. *PPR* is a refereed journal and is distributed in 48 countries. In addition, he served for four years as the editor in chief of the *Professional Issues in Criminal Justice Journal*.

He has authored or coauthored over 50 books and texts on legal subjects. His books include the following:

Cliff Roberson, Harvey Wallace, and Gilbert Stuckey (2009), *Procedures in the Justice System*, 9th ed. (Upper Saddle River, NJ: Pearson)
Cliff Roberson (2009), *Constitutional Law and Criminal Justice* (Boca Raton, FL: Taylor & Francis)
Harvey Wallace and Cliff Roberson (2008), *Principles of Criminal Law*, 4th ed. (Boston: Allyn & Bacon)
Michael Birzer and Cliff Roberson (2008), *Police Field Operations: Theory Meets Practice* (Boston: Pearson)
Cliff Roberson and Dilip Das (2008), *An Introduction to Comparative Legal Models of Criminal Justice* (Baca Raton, FL: Taylor & Francis)
Cliff Roberson and Scott Mire (2010, at printer), *Ethics and Criminal Justice* (Boca Raton, FL: Taylor & Francis)
Harvey Wallace and Cliff Roberson (in publication), *Family Violence* (Boston: Pearson)

His previous academic experiences include Associate Vice-President for Academic Affairs, Arkansas Tech University; Dean of Arts and Sciences, University of Houston, Victoria; Director of Programs, National College of District Attorneys; Professor of Criminology and Director of Justice Center, California State University, Fresno; and Assistant Professor of Criminal Justice, St. Edwards University.

Dr. Roberson's nonacademic experience includes US Marine Corps service as an infantry officer, trial and defense counsel, and military judge as a marine judge advocate; and Director of the Military Law Branch, US Marine Corps. Other legal employment experiences include Trial Supervisor, Office of State Counsel for Offenders, Texas Board of Criminal Justice and judge pro-tem in the California courts. Cliff is admitted to practice before the US Supreme Court, US Court of Military Appeals, US Tax Court, Federal Courts in California and Texas, Supreme Court of Texas, and Supreme Court of California.

His educational background includes Ph.D. in Human Behavior, US International University; L.L.M., in Criminal Law, Criminology, and Psychiatry, George Washington University; J.D. American University; B.A. in Political Science, University of Missouri; and one year of postgraduate study at the University of Virginia School of Law.

Frank DiMarino, J.D., L.L.M., is the Dean of the Kaplan University School of Legal Studies and the former Dean of the School of Criminal Justice. DiMarino was appointed dean in 2006 after serving on the University's undergraduate and graduate faculty for two years. DiMarino has used his more than 20 years as a federal prosecutor and his academic experience to develop undergraduate and graduate degree programs that emphasize practical applications for criminal justice and legal studies students.

As a career prosecutor prior to joining Kaplan University, DiMarino served as an Assistant United States Attorney prosecuting offenses involving financial institution fraud, mail and wire fraud, income tax fraud, credit card fraud, government procurement fraud, public corruption, labor union embezzlements, money laundering, drug conspiracies, firearms, and environmental crimes. He has led undercover, electronic surveillance, and complex grand jury investigations. Besides having tried more than 200 jury trials, including a federal death penalty trial, he has argued criminal appeals before the Eleventh Circuit Court of Appeals.

In Washington, District of Columbia, he served as a Senior Trial Attorney in the Division of Enforcement at the Commodity Futures Trading Commission in the Multi-District Fraud Unit. As an Army officer in the Judge Advocate General's Corps, DiMarino was the Chief of the Criminal Law Division at Fort Stewart, Georgia, during Desert Storm as well as an appellate counsel and branch chief for the US Army Legal Services Agency. He has argued cases before the Court of Military Appeals. He began his criminal justice career in Nuremberg, Germany, as a trial defense counsel and later as a prosecutor in military courts-martial.

For 20 years of his career, DiMarino also served as an adjunct instructor of Criminal Law and Procedure, Evidence, Constitutional Law, Business Law, International Law, criminal justice, and legal studies at Boston University, the University of Maryland, Georgia Southern University, Central Texas College, South University, and Armstrong Atlantic University. He also has been a visiting lecturer in money laundering, customs fraud, and complex criminal investigations at the Federal Law Enforcement Training Center.

DiMarino began publishing in 1983, writing articles for *The Advocate*, a publication for Judge Advocate General's counsel, and has coauthored several criminal justice texts with his friend and mentor, Dr. Clifford Roberson.

He earned his Masters of Law degree from George Washington University, a Juris Doctor degree from Case Western Reserve University, and a Bachelor's degree in Government and International Relations from Georgetown University. DiMarino is admitted to practice law before the Supreme Courts of Ohio, Pennsylvania, and Georgia, as well as the United States Supreme Court.

Introduction to the Study of White-Collar Crime

1

Chapter Objectives

After studying this chapter, the reader should be able to or understand the following:

- The meaning of the phrase "white-collar crime."
- The extent of white-collar crime in the United States.
- Public perception of white-collar crime.
- How the white-collar crime concept developed.
- How white-collar crime differs from street crime.
- The fact that white-collar crime existed prior to Sutherland's coining of the phrase.
- The victimization that is attached to white-collar crime.
- Who is a white-collar criminal?
- How does the white-collar criminal differ from the street criminal?
- Some of the problems involved in prosecuting white-collar criminals.
- The existence of the National White Collar Crime Center (NW3C).
- The U.S. Attorney General's policy on prosecuting white-collar criminals.

Introduction

The introduction of the concept of white-collar crime into the study of criminal behavior revolutionized the thinking of the field by making it no longer possible to employ class-specific explanations to interpret such behavior. [Gilbert Geis and Colin Goff.*]

The surge in incarceration since 1980 has been fueled in part by the mistaken belief that the population can be divided neatly into "good guys" and "bad guys." In fact, crime rates are not determined by the number of at-large criminals, any more than farm production is determined by the number of farmers. Crime is a choice, a choice that is influenced by available opportunities as much as by character. This perspective, drawn from economic theory, supports a multifaceted approach to crime control.†

---

* Gilbert Geis and Colin Goff. (1983). "Introduction." In: Edwin H. Sutherland. *White Collar Crime: The Uncut Version.* New Haven, CT: Yale University Press. Page xxx1.
† Philip J. Cook. (December 10, 2011.) "Economical crime control: Perspectives from both sides of the ledger." *NIJ Seminar.* Washington, DC: Duke University.

FRAUD CASES RARELY PENALIZE EXECUTIVES WHO CAUSED THE FRAUD

According to a statement issued by U.S. Senator Jack Reed of Rhode Island, people on the street wonder how a company can commit serious violations of federal law and yet "no individuals seem to be involved."[*] Senator Reed noted that in the first eight months of the calendar year 2012, pharmaceutical companies, banks, military contractors, and other corporations were on track to pay over $8 billion dollars to resolve charges of defrauding the U.S. Government. The amount exceeds the total assessed for any prior complete year. The billions were for civil charges of fraud against the Government. Reed questioned why company executives who are involved in the fraud against the U.S. Government are not also prosecuted.

One reason for this lack of attack on the individual executives may because of the difficulties of prosecuting them. In July 2012, for example, a federal jury in New York City acquitted a bank manager who had been involved in selling an exotic financial security consisting of residential mortgages. The manager had been charged with falsely describing the company's role in selecting the assets and failing to disclose that the bank group was betting against the investment.[†]

According to the Securities and Exchange Commission's (SEC) complaints, filed in the U.S. District Court for the Southern District of New York (SDNY), in October 2006, personnel from a bank group's collateralized debt obligation (CDO) trading and structuring desks had discussions about possibly having the trading desk establish a short position in a specific group of assets by using credit default swaps (CDS) to buy protection on those assets from a CDO that the bank group would structure and market. Following the institution of discussions with Credit Suisse Asset Alternative Capital, LLC (CSAC) about having CSAC act as the collateral manager for a proposed CDO transaction, Stoker sent an e-mail to his supervisor in which he stated that he hoped that the transaction would go forward and described the transaction as the bank group's trading desk head's "prop trade (don't tell CSAC). CSAC agreed to terms even though they don't get to pick the assets." The New York federal jury found the defendant not guilty in July 2012.

---

[*] Statement of Senator Jack Reed on the floor of the U.S. Senate as reported by Houston Chronicle on August 8, 2012. Page E-1.

[†] *Securities and Exchange Commission v. Brian H. Stoker,* 11-Civ.-7388 (S.D.N.Y. filed October 19, 2011).

Many attorneys contend that the federal government is more likely to go after the companies than the executives because of the companies' deep pockets. One SEC attorney noted that for every $1 the government spends on a civil fraud case, the government gets a return of $15, whereas the government almost never makes money when prosecuting an executive in a criminal action. In addition, it is noted that it is often difficult and expensive to build a criminal case against a corporate executive because senior executives are often insulated from day to day decisions of the business.* Note: The above referenced trial proceedings that resulted in a not guilty finding started in 2006 and ended with a jury verdict in 2012.

* *Securities and Exchange Commission v. Citigroup Global Markets Inc.*, 11-Civ.-7387 (Rakoff, J.) (S.D.N.Y. filed October 19, 2011).

One of the first problems in any discussion of white-collar crime is defining the concept of white-collar crime. As will be noted later in this chapter, the definition is not simple. As pointed out by Peter Henning, most crimes in the United States fall into the category of street crimes, which range from property offenses to episodic violence that involves a single or limited number of victims at a specific point in time. The content of the phrase "white-collar crime" is difficult to pin down. Generally, when we refer to white-collar crime, we are referring to offenses where there is a family resemblance to some type of concept of untruthfulness such as perjury, fraud, false statements, obstruction of justice, bribery, extortion and blackmail, insider trading, tax evasion, and certain regulatory offenses. According to Henning, what sets white-collar crime apart from traditional crime is that white-collar crimes are the product in many ways of an advanced economy with high-speed communications, a large administrative apparatus, and a pervasive legal system that makes enforcement of the law a priority. He also noted that while many crimes have their roots in common law, such as larceny by trick or perjury, white-collar crime generally encompasses the right of honest services that permits prosecution of public officials and corporate employees for breaching their judiciary duties.*

* Peter J. Hennings. (Spring 2008). "The DNA of a white-collar crime." *New Criminal Law Review.* Vol. 11. Pages 323–338.

According to the Federal Bureau of Investigation (FBI), white-collar crime costs the United States more than $300 billion each year. Approximately one-third of Americans are victims of white-collar crime. Following the loss of much of his life savings in a 2011 investor scheme, one victim, a retired person, described his feeling of a "deep depression" with "no desire to live, no prospect of earning a living, and no way to pay the bills."* In Europe, 42.5% of the larger companies have been victimized by white-collar criminals, with embezzlement and breach of trust being the prevalent modes involved.†

White-collar crimes are prosecuted under either federal or state law, depending upon the type of crime or the offender. Some of the white-collar crimes that are listed by the FBI include securities fraud, racketeering-influenced and choral organization violations, embezzlement, insider trading, identity theft, computer crimes, public corruption, pension fund crimes, perjury, counterfeiting, bribery, extortion, environmental violations, and obstruction of justice.‡ Sociologist Edwin H. Sutherland argued that white-collar criminals inflict more harm on the U.S. society than burglars or robbers, but the criminal justice system treats white-collar offenders with more leniency and less consistency than street criminals.§

Definition of White-Collar Crime

For most people, the term "white-collar crime" brings up images of corporate executives contriving in their way to fortune, but this is not really an accurate picture of the concept.¶ White-collar crime is generally committed by individuals at all economic levels. The term was originally intended as a classification of offenders, but has since expanded to include a broad range of nonviolent offenses where cheating and dishonesty in normally legal business transactions are the central element.

The Department of Justice defines white-collar crime as offenses classified as nonviolent illegal activities that principally involve traditional notions of deceit, deception, concealment, manipulation, breach of trust, subterfuge, or illegal circumvention.** Does this mean that the young teenager who shares

---

* Marilyn Price and Donna Norris. (2009). "White-collar crime: Corporate and securities and commodities fraud." *Journal of the American Academy of Psychiatry and the Law.* Vol. 37. Pages 538–544.
† Price and Norris (2009), p. 538.
‡ Cliff Roberson. (2010). *RICO, 15th ed.* Ft. Worth: Knowles Publishing. Pages 1–4.
§ Edwin H. Sutherland. (1950). *White-Collar Crime.* New Haven, CT: Yale University Press. Page 32.
¶ Jane McGrath. (2010). "How white-collar crime works." Posted at http://money.howstuffworks.com [Accessed on January 8, 2011].
** World Wide Legal web site. (2010). "White collar crime." Posted at http://www.hg.org/white-collar-crime.html [Accessed on January 9, 2011].

WHITE-COLLAR CONVICT AWARDED $104 MILLION BY THE U.S. GOVERNMENT FOR WHISTLE BLOWING ON SWISS BANKS

According to a September 11, 2012, New York Times edition, Bradley Birkenfeld, a former banker at UBS who served two and a half years in prison for conspiring with a wealthy California developer to evade U.S. income taxes, has been awarded $104 million dollars by the Internal Revenue Service (IRS). A spokesperson for the IRS stated that the information Birkenfeld provided was very helpful. He revealed the secrets of the Swiss banking system. By divulging schemes that banks used to encourage American citizens to dodge their taxes, he led to an investigation that greatly diminished Switzerland's status as a secret haven for American tax cheats and allowed the Treasury to recover billions in unpaid taxes.

The Swiss bank was required to pay $780 million to avoid criminal prosecution and turned over account information regarding more than 4,500 American clients. The disclosure of Swiss banking information set off such a panic among wealthy Americans that more than 14,000 joined a tax amnesty program. IRS officials say the amnesty program has helped recover more than $5 billion in unpaid taxes. The award is the largest ever paid by the IRS. Note: The reward is subject to federal income taxes.

Source: David Kocieniewski. (September 12, 2012). "Whistle-blower awarded $104 million by I.R.S." *The New York Times.* Page B-1.

copyrighted material by burning a music CD and giving it to a friend, a federal crime, is a white-collar criminal? Or what about the senior citizens, living near the Mexican or Canadian borders, who travel to Mexico or Canada to get cheaper medications?

The National White Collar Crime Center (NW3C) defines white-collar crime as "illegal or unethical acts that violate fiduciary responsibility or public trust for personal or organizational gain."[*] The Federal Bureau of Investigation (FBI) defines white-collar crime as

> Illegal acts which are characterized by deceit, concealment, or violation of trust and which are not dependent upon the application or threat of force or violence. Individuals and organizations commit these acts to obtain money, property, or services, to avoid payment or loss of money or to secure personal or business advantage.[†]

---

[*] John Kane and April Wall. (2006). *2005 National Public Survey on White-Collar Crime.* Fairmont, VA: National White-Collar Crime Center. Page 1.

[†] Federal Bureau of Investigation. (1989). *White-Collar Crime: A Report to the Public.* Washington, DC: U.S. Department of Justice. Page 3.

IN DEFINING "WHITE-COLLAR" CRIME, SHOULD WE USE AN OFFENSE-BASED OR OFFENDER-BASED DEFINITION?

Sutherland first defined the concept of white-collar crime as crime committed by person of respectability and high social status in the course of his occupation.* Thus, he used an offender-based definition. Presently, many researchers tend to define the concept using an offense-based definition. Former federal prosecutor Herbert Edelhertz opined that Sutherland was rather casual in his conceptualization of white-collar crime, at times stressing social status, at times behavior carried out in an occupational role, and at times crime committed by organizations or by individuals acting in organizational capacities. Edelhertz, in an attempt to overcome his perception of Sutherland's faults, defined white-collar crime as "an illegal act or series of illegal acts committed by nonphysical means and by the concealment or guile to obtain money or property, to avoid the payment or loss of money or property, or to obtain business or personal advantage."† Edelhertz's definition is an offense-based definition.

Note that the offense-based definition provides a wider definition of white-collar crime than does the offender-based. For example, consider identify theft and counterfeiting. Under the offense-based definition, these two crimes would be considered as white-collar crimes, whereas under Sutherland's offender-based definition, they may not be.

Edelhertz stated in testifying before a U.S. Congress, House Subcommittee on Crime on December 1, 1978, that white-collar crime is a widespread example of antisocial behavior that is financially or materially motivated and occurs as ad hoc violations, abuses of trust, collateral business crimes, and con games. Such insidious behavior is often rationalized by those who say that the acts involved are not street crimes, that the government does not understand the marketplace, and that everyone is doing it. These blurred distinctions between illicit and legal behavior will continue if adequate enforcement of existing laws is lacking, if the same acts are made the subject of optional criminal or civil action, if the white-collar offender is treated more leniently even after criminal prosecution and conviction, and if remedies for the victims of economic crimes are inadequate. Estimates of dollar losses from white-collar crime range from $3 to $60 billion per year, depending upon what crimes are included; estimates of the impact of such crimes on people,

* Edwin Sutherland. (1983). *White Collar Crime: The Uncut Version.* New Haven, CT: Yale University Press. Page 7.
† H. Edelhertz. (1970). *The Nature, Impact, and Prosecution of White-Collar Crime.* Washington, D.C.: U.S. Government Printing Office. Page 3.

quality of life, business operations, and public trust are immense and far more significant than mere dollar losses. Because the integrity issue is the most important issue posed by white-collar crime, the moral tone of society will continue to erode unless such crime is more effectively curbed. White-collar crime enforcement on the federal level has been impeded by structural and resource problems (legal jurisdiction, lack of resources, and enforcement policies).

Edelhertz stated that the federal government could act to deter white-collar crime by setting and enforcing standards of integrity in business conduct; analyzing and reorganizing federal efforts to detect, investigate, and prosecute white-collar crimes; making white-collar crime unprofitable for businesses; and providing supplementary services and facilities to local and state law enforcement agencies.*

* As reported at http://www.ncjrs.gov/App/Publications [Accessed on March 4, 2012].

Public Perception of White-Collar Crime

As noted by Price and Norris, traditionally, the public's attention to crime has focused on violent crime prevention and enforcement. Most individuals assume that white-collar crime is less damaging to society and to the individual. For example, a 2005 National Public Survey of 402 households attempted to measure public perception of the criminal justice system's response to white-collar crime versus street crime. Respondents were asked to compare two situations: one involving a street crime where an individual was robbed of $1,000 and one involving white-collar crime such as the embezzlement of $1,000. The results were that about 63% of the respondents believed that the street crime offenders such as the robber in the example were more likely to be apprehended, and about 67% of the respondents concluded that the street criminals were more likely to receive stiffer penalties. Other findings included that about 66% of the respondents opined that the street criminals should receive stiffer punishments. However, about 61% concluded that the federal government should devote equal or more resources to enforcing and preventing white-collar crime.*

Development of the Concept

The concept of white-collar crime is generally traced back to Edwin H. Sutherland. Professor Sutherland, at the time a faculty member at Indiana

* K. Holtfreter, S. Van Slyke, and J. Bratton. (2008). "Public perceptions of white-collar crime and punishment." *Journal of Criminal Justice*. Vol. 36. Pages 50–60.

University and president of the American Sociological Association, delivered the 34th annual presidential address in Philadelphia, PA, on December 27, 1939. It was in this address that the definition of "white collar" was first publicly used. Sutherland stated,

> The "robber barons" of the last half of the nineteenth century were white-collar criminals, as practically everyone now agrees. Their attitudes are illustrated by the statements: Col. Vanderbilt asked, "You don't suppose you can run a railroad in accordance with the statutes, do you?" A.B. Stickney, a railroad president, said to 16 other railroad presidents in the home of J. P. Morgan in 1890, "I have the utmost respect for you gentlemen, individually, but as railroad presidents I wouldn't trust you with my watch out of sight.".…
>
> The present day white-collar criminals, who are more swallowed and deceptive than the robber barons, are represented by Krueger, Stavisky,… and many other merchant princes and captains of finance and industry, and by a host of lesser followers. Their criminality has been demonstrated again and again in the investigation of land offices, railways, insurance, munitions, banking, public utilities, stock exchanges, the oil industry, real estate, reorganization committees, receiverships, bankruptcies, and politics.… White-collar criminals are found in ever occupation, as can be discovered readily in casual conversation with a representative of an occupation by asking him, "What crooked practices are found in your occupation?"[*]

Sutherland concluded his famous speech with a brief and general description of white-collar criminality, which he stated in the following propositions[†]:

- White-Collar criminality is real criminality, being in all cases violations of the criminal law.
- White-collar criminality differs from lower-class criminality principally in an implementation of the criminal law which segregates white-collar criminals administratively from other criminals.
- The theories of criminologists that crime is due to poverty or to psychopathic and sociopathic conditions statistically associated with poverty are invalid because, first, they are derived tables which are grossly biased with respect to socioeconomic status; second, they do not apply to white-collar criminals; and third, they do not even explain the criminality of the lower class, since the factors are not related to a general process characteristic of all criminality.

[*] Edwin H. Sutherland. (February 1940). "White-collar criminality." *American Sociological Review.* Vol. 5. No. 1. Pages 1–12.
[†] Sutherland (1940), p. 12.

- A theory of criminal behavior which will explain both white-collar criminality and lower-class criminality is needed.
- A hypothesis of this nature is suggested in the terms of differential association and social disorganization.*

It is interesting to note that Sutherland attempted to redefine crime according to the defendant's socio-economic class, rather than what the criminal did. Sutherland disregarded traditional principles of our criminal law system by arguing that the presumption of innocence and the require-ment of *mens rea* should not apply to white-collar crime. According to John Baker, the results of Sutherland's efforts were to criminalize social and economic conduct not because of the wrongful nature of the conduct, but because of fidelity to a long-discredited class-based view of society.†

Since Sutherland first coined the phrase "white-collar crime," the defi-nition of what constitutes white-collar crime has been expanded by many researchers, lawmakers, and law enforcers to include almost any crime moti-vated by profit. Sutherland's original definition of white-collar crime was "a crime committed by a person of respectability and high social status in the course of his occupation."‡ A 2008 research report published in the St. John's Law Review indicated that participants in a study of white-collar crime, almost without exception, defined white-collar criminal as someone who commits a nonviolent, business-related crime.§

Stuart P. Green noted that the meaning of white-collar crime, like most other abstract terms in legal and social science, is deeply contested. He noted that the definitions vary across and within disciplines. According to Green, white-collar crime scholars who have sought to find an agreed-upon mean-ing of the term are looking for substitutes, but none of their efforts have been successful in that there is no general acceptance of the definition of white-collar crime. Yet the term is so deeply embedded within our legal, moral, and social science vocabularies that it can hardly be abandoned. Green concludes that the term "white-collar crime" persists and proliferates not so much in spite of its lack of definitional precision, but because of it. He asserts that law-makers, law enforcers, and scholars attribute to the term's meanings concepts that correspond to their own particular analytical or ideological concerns. Green notes that even Sutherland, who was probably the most influential

---

* The theories of differential association and social disorganization are discussed in Chapter 2.
† John S. Baker. (October 4, 2004). "The sociological origins of white-collar crime." *Legal Memorandum of the Heritage Foundation*. No. 14.
‡ Sutherland (1950), p. 7.
§ Pamela Bucy, Elizabeth Formby, Marc Raspanti, and Kathryn Rooney. (2008). "Why do they do it?: The motives, mores, and character old white-collar criminals." *St. John's Law Review*. Vol. 82. Pages 401–440.

SALE OF THE EIFFEL TOWER

Victor Lustig (1890–1947) was clearly an early white-collar criminal. He became famous as "the man who sold the Eiffel Tower." Lustig could speak five different languages and is known to have used 45 aliases.

In the spring of 1925, Lustig noted an article in a Paris newspaper stating that the French government was having problems maintaining the Eiffel Tower and was considering to have it dismantled. Using fake French government stationery, he invited six of France's leading scrap-metal dealers to a meeting at the Hotel de Crillon in Paris. At the meeting, he introduced himself as a deputy minister in France's Ministry of Posts and Telegraphs. He invited the six dealers to bid on buying the tower for scrap metal. Not only did he get paid from one of the dealers, but he also accepted a bribe from the buyer for giving him the inside track on the bids.[*]

[*] Cliff Roberson. (2009). *Identify Theft Investigations*. New York: Kaplan Publishing. Pages 12–13.

American criminologist of his day, was famously vague and inconsistent when using the term, and that the concept that Sutherland was first to put a label on is so inherently complex and multifaceted that it seems unlikely that one single definition will ever prevail.

Green also notes that some researchers have used the term "elite deviance." He notes that that term is highly problematic because not all deviant behavior is criminalized and, in some cases, criminal behavior is not generally regarded as deviant. He asserts that "elite deviance" could be used to indicate misconduct at Wimbledon during a tennis match, and that conduct certainly would not be considered as criminal.[*]

In this text, when the authors refer to the phrase white-collar crime, generally they are referring to crimes committed by individuals or organizations usually in the course of business activity and usually characterized by fraud or falsehood and by complexity. This definition was taken from Abraham Goldstein's article on white-collar crime and civil sanctions.[†] Although the phrase white-collar crime is considered to have originated with Sutherland in 1939, embezzlers, counterfeiters, stock swindlers, and con men have practiced their crimes for many centuries.

[*] Stuart P. Green. (2004). "White-collar criminal law in comparative perspective: The Sarbanes–Oxley Act of 2002." *Buffalo Criminal Law Review*. Vol. 8. Pages 1–11.
[†] Abraham S. Goldstein. (June 1992). "White-collar crime and civil sanctions." *Yale Law Journal*. Vol. 101. Pages 1895–1899.

American as Apple Pie

Often, individuals think of white-collar crime as primarily an American crime. As noted in the earlier discussion on the sale of the Eiffel Tower, this is not the case. As noted by Jon S.T. Quah, corruption and bribery were introduced to the Philippines several centuries prior to the American takeover in 1898. Quah contended that corruption was introduced to the Philippines by the Spanish based on the low salaries and poor working conditions of the bureaucrats that ran the country. Similar conditions existed in many other countries, including South Korea.*

Victims of White-Collar Crime

Many white-collar criminals contend that there are no victims in white-collar crime, only organizations. The victim of the Madoff scheme who was quoted earlier in this chapter would not agree. Although white-collar crime is not as violent a danger as being robbed, these crimes have far-reaching effects. As noted by Price and Norris, these crimes undermine investor confidence, affect the economic health of corporations and of their employees, depress stock and bond values, affect bank loan delinquencies, and contribute to the financial devastation of the individual investor through declines in retirement and investment portfolios.†

In a study of a random sample of U.S. citizens with regard to victimization, reporting behaviors, and perceptions of crime seriousness, results found that‡

- Nearly one in two households was victimized by white-collar crime within the past year.
- Well over half of the individuals surveyed have been victimized by white-collar crime within their lifetimes.
- There has been an increase in crimes involving technology.
- Few reports of victimization reach law enforcement agencies.
- White-collar crime is being seen as more serious than in the past.
- The government is not allocating enough resources to combat white-collar crime.

The results of the random sample indicated that white-collar crime victimizations are more prevalent than in the past. Household victimization

---

* J.S.T. Quah. (1982). "Bureaucratic corruption in the ASEAN countries: A comparative analysis." *Journal of South-east Asian Studies*. Vol. 12. Issue 1. Pages 153–177.
† Price and Norris (2009), pp. 538–539.
‡ Kane and Wall (2006), p. 19.

(46.5%) increased from earlier surveys. Furthermore, 36.0% of respondents had been victimized within the previous year, whereas a staggering 62.5% reported being victimized at least once within their lifetimes. These results, when applied to the U.S. population, indicate that over 130 million Americans have potentially been victimized by white-collar crime at least once during their lives.[*]

White-Collar Criminal

Why do talented, bright, highly educated, successful people who have "made it" risk it all by lying, stealing, and cheating, especially when what they are stealing is not much compared to what they have? The simple answer is "because they can."[†]

As noted by Paul Henning, some of the most famous crimes in history have involved the question of identity—has the real killer been found? He noted that speculation still surrounds the identity of Jack the Ripper and the zodiac killer.[‡] Few white-collar crime cases, however, involve the identity of the perpetrator, or whether or not the perpetrator had an alibi. Henning states that white-collar crimes are fundamentally crimes of intent because the defendants in such cases freely acknowledge their involvement in the transactions or events. The issue is generally what the defendant knew, or wanted, or failed to disclose, which raises an issue as to whether a crime actually took place. For example, Jeffrey Skilling denied his role as the leader of Enron and claimed that he had no intent to violate the law and, indeed, he had done no wrong. A similar situation existed with Martha Stewart, who was convicted of perjury based on the testimony of her broker and co-conspirator during an SEC deposition.

A frequent defense used in defending street crime criminals is SODDIT, which is slang for "some other dude did it." The white-collar criminal generally proclaims his or her innocence, not because the prosecution got the wrong guy, but because the defendants purportedly did not intend to commit a crime.[§] Often, the defense counsel asserts that the pending issue was not really a criminal case but was really a civil matter. This defense would never be used in an ordinary street crime case. The popular notion that the criminal's background includes broken homes, poor education, and other presumptive handicaps also does not apply to the white-collar criminal.

---

[*] Kane and Wall (2006), p. 20.
[†] Bucy et al. (2008), pp. 401–438.
[‡] Hennings (2008), p. 328.
[§] Hennings (2008), p. 329.

IS A PERSON A CRIMINAL WHO HAS NOT BEEN CONVICTED OF A CRIME?

In 1946, Paul Tappan submitted an article to the *American Journal of Sociology* in which he defined who a criminal is. The journal editor submitted the article to Edwin Sutherland for review. Sutherland deplored Tappan's definition that implied that only convicted persons should be considered as criminals. Sutherland contended that a criminal conviction was not important in a definition of criminal behavior. Based on Sutherland's recommendation, the article was rejected by the *American Journal of Sociology* but was later published in the *American Sociological Review.** In this text, when the authors refer to white-collar criminals, they are referring to individuals involved in white-collar criminal conduct, and like Sutherland, a conviction is not necessary.

* Geis and Goff (1983), p. xxix.

Professor Bucy and her research team explored the traditionally held views about white-collar criminals. Her research team tested the following hypotheses:

- Most white-collar criminals fall into two categories: leaders or followers.
- Those in each category display distinct personality profiles.
- Accordingly, the method of deterring crime differed for each category.*

Bucy's research team concluded that the three hypotheses were mostly accurate. Her team noted that the concepts that white-collar criminals were either leaders or followers were strongly supported in the Federal Sentencing Guidelines. They based this decision in part because the guidelines recommended sentences that are based on two factors: the offense conduct and defendant's criminal history. They noted that the guidelines provided stiffer sentences for those criminals who actually commit the crimes as compared to those who only aided and abetted in the commission of the crimes. The researchers concluded that some white-collar criminals wander into crime schemes, never realizing that they are violating the law, and sometimes, the line between leaders and followers is blurred depending on the nature of the

* Bucy et al. (2008), p. 401.

investigation and the charges brought against the criminal. In addition, some criminals may start out as followers and morph or graduate into leaders.*

The Bucy research team noted that the most cited reason by study participants (federal prosecutors and an experienced defense counsel) as to why leaders engage in white-collar criminal acts was greed. Money or financial gain was cited by almost all participants in their study. This book's authors, DiMarino and Roberson, were amazed by the fact that only 5% of the federal prosecutors and the defense counsel expressed the view that the criminals committed the crime because they were "amoral" or "evil." The research team also noted that convicted white-collar criminals confirmed those views.† DiMarino and Roberson believe that if similar questions were asked to the prosecutors and the defense counsel regarding street criminals, a significantly higher percentage of respondents would assign the reason that the criminals were amoral or evil. This raises the interesting issue as to why we generally do not see white-collar criminals as amoral or evil as we do the rapist or the convenience store robber.

The Bucy research team found that the respondents (federal prosecutors and the defense counsel) assigned one of four motives for the followers to commit white-collar crime. Those motives assigned to the followers were as follows:

- They were weak people who trailed behind someone else.
- They were convinced of the rightness of their criminal schemes or that no harm was caused by their behavior.
- They were interested in making more money or getting a "piece of the action."
- They were motivated by the fear of losing their job or of physical harm.‡

The Bucy research team concluded that the personalities of the leaders were classified as "Type A" personalities and that the leaders were intelligent, arrogant, cunning, successful, greedy, and prone to take risks. The followers were described by the researchers as less confident, less aggressive, less ambitious, and gullible.§

---

* Bucy et al. (2008), p. 406.
† Bucy et al. (2008), p. 407.
‡ Bucy et al. (2008), p. 409.
§ Bucy et al. (2008), p. 412.

EDWIN HARDIN SUTHERLAND 1883–1950

Edwin Sutherland was born in Gibeon Nebraska. He grew up and was educated in Ottawa, Kansas, and Grand Island, Nebraska. In 1904, he received his Bachelor of Arts degree from Grand Island College, where he majored in history with a minor in sociology. After graduation, he taught Latin and Greek history and shorthand for two years at Sioux Falls College in South Dakota. During this period, he took a correspondence course in sociology offered by the University of Chicago. He needed the course to meet a requirement to attend their graduate school. He received his PhD in sociology from the University of Chicago in 1913.[*]

After completing his graduate studies, he became a professor at the University of Minnesota from 1926 to 1929. During this period, his focus was on sociology as a scientific enterprise whose goal was the understanding and control of social problems, including crime. It was at the University of Minnesota that he established his reputation as a leading criminologist. In 1930, he accepted a position at the University of Chicago and later moved to the University of Indiana.

Prior to developing his theory of differential association, Sutherland spent most of his time modifying the central aspects of the social disorganization perspective. Later, Sutherland shifted from sociology to criminology. Several researchers have contended that he switched because of his fear that he might not achieve professional recognition as a sociologist.

In 1939, Sutherland formally presented his theory of differential association in which he relied heavily upon the works of Shaw and McKay. Although Sutherland was an extremely brilliant researcher, his students considered him a below average professor. As one student remarked, it was difficult to listen to Sutherland's lectures because he mumbled.[†]

As noted by Masters and Roberson, Sutherland's theory of differential association was developed in an effort to explain the behavior of career criminals. Masters and Roberson (1990) conclude that

---

[*] Information on Sutherland taken from Albert Cohen, Alfred Lindesmith, and Karl Schuessler (Eds.). (1955). *The Sutherland Papers.* Blooming, IN: University of Indiana; Mark S. Gaylord. (1986). *Edwin Sutherland and the Origins of Differential Association Theory.* Ann Arbor, MI: University Microfilms International; and Sawyer F. Sylvester. (1972). *The Heritage of Modern Criminology.* Cambridge, MA: Schenkman Pub.

[†] Ibid.

differential association is not a good description for his theory. The title makes his theory sound as though it refers to individuals in association, but it does not say who associates with whom. What Sutherland is referring to as differentially associated are definitions of situations.*

Sutherland was clearly the most influential American Criminologist of the twentieth century. He had a conflict orientation to society. According to Sutherland, an individual has a number of societal values from which he or she can choose from, and the individual's choice is influenced by our associations and situational definitions. In short, we learn to commit crime like we learn to play baseball or basketball.

* Ruth Masters and Cliff Roberson. (1990). *Inside Criminology*. Upper Saddle River, NJ: Prentice-Hall. Pages 200–201.

Prosecuting White-Collar Criminals

It is difficult to (if not impossible) to demonstrate that the threat of criminal sanctions deters white-collar crime. Clearly, given the pervasiveness of such crime, a great deal of it has not been deterred. Furthermore, the perceived improbabilities of detection and punishment of white-collar offenders surely compromises any deterrent effect. [David Friedrichs*]

Societal interest in white-collar crime and the prosecution of it grew rapidly in the 1970s. Since that time, prosecutors have assigned the higher priority to prosecuting those crimes, which was previously reserved only for violent street crimes. Also, since the 1970s, there has been an increased emphasis on the dangers that white-collar crime does to society.

The decision to prosecute is unavoidably discretionary. According to Baker, when the people advocate the prosecution of white-collar criminals, they are not advocating the locking up of those who copy music CDs, or who purchase medicine from neighboring countries, despite the fact that such crimes defraud pharmaceutical and music companies and their shareholders of billions of dollars, but the locking up of senior corporate executives. Baker noted that while the U.S. Justice Department's definition of white-collar crime disregards social class or economic status, the truth is that in white-collar cases, such distinctions do influence decisions about whether or not to prosecute. He also concludes that the government prosecutors are far more

* David O. Friedrichs. (1995). *Trusted Criminals*. Belmont, CA: Wadsworth. Page 341.

likely to indict individuals in the upper socio-economic classes. Accordingly, Baker concludes that the war against white-collar crime embraces a class-based sociological concept of crime.*

Abraham Goldstein reports that the prosecution of white-collar crime is being transformed. He concludes that criminal law is now being used by prosecutors not only to imprison the offenders but also to provide the basis for financial remedies and that probation is being used in white-collar criminal cases to impose conditions on businessmen and corporations, making it the functional counterpart of injunctive remedies. Goldstein notes that the conduct considered as white-collar crime is under attack in all ways available to the regulatory state—through criminal, civil, and administrative law. Goldstein sees this as an erosion of the formal distinctions between "criminal" and "civil" actions.†

In many cases, the white-collar criminal is prosecuted for an offense other than the white-collar crime. For example, in *Bronston v. United States*,‡ Bronston was convicted of perjury, under 18 U.S.C.S. § 1621, for giving an answer, while under oath during a bankruptcy hearing, that was literally true but not responsive to the question asked and arguably misleading by negative implication. The Supreme Court reversed the petitioner's conviction for perjury because although the petitioner gave a response under oath that was unresponsive to the question posed, and was arguably false by negative implication, the petitioner believed his statement to be true and thereby evaded criminal liability under the language of the federal statute. A quick look at the Bronston case provides an example of how complex the white-collar crimes are.

The petitioner (Bronston) was the sole owner of Samuel Bronston Productions, Inc., a company that produced motion pictures in various European locations between 1958 and 1964. For these enterprises, Bronston Productions opened bank accounts in a number of foreign countries; in 1962, for example, it had 37 accounts in five countries. As president of Bronston Productions, the petitioner supervised the transactions involving foreign bank accounts. This case is an illustration of how difficult most white-collar prosecutions are.

In June 1964, Bronston Productions petitioned for an arrangement with creditors under Chapter XI of the Bankruptcy Act, 11 U. S. C. § 701. On June 10, 1966, a referee in bankruptcy held a hearing to determine, for the benefit of the creditors, the extent and location of the company's assets. The petitioner's perjury conviction was founded on the answers he gave as a witness

---

* Baker (2004), p. 2.
† Goldstein (1992), pp. 1895–1900.
‡ 409 U.S. 352, 354–355 (U.S. 1973).

at that bankruptcy hearing and, in particular, on the following colloquy with a lawyer for a creditor of Bronston Productions:

Q: "Do you have any bank accounts in Swiss banks, Mr. Bronston?" [Note: On the day of the hearing, Bronston did not have any Swiss bank accounts.]
A: "No, sir."
Q: "Have you ever?"
A: "The company had an account there for about six months, in Zurich." [Note: Bronston did not answer this question.]
Q: "Have you any nominees who have bank accounts in Swiss banks?"
A: "No, sir."
Q: "Have you ever?"
A: "No, sir."

It is undisputed that for a period of nearly five years, between October 1959 and June 1964, the petitioner had a personal bank account at the International Credit Bank in Geneva, Switzerland, into which he made deposits and upon which he drew checks totaling more than $180,000. It is likewise undisputed that the petitioner's answers were literally truthful.

(a) Petitioner did not at the time of questioning have a Swiss bank account.
(b) Bronston Productions, Inc., did have the account in Zurich described by the petitioner.
(c) Neither at the time of questioning nor before it did the petitioner have nominees who had Swiss accounts.

The Government's prosecution for perjury went forward on the theory that in order to mislead his questioner, the petitioner answered the second question with literal truthfulness but unresponsively addressed his answer to the company's assets and not to his own—thereby implying that he had no personal Swiss bank account at the relevant time.

Chief Justice Warren Burger noted in the court's opinion that it is no answer to say that here the jury found that the petitioner intended to mislead his examiner. The chief justice stated,

A jury should not be permitted to engage in conjecture whether an unresponsive answer, true and complete on its face, was intended to mislead or divert the examiner; the state of mind of the witness is relevant only to the extent that it bears on whether he does not believe his answer to be true. To hold otherwise would be to inject a new and confusing element into the adversary testimonial system we know. Witnesses would be unsure of the extent of their responsibility for the misunderstandings and inadequacies of examiners, and might well fear having that responsibility tested by a jury under the vague rubric of "intent to mislead" or "perjury by implication." The seminal modern treatment of the history of the offense concludes that one consideration of policy overshadowed all others during the years when perjury first emerged as a common-law offense.

NATIONAL WHITE COLLAR CRIME CENTER

VISION

The National White Collar Crime Center (NW3C) is designed to be the national and international leader in the prevention, investigation, and prosecution of economic and high-tech crime.

MISSION

The mission of the NW3C is to provide training, investigative support, and research to agencies and entities involved in the prevention, investigation, and prosecution of economic and high-tech crime.

WHAT THEY DO

NW3C is a nonprofit membership organization that has been continuously funded through competitive grants for over three decades. Through a combination of training and critical support services, we equip state, local, tribal, and federal law enforcement agencies with skills and resources they need to tackle emerging economic and cyber crime problems.

HISTORY OF THE CENTER

Started in 1980, NW3C has been funded by an annual congressional appropriation through the Bureau of Justice Assistance. NW3C is a nonprofit membership affiliated organization composed of state and local law enforcement, prosecutorial, and regulatory agencies. It provides a nationwide support system to state and local law enforcement for the prevention, investigation, and prosecution of economic and high-tech crime. NW3C membership expands across all 50 states, the U.S. Territories, and foreign countries.

MEMBERSHIP QUESTIONS

Membership is FREE; there are no application fees or yearly dues. There are two types of membership, voting and associate. Voting member agencies have full rights and privileges to participate in NW3C activities and a right to vote for representation on NW3C's Board of Directors. Associate member agencies have limited access to NW3C services, have full rights and privileges to literature and networking opportunities, and are charged a nominal fee for NW3C-sponsored training. NW3C does not offer membership to individuals or private companies, only to eligible agencies.

To be eligible for membership, agencies must have a nexus to the prevention, investigation, or prosecution of economic crime, cyber crime, or terrorism, and must meet the criteria of one of the following types:

Voting Membership
  State and local law enforcement agencies;
  State and local prosecutors; or
  State agencies with criminal investigative authority.

Associate Membership
  Any law enforcement agency or division of a federal or foreign
    government;
  State or local government agency with no statutory criminal
    investigative authority; or
  Duly constituted permanent task force comprised of two or
    more of the above agencies (voting or associate).

FREQUENTLY ASKED QUESTIONS OF NW3C

What is NW3C?

The mission of NW3C is to provide a nationwide support system for agencies involved in the prevention, investigation, and prosecution of economic and high-tech crimes and to support and partner with other appropriate entities in addressing homeland security initiatives, as they relate to economic and high-tech crimes.

What type of information is available?

Members of the media may use the public website, under the "Research" tab, to access NW3C's recent initiatives, papers, publications, reports, and The White Collar Crime Research Consortium. Many of the most frequently asked media questions can be answered with information you can easily find in these pages.

Can you discuss current investigations?

NW3C does not answer questions about current, ongoing investigations. Once an NW3C-assisted case has completely worked its way through the law enforcement and judicial system, researchers may be able to discuss those cases, under some circumstances. Requests involving such cases will be considered on a case by case basis. NW3C reserves the right to refuse any interview request at anytime, without citing its reason for doing so.

How can I find statistics on white-collar crime in my area?

Most of the crime information you will find on the Web site quotes national trends and statistics. NW3C is the "National White Collar Crime Center," and most of the information we deal with involves nationwide statistics. You may be able to access FBI statistics, released on a yearly basis, for state by state information.

May I interview a researcher or fraud analyst?

In some cases, media members may be able to interview one of NW3C's analysts, according to the type of story or report. Such requests will be considered on a case by case basis, and NW3C reserves the right to deny requests, without stating a specific reason.

Where can I learn more about NW3C-sponsored programs?

NW3C is a nonprofit membership organization that has been continuously funded through competitive grants for over three decades. Get an overview of NW3C programs from the NW3C Web site.

What support services does NW3C make available?

Specifically for a law enforcement audience, NW3C support services include training on financial investigations and cyber crime, investigative support, Internet crime complaint referrals, outreach programs, and research. Learn more about NW3C services and the benefits of membership from the NW3C Web site.

What kind of law enforcement training is available to my agency?

NW3C trainings have been delivered to enforcement officers nationwide. Find a list of our onsite classroom and computer-based trainings at the NW3C Web site.

I want to file an Internet crime complaint. Where do I go for help?

The Internet Crime Complaint Center (IC3) is an alliance between our organization and the FBI. IC3's mission is to serve as a vehicle to receive, develop, and refer criminal complaints regarding the rapidly expanding arena of cyber crime. IC3 gives the victims of cybercrime a convenient and easy-to-use reporting mechanism that alerts authorities of suspected criminal or civil violations. For law enforcement and regulatory agencies at the federal, state, local, and international level, IC3 provides a central referral mechanism for complaints involving Internet-related crimes.

You can complete an online complaint form at http://www.ic3.gov. The analysts at IC3 will determine which law enforcement agency should handle your complaint and will refer the complaint information on your behalf.

I need current statistics on Internet fraud and economic crime. Where can I find the latest?

NW3C research has provided empirical data crucial to the support of consumer education efforts being deployed by state agencies. Obtain the latest information at http://www.ic3.gov.

Where can I learn more about employment opportunities with NW3C?

Available positions are listed online. If you are applying for a position, please be sure to complete an application package. Materials can be found on the Web site in PDF format.

MORTGAGE FRAUD

CONSIDER THE FOLLOWING SCENARIO:

1. You own a home in a depressed area. You owe more on your mortgage ($200,000) than the fair market value of the home ($150,000).
2. Your friend approaches you and informs you that she has a friend who is a qualified real estate appraiser and that the appraiser will give you a very low (well below market value) appraisal of your home. You hire the appraiser at a higher than normal fee, and the appraiser provides you with a certified appraisal stating that your home's market value is $100,000.

3. You approach your mortgage company with the artificially low appraisal and get the mortgage company to reduce your mortgage balance to $100,000. You then sell the home for $125,000.

QUESTIONS

1. Have you committed a white-collar crime? Explain your answer. Did you use an offender-based definition or an offense-based definition?
2. Has the appraiser committed a white-collar crime? Explain your answer.

HISTORY OF MORTGAGE FRAUD

Mortgage fraud was not tracked until 1996, when the U.S. Treasury Department's Financial Crimes Enforcement Network began tracking the fraud. In 2001, there were 4,695 reports of mortgage fraud. At the height of the U.S. housing boon in 2006, there were more than 37,000 cases reported. During the economic downturn or housing bust era of 2009, there were 67,507 cases reported, and for 2010, there were 70,472 cases reported. While those two years had the highest reported cases, the Financial Crimes Enforcement Network indicated that a high percentage of the cases occurred earlier but were not discovered until the downturn in housing.[*]

[*] Robbie Whelan. (May 10, 2011). "Mortgage-fraud reports rise." *Wall Street Journal*. Page A2.

Required Criminal Conduct

One of the problems in prosecuting white-collar criminals is establishing a factual determination of the defendant's intent at the time of the acts in issue. The type of conduct required to convict is generally divided into four levels. This statute or act that prescribes the conduct as criminal will generally indicate which of the four levels is required to convict a defendant.

- Willful intent—this level describes the conscious desire of the dependent to commit the criminal act.
- Knowledge—this refers to the fact that the defendant is aware that his sins may result in predictable harm to the victim.

- Recklessness—based on a conscious decision to commit a certain action regardless of the consequences.
- Negligence—refers to the situation wherein a person fails to meet a reasonable standard of behavior.

Most white-collar crime statutes require a willful intent. Frequently, the issue as to whether or not the defendant committed the act is not the question, but the intent of the defendant.

EXCERPTS FROM THE U.S. ATTORNEY GENERAL'S CRIMINAL RESOURCE MANUAL, 9-28.300 REGARDING THE DETERMINING WHETHER OR NOT TO PROSECUTE A CORPORATION

[REFORMATTED TO ENHANCE READABILITY]
9-28.300 Factors to Be Considered

General Principle: Generally, prosecutors apply the same factors in determining whether to charge a corporation as they do with respect to individuals. Thus, the prosecutor must weigh all of the factors normally considered in the sound exercise of prosecutorial judgment: the sufficiency of the evidence; the likelihood of success at trial; the probable deterrent, rehabilitative, and other consequences of conviction; and the adequacy of noncriminal approaches.... However, due to the nature of the corporate "person," some additional factors are present. In conducting an investigation, determining whether to bring charges, and negotiating plea or other agreements, prosecutors should consider the following factors in reaching a decision as to the proper treatment of a corporate target:

- The nature and seriousness of the offense, including the risk of harm to the public, and applicable policies and priorities, if any, governing the prosecution of corporations for particular categories of crime.
- The pervasiveness of wrongdoing within the corporation, including the complicity in, or the condoning of, the wrongdoing by corporate management.
- The corporation's history of similar misconduct, including prior criminal, civil, and regulatory enforcement actions against it.
- The corporation's timely and voluntary disclosure of wrongdoing and its willingness to cooperate in the investigation of its agents.

- The existence and effectiveness of the corporation's preexisting compliance program.
- The corporation's remedial actions, including any efforts to implement an effective corporate compliance program or to improve an existing one, to replace responsible management, to discipline or terminate wrongdoers, to pay restitution, and to cooperate with the relevant government agencies.
- Collateral consequences, including whether there is disproportionate harm to shareholders, pension holders, employees, and others not proven personally culpable, as well as impact on the public arising from the prosecution.
- The adequacy of the prosecution of individuals responsible for the corporation's malfeasance and the adequacy of remedies such as civil or regulatory enforcement actions.

Comment: The factors listed in this section are intended to be illustrative of those that should be evaluated and are not an exhaustive list of potentially relevant considerations. Some of these factors may not apply to specific cases, and in some cases, one factor may override all others. For example, the nature and seriousness of the offense may be such as to warrant prosecution regardless of the other factors. In most cases, however, no single factor will be dispositive. In addition, national law enforcement policies in various enforcement areas may require that more or less weight be given to certain of these factors than to others. Of course, prosecutors must exercise their thoughtful and pragmatic judgment in applying and balancing these factors, so as to achieve a fair and just outcome and promote respect for the law.

In making a decision to charge a corporation, the prosecutors generally have substantial latitude in determining when, whom, how, and even whether to prosecute for violations of federal criminal law. In exercising that discretion, prosecutors should consider the following statements of principles that summarize the considerations they should weigh, and the practices they should follow, in discharging their prosecutorial responsibilities. In doing so, prosecutors should ensure that the general purposes of the criminal law—assurance of warranted punishment, deterrence of further criminal conduct, protection of the public from dangerous and fraudulent conduct, rehabilitation of offenders, and restitution for victims and affected communities—are adequately met, taking into account the special nature of the corporate "person."

Major White-Collar Crimes*

The figure below reflects the number of securities and commodities fraud cases that were being investigated by the FBI during the respective fiscal years. [From http://www.fbi.gov/stats-services/publications/financial-crimes-report-2009, accessed on January 24, 2011.]

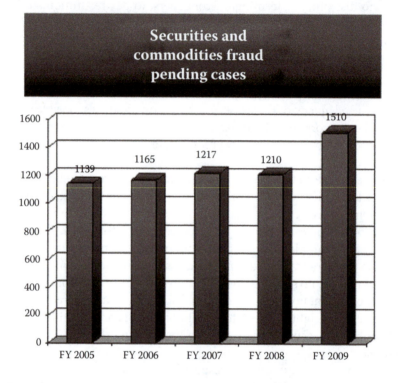

Securities and commodities fraud pending cases

Significant Recent White-Collar Crime Cases

Bernard L. Madoff Investment Securities (New York)

This investigation centered on Bernard L. Madoff, founder of BLM Investment Services LLC (BLMIS), who was arrested in December 2008 on charges of securities fraud. The complaint charged Madoff with running a $64 billion Ponzi scheme. Madoff is the founder of BLMIS, a securities broker dealer, and former Chairman of the NASDAQ Stock Market. Madoff made statements to his employees that his business was a giant Ponzi scheme and that the business had been insolvent for years. Madoff provided clients with monthly investment statements and trade confirmation for transactions that

---

* Material for this section was taken from the FBI Web site at http://www.fbi.gov/stats-services/publications/financial-crimes-report-2009 [Accessed on January 24, 2011].

never actually occurred. For decades, Madoff has utilized new client funds to pay profits and redemptions to existing clients. Madoff pleaded guilty to the indictment and was sentenced to 150 years in prison in June 2009. Thus far, nearly $1 billion in property and assets have been seized, of which approximately $750 million have been forfeited.

Richard Monroe Harkless, d/b/a MX Factors LLC (Los Angeles)

This investigation centered on Richard Monroe Harkless, who operated a Ponzi scheme from 2000 to 2003 via his company MX Factors. Harkless informed clients that he was investing their money in government-guaranteed construction loans, which provided returns as high as 14% every three months. In reality, Harkless diverted the investor funds to Belize and Mexico to pay for personal expenses. Hundreds of individuals invested more than $60 million, with losses in excess of $39 million. The losses by individual investors ranged from $10,000 to more than $500,000. In September 2009, Harkless was sentenced to more than 100 years in prison. This investigation was worked jointly with the IRS and the U.S. Postal Inspection Service (USPIS).

Curtis Somoza (Los Angeles)

This investigation centered on Curtis Somoza, who ran an investment scheme whereby 63 California and Texas investors were defrauded out of $64 million. Somoza guaranteed large returns for investments in a bond-trading program and life insurance pool that would benefit churches in south Los Angeles. Somoza was convicted in 2008 and was sentenced in November 2009 to 25 years in prison for his involvement in this large investment scheme.

Health Care Fraud

The FBI's mission in the area of health care fraud (HCF) is to oversee the FBI's HCF initiatives by providing national guidance and assistance to support HCF investigations targeting individuals and organizations who are defrauding the public and private health care systems. The FBI, along with its federal, state, and local law enforcement partners, the Centers for Medicare and Medicaid Services (CMS), and other government and privately sponsored program participants, work closely together to address vulnerabilities, fraud, and abuse.

All health care programs are subject to fraud; however, Medicare and Medicaid programs are the most visible. Estimates of fraudulent billings to health care programs, both public and private, are estimated to be between 3% and 10% of total health care expenditures. The fraud schemes are not specific to any area, but they are found throughout the entire country. The schemes target large health care programs, public and private, as well as beneficiaries. Certain schemes tend to be worked more often in certain geographical areas, and certain ethnic or national groups tend to also employ the same fraud schemes. The fraud schemes have, over time, become more sophisticated and complex and are now being perpetrated by more organized crime groups.

Mortgage Fraud

In 2009, the continuing deterioration of the real estate market and the dramatic rise in mortgage delinquencies and foreclosures helped fuel the financial crisis and exposed fraudulent practices that were prevalent throughout the mortgage industry. Weak underwriting standards and unsound risk management practices, which had allowed mortgage fraud perpetrators to exploit lending institutions and avoid detection, became evident once the housing market began declining in 2006.

Mortgage fraud schemes employ some type of material misstatement, misrepresentation, or omission relating to the property or potential borrower, which is relied on by an underwriter or lender to fund, purchase, or insure a loan. These misstatements, misrepresentations, or omissions are indicative of mortgage fraud and include the following:

- Inflated appraisals
- Fictitious/Stolen identities
- Nominee/Straw buyers
- False loan application
- Fraudulent supporting loan documentation
- Kickbacks

Insurance Fraud

Insurance fraud continues to be an investigative priority for the FBI, due in large part to the insurance industry's significant role in the U.S. economy. The U.S. insurance industry consists of thousands of companies and collects nearly $1 trillion in premiums each year. The size of the industry, unfortunately, makes it a prime target for criminal activity; the Coalition Against Insurance Fraud (CAIF) estimates that the cost of fraud in the industry is as high as $80 billion each year. This cost is passed on to consumers in the form of higher premiums.

The downturn in the U.S. economy due to the financial crisis has led to an increase in insurance fraud. The FBI continues to identify the most prevalent schemes and the top echelon criminals defrauding the insurance industry in an effort to reduce insurance fraud. The FBI works closely with the National Association of Insurance Commissioners, National Insurance Crime Bureau (NICB), and CAIF, as well as state fraud bureaus, state insurance regulators, and other federal agencies to combat insurance fraud. In

DIRTY TRUTHS ABOUT WHITE-COLLAR CRIME

Myth: White-collar crime is nonviolent. "Not true" states attorney Frank Perri. He states that the white-collar criminal will not hesitate to use violence to cover up crime. According to Perri, white-collar criminals tend to show a sense of entitlement, a need for control, and a lack of empathy.

Myth: Most white-collar criminals are highly paid. According to a study conducted by the University of Alabama School of Law researchers, only the head honcho is successful in obtaining riches. They say that most need a gaggle of lower-paid followers to commit the crimes.

Myth: White-collar criminals are otherwise upstanding citizens. Almost 40% have a previous criminal record according to a 1999 study, and some have even more checkered pasts than street criminals. The study indicated that individuals convicted of mail fraud averaged more previous arrests than individuals convicted of narcotic charges.

Myth: It's all about cash. Often individuals commit white-collar crimes where the benefits are small. For example, Martha Stewart, whose net worth was estimated at about $650 million, saved less than $50,000 in stock losses.

[Information adapted from Mary Diduch. (April 2012). "In Cold Blood." *Scientific American*. 45–46.]

addition, the FBI is a member of the International Association of Insurance Fraud Agencies, an international nonprofit organization whose mission is to maintain an international presence to address insurance and insurance-related financial crimes on a global basis.

Mass Marketing Fraud

Mass marketing fraud is a general term for frauds that exploit mass-communication media, such as telemarketing, mass mailings, and the Internet. Since the 1930s, mass marketing has been a widely accepted and exercised practice. Advances in telecommunications and financial services technologies have further served to spur growth in mass marketing, both for legitimate business purposes and for the perpetration of consumer frauds.

While these fraud schemes may take a wide variety of forms, they share a common theme: the use of false and/or deceptive representations to induce potential victims to make advance fee-type payments to fraud perpetrators. Although there are no comprehensive statistics on the subject, it is estimated that mass marketing frauds victimize millions of Americans each year and generate losses in the hundreds of millions of dollars. The following is a brief description of some of the key concepts and schemes associated with the mass marketing/advance fee fraud crime problem.

FEDERAL CRIME LIST INCREASES

When you visit a federal prison, you will generally note that there are two broad types of criminals: those involved in illegal substance crimes and those involved in white-collar crime. Under our federal system of government, most ordinary crimes are handled by state criminal justice systems. The federal government has limited jurisdiction, and crimes such as homicide, rape, and battery must have a federal connection before the federal criminal justice system has jurisdiction. Generally, the federal system is involved with crimes that occur on federal property or involve federal property, interstate commerce, federal taxes, or civil rights violations. A significant number of those federal crimes are considered as white-collar crimes. Accordingly, this increase in crimes results in an increase in the number of crimes that fit within the white-collar crime definition.

A bedrock principle of federal criminal law has been the need for *mens rea*, which is Latin for "guilty mind." Stated in a different way, it means that people must know they are doing something wrong before they can be found guilty by a court. This principle is slowly being eroded in federal criminal law; as the list of federal crimes grows, the threshold of guilt declines. To convict a person of theft or larceny, the prosecutor must prove not only that the suspect took the goods in question but that he or she knew that the taking was wrong. A classic example of this is that taking someone else's book by mistake is not a crime as long as the mistake was honest.

In recent decades, the U.S. Congress has repeatedly crafted crimes that do not require a guilty mind or lessen the requirement.* For example, an exception to the Marine Protection Act, coastal native Alaskans are allowed to trap and hunt species that other people are not allowed to trap or hunt. In 2003, Wade Martin, a native Alaskan living in Sitka, Alaska, trapped 10 sea otters. This action was legal. A different section of the law, however, requires that the sale of animals taken

---

* Gary Fields and John R. Emshwiller. (September 27, 2011). "As federal crime list grows, threshold of guilt declines." *The Wall Street Journal*. Page 1A.

under this exception to nonnative Alaskans must first be converted into handicrafts. Wade sold the 10 otters to a nonnative for $50 each. When Wade admitted selling the otters but told federal magistrate judge John Roberts that he did not know of this restriction, the judge stated, "You're responsible for the actions you take."*

The Sarbanes–Oxley Act discussed in Chapter 4 provides that it is a crime to destroy any material that might be part of any future investigation. With the present wide range of government investigations from whether or not a baseball player took steroids to the price per gallon of gasoline, a lot of material is covered under this provision. With congressional committees always investigating various aspects of student financial aid, many universities have restrictions on what emails professors and administrators may delete.

In 1790, there were 20 federal crimes. Today there are over 4,500 federal crimes. The crimes are scattered in 42 of the 51 titles of the U.S. Code. In addition, there are also federal crimes embedded in the federal regulations.

* Fields and Emshwiller (2011), p. A12.

Summary

One of the first problems in any discussion of white-collar crime is defining the concept of white-collar crime. Generally, when we refer to white-collar crime, we are referring to offenses where there is a family resemblance to concepts such as perjury, fraud, false statements, obstruction of justice, bribery, extortion and blackmail, insider trading, tax evasion, and certain regulatory offenses.

According to the FBI, white-collar crimes cost the United States more than $300 billion each year, and approximately one third of Americans are victims of white-collar crime. White-collar crimes are prosecuted under either federal or state law, depending upon the type of crime or the offender. Some of the white-collar crimes that are listed by the FBI include securities fraud, racketeering-influenced and choral organization violations, embezzlement, insider trading, identity theft, computer crimes, public corruption, pension fund crimes, perjury, counterfeiting, bribery, extortion, environmental violations, and obstruction of justice.

The Department of Justice defines white-collar crime as offenses classified as nonviolent illegal activities that principally involve traditional notions of deceit, deception, concealment, manipulation, breach of trust, subterfuge, or illegal circumvention. The concept of white-collar crime is generally traced back to Edwin H. Sutherland. He referred to the "robber barons" of the last half of the nineteenth century as white-collar criminals.

Sutherland attempted to redefine crime according to the defendant's socio-economic class, rather than what he or she did. He disregarded traditional principles of our criminal law system by arguing that the presumption of innocence and the requirement of *mens rea* should not apply to white-collar crime.

Since Sutherland first coined the phrase "white-collar crime," the definition of what constitutes white-collar crime has been expanded by many researchers, lawmakers, and law enforcers to include almost any crime motivated by profit. Sutherland's original definition of white-collar crime was "a crime committed by a person of respectability and high social status in the course of his occupation." When the authors refer to the phrase white-collar crime, generally they are referring to crimes committed by individuals or organizations usually in the course of business activity and usually characterized by fraud or falsehood and by complexity.

Few white-collar crime cases involve the identity of the perpetrator, or whether or not the perpetrator had an alibi. Henning states that white-collar crimes are fundamentally crimes of intent because the defendants in such cases freely acknowledge their involvement in the transactions or events. The issue is generally what the defendant knew, or wanted, or failed to disclose, which raises an issue as to whether a crime actually took place.

The Bucy research team noted that the most cited reason by study participants (federal prosecutors and an experienced defense counsel) as to why leaders engage in white-collar criminal acts was greed. Money or financial gain was cited by almost all participants in their study.

Societal interest in white-collar crime and the prosecution of it grew rapidly in the 1970s. Since that time, prosecutors have assigned the higher priority to prosecuting those crimes, which was previously reserved only for violent street crimes. Also, since the 1970s, there has been an increased emphasis on the dangers that white-collar crime has on society.

QUESTIONS IN REVIEW

1. How would you define white-collar crime?
2. Should white-collar criminals be sentenced as severely as street criminals?
3. Explain the development of the concept of white-collar crime.
4. How are white-collar crimes different from street crimes?
5. What is the U.S. Attorney's policy on prosecuting white-collar criminals?

6. Why is "intent" rather than "identity" an issue in prosecuting white-collar criminals?"
7. Explain the history of NW3C.
8. What is the FBI's role in health care fraud?

Practicum

Rate the following 10 crimes as to seriousness of the crime to society, with the most serious crime listed as 1 and the least serious listed as 10. Then, add the scores for the street or nonwhite-collar crimes and the scores for white-collar crimes. What is the difference in the sum of the two groups? Which group did you assign as the most serious group? [Note: Questions were taken from Kane and Wall's survey.*]

1. A bank teller becomes friends with a customer and embezzles $10,000 out of his personal account over the course of two years.
2. A small factory, in order to cut costs and sustain the town's job market, knowingly disposes of toxic waste that pollutes the community's water supply. As a result, several residents fall ill.
3. A teenager attacks a jogger in the park and robs him of $100. The man is taken to the hospital but is not seriously injured.
4. A corporation reports false quarterly earnings to increase the value of their stock.
5. A pharmaceutical company releases a new drug but hides information revealing important health and safety issues for consumers.
6. A person sells one antique bracelet through an online auction to 50 consumers, collects payment from each person, and does not deliver the item to anyone.
7. A man carjacks the vehicle of a teenager, shooting and killing one of the car's passengers in the process.
8. A burglar steals $500 worth of jewelry from an elderly couple's home while they are on vacation.
9. During a bar room fight, one patron attacks another with a broken beer bottle. The man is seriously injured and requires rehabilitation as a result.
10. A college student has forced sexual intercourse with his date.

* Kane and Wall (2006), Appendix B.

Resources

FBI Web Site on White-Collar Crime (http://www.fbi.gov/about-us/investigate/white_collar/whitecollarcrime).

Financial Crimes Enforcement Network (or FinCEN) is a bureau of the U.S. Department of Treasury, which collects and analyzes information on financial crimes (http://www.fincen.gov).

National White Collar Crime Center (http://www.nw3c.org).

Traditional Explanations of White-Collar Crime

2

Chapter Objectives

After reading this chapter, you should be able to do or understand the following:

- The causes of white-collar crime as explained by the control theorists.
- The role of anomie in white-collar crime causation.
- The traditional explanations of why individuals commit white-collar crimes.
- How Sutherland used the concept of differential association to explain white-collar crimes.
- How do social theories explain white-collar crime?
- Discuss whether white-collar crime is caused by societal or organizational pressures.
- Is white-collar crime caused by organizational-specific pressures?
- Why do social control theorists contend that individuals are by nature amoral and will commit deviant acts if they have the chance?
- Explain the social disorganization theories.

Introduction

As noted in Chapter 1, Sutherland coined the phrase "white-collar crime" in 1939; however, the first reported American case in which the term was used was in 1955 in a New York State court discussing the Sherman Anti-Trust Act of 1890.* This fact does not mean that there were no white-collar crimes prosecuted prior to 1955; only that it was not until then that the courts begin using the term.

In this chapter, we will examine the traditional explanations of why individuals commit white-collar crime. Any discussion of crime causation involving this area of criminal law should naturally begin with Edwin Sutherland's concept of differential association (DA). As noted by the famous

---

* *United States v. Standard Ultramarine & Color Co.*, 137 F. Supp. 167, 174 (D.N.Y. 1955).

EXCERPTS FROM *UNITED STATES V. STANDARD ULTRAMARINE & COLOR CO.*, 137 F. SUPP. 167, 168–173 (D.N.Y. 1955)

[**Note:** This is the first reported case in which the term "white-collar crime" was used.]

The defendants, six corporations, were charged in a single-count indictment with conspiracy to violate the Sherman Anti-Trust Act. They are manufacturers of dry colors that are used in the paint, printing inks, paper, plastic, and many other industries. The indictment charged that over a nine-year period, the defendants combined and conspired (a) to fix and maintain prices, (b) to adopt uniform and noncompetitive methods of pricing, and (c) to adopt uniform and noncompetitive terms of sale. It was alleged that the defendants sold $30,000,000 of dry colors in 1954, representing approximately 37.5% of the $80,000,000 volume of business in that year in the United States. Defendant corporations moved for leave to withdraw a previous plea of not guilty and to enter a plea of *nolo contendere* in a criminal action brought under the Sherman Anti-Trust Act, 15 U.S.C.S. § 1. The government opposed the change of plea.

The defendants urged acceptance of the plea on the ground that it is in the interest of the sound administration of justice. First, they claimed that the plea of *nolo contendere* fully vindicates the public interest since it was tantamount to a plea of guilty for the purposes of the case and permitted the imposition of the same fine as may be imposed following a protracted and expensive trial, assuming a verdict of guilty. Second, if the plea was not accepted, they would of necessity defend the prosecution rather than plead guilty and thus burden the Court with a lengthy trial, adding to an already congested calendar and depriving other litigants of prompter trials. Last, they asserted that the plea conformed to congressional policy as enunciated in the Clayton Act and in the Federal Rules of Criminal Procedure.

The court noted that while the defendants' arguments were couched in terms of concern for public interest, acceptance of the plea would carry with it definite and incalculable advantages to the defendants. The plea would avoid trial with its attendant expense and adverse publicity in the event of conviction. Further, it would, and this the defendants acknowledge as an overriding consideration, eliminate the impact of § 5 of the Clayton Act, which would follow in the event of a conviction, thereby reducing the risks to them of private treble damage suits. And it is exactly for this reason that the Government contended that a plea of *nolo contendere* in this case would defeat rather than promote public interest. This reflects the hard core of the issue presented to the Court.

Under § 5 of the Clayton Act, a private litigant may introduce a prior final criminal judgment and equity decree entered against a defendant in Government antitrust suits as prima facie evidence of all matters necessarily determined by the judgment or decree. However, a *nolo contendere* plea is exempt from the application of § 5. Although equivalent to a plea of guilty in the particular case, a defendant is not estopped in any other action to deny the facts upon which the prosecution was based. Further, it cannot be used as an admission in a civil case grounded upon the same facts.

It is true that in the event of a long trial, the fine that might be imposed if there were a conviction would be no greater than under a *nolo contendere* plea—a maximum of $5,000. It is also true that the Government would be saved the expense of further prosecution and a protracted trial avoided. However, do payment of a fine and the elimination of a trial and its cost really vindicate public interest? This in turn poses the basic question: whether under the circumstances of this case it is in the public's interest to deprive private parties of the benefits of the prima facie case under § 5 if the defendants should be found guilty upon trial.

We need not tarry long on the issue of the elimination of expense to the Government. It has already been put to great expense in the investigation and preparation of the matter to date. The fact that it was presented to a grand jury suggests that the violations charged were deemed by the Attorney General to be of a "flagrant" nature. The suggestion that the Government forego its right, and indeed its duty, to uphold the integrity of our laws because of the heavy cost of prosecution falls of its own weight. Cost of enforcement in terms of manpower and money is of little consequence when necessary to assure decent respect for, and compliance with, our laws.

We move on to the fundamental issue that is at the heart of the controversy. The antitrust statutes, as has so often been emphasized, are aimed at assuring that our competitive enterprise system shall operate freely and competitively. They seek to rid our economy of monopolistic and unreasonable restraints. Upon their vigorous and constant enforcement depends the economic, political, and social wellbeing of our nation. The concept that antitrust violations really are "minor" and "technical" infractions, involve no wrongdoing, and merely constitute "white-collar" offenses has no place in the administration of justice.

Ever since the passage in 1890 of the Sherman Anti-Trust Act, referred to by Mr. Chief Justice Hughes as a "charter of freedom," Congress has shown constant and increasing concern over practices that destroy economic competition.

Congress, to secure effective enforcement of the antitrust laws, provided both criminal and civil sanctions through governmental agencies. However, it was not content to rely solely upon official action. It sought to encourage individuals to aid in the policing, and to help achieve the broad objectives of the Act, the treble damage action was authorized in favor of those who had been injured by the condemned conduct. Its purpose was not only the redress of private wrong but also the protection of public interest, and "Congress intended to use private self-interest as a means of enforcement...when it gave to any injured party a private cause of action...." Another purpose in permitting an injured party to recover threefold his actual damage was that substantial verdicts against the wrongdoer would constitute punitive sanctions—to act as a deterrent against any repetition of the offense and to serve as a warning to potential violators.

However, even this auxiliary policing method did not altogether fulfill its purpose. The years that followed the enactment of the treble damage provision revealed that few private litigants had the resources or staying power to conduct a protracted and difficult antitrust case, and those who were able and willing to assume the staggering cost of litigation were frequently worn out by their opponents by sheer attrition. The disparate situation between victim and violator was sharply pointed out by President Wilson, when he urged Congress to enact what ultimately became § 5 of the Clayton Act. A reading of the interesting debates that followed shows that the unmistakable purpose of the Congress in enacting § 5 in response to the Presidential message was "to minimize the burdens of litigation for injured private suitors by making available to them all matters previously established by the Government in antitrust actions." The defendants urge that there is no obligation upon the Government to assist or encourage litigants, but a fair reading of the debates and the Committee Reports indicates that such was the very purpose of the clause. It was fashioned as a powerful weapon to aid private litigants in their suits against antitrust violators by reducing the almost prohibitive costs and staggering burdens of such litigation in making available to him the results of the Government's successful action, whether an equity suit or a criminal prosecution, and the hoped-for by-product of the benefit to a plaintiff was increased law enforcement.

It is against this legislative background that defendants' motions must be considered. The various District Court rulings cited by the parties denying or granting motions for leave to plead *nolo contendere* cannot serve as precedents and are of little aid in the matter. In deciding whether public interest will be better served by acceptance or rejection of the plea, each case must be governed by its own facts. Some, but by no means all, of the factors to be considered, or at least those which this Court deems relevant, are as follows: the nature of the claimed violations, how long they persisted, the size and power of the defendants in the particular industry, the impact of the condemned conduct upon the economy, and whether a greater deterrent effect will result from conviction rather than from acceptance of the plea—obviously these will vary from case to case. Another circumstance to be given relative, but by no means, controlling weight is the view of the Attorney General. As chief enforcement officer, his judgment, that from an overall national viewpoint the prospect of conviction rather than a *nolo* plea will more readily vindicate the public interest, should be considered.

The violations here are alleged to have extended over a nine-year period; the offense charged is price fixing, a per se violation and deemed one of the more serious infractions of the law. The volume of business of the defendants is substantial: $30,000,000 out of a total national sales volume of $80,000,000.

I am satisfied, after taking into account all significant factors, the motion is denied. The balance, if the defendants were permitted to plead *nolo contendere*, would be disproportionately in their favor, without countervailing benefit to public interest. Such a plea, apart from yielding to a defendant the decided advantages already noted, gains for him the tremendous advantage of depriving parties allegedly injured by his conduct of the benefits of the prima facie case under § 5. If violators may expiate their wrongdoing by payments of token fines—by accepting the proverbial "slap on the wrist"—and to boot, avoid the impact of § 5, then a powerful deterrent to law violation has been removed. Government officials have readily acknowledged that the financial pinch on an antitrust defendant achieved through the treble damage action is a "substantial deterrent."

If a defendant in fact has violated the antitrust laws, it would not be in the public's interest that he would have the aid of the Court to add to the admittedly heavy burden of the victim seeking redress, thereby decreasing the prospect of private treble damage recovery with its punitive value and possible deterrent effect. Instead of the heavy burden being lightened, it would be rendered more difficult. Instead of the victim having, as Congress intended, "as large an advantage as the estoppel doctrine would afford had the Government brought suit," the advantage would go to the wrongdoer. Such a course not only fails to carry out the congressional purpose but would also tend to diminish rather than increase respect for law. Accordingly, it should not have the sanction of the Court.

The defendants suggest no consideration that would not be present in any other antitrust proceeding for the acceptance of the *nolo* plea. With compelling factors absent, to grant the motion is virtually to rule that a defendant in an antitrust proceeding is entitled to plead *nolo contendere* as a matter of right. The discretion of the Court should be exercised favorably only when special considerations are present.

The defendants urge that Congress, by the proviso in § 5, that it "shall not apply to consent judgments or decrees entered before any testimony has been taken," intended to encourage defendants to capitulate to the Government charges without a trial whether the proceeding was criminal or civil. Hence, they say that it would conform to congressional policy for the Court to give weight to this inducement and permit them to enter the *nolo* plea. It is far from clear, despite judicial authority supporting the view, that the exception in § 5 was intended to apply to criminal prosecutions as well as to equity suits. As has been recognized, a "consent judgment or decree" in a criminal prosecution is an anomaly.

Question: Why does the judge feel that it would be in the best interests of the public to require the defendants either to plead guilty or conduct a trial?

British criminologist, Hermann Mannheim, "if there were a Nobel Prize in Criminology, Sutherland undoubtedly would have been awarded it."[*] As noted by Sutherland, the traditional concept that crime is caused by poverty or the psychopathic and sociopathic conditions associated with poverty is discredited because that concept omits almost entirely the behavior of white-collar criminals. In addition, Sutherland noted that with a small number of expectations, the generalization that criminality is closely associated with poverty does not apply to white-collar criminals. He concludes that white-collar criminality, like other criminality, is learned.[†]

[*] Harvey W. Kushner. (Summer 1984). "Book review: White collar crime: The uncut version." *Journal of Criminal Law and Criminology*. Vol. 75. Pages 508–510.
[†] Edwin H. Sutherland. (February 1940). "White-collar criminology." *American Sociological Review*. Vol. 5. No. 1. Pages 1–12.

DOES AN INDIVIDUAL'S ECONOMIC LEVEL DETERMINE NOT WHETHER HE OR SHE WILL BE A CRIMINAL BUT, INSTEAD, THE TYPE OF CRIME THE INDIVIDUAL WILL COMMIT?

We were taught as kids that stealing is bad. Dan Ariely, a professor of behavioral economics at Duke University in his book *Predictably Irrational*,* contends that people are more ethical when dealing with paper money than when dealing with other items that have the same dollar value. Ariely placed six-packs of soda in refrigerators located in a common area of a college dormitory. He also placed in other refrigerators at similar locations six $1 bills. After 72 hours, all the sodas were gone, but not the bills. He opined that this revealed hidden biases that we all have to some degree. He also opined that office workers were more likely to steal office pens and pencils than they were likely to steal from the petty cash drawer. Another conclusion of Ariely was that people were more dishonest when the reward was something other than money.

While other researchers agree with him, I have often wondered what I would do if I opened a refrigerator in my college dorm and there were six $1 bills. Since, unlike sodas, $1 bills are not usually found in a refrigerator, I would be hesitant to touch them thinking it was some type of trap. You would naturally assume that the greenbacks were a weird thing to be in a refrigerator unless you were a former congressman from Louisiana who hid his bribe money in one. Ariely contends that we will cheat by a factor bigger than we could ever imagine if the rewards are something other than cash. For example, according to Ariely, the white-collar criminal rarely steals money; more often, it is stocks, etc.

---

* Dan Ariely. (2009). *Predictably Irrational: The Hidden Forces That Shape Our Decisions*. New York: Harper-Collins.

Is white-collar crime caused by societal or organizational pressures? Is the crime caused by organizational-specific pressures? Executives are prone to overstate the earnings and understate the liabilities of their companies because they are judged by the profit margin during their stewardship. Are certain personality characteristics more associated with white-collar criminals? For example, is an individual with a competitive personality more likely to commit white-collar criminality than an individual who does not have that personality? Each of these questions will be discussed in the following sections.

SUTHERLAND ON CAUSATION

[Excerpts from Edwin H. Sutherland, "White-Collar Criminality"]*

The theory that criminal behavior in general is due either to poverty or to the psychopathic and sociopathic conditions associated with poverty can now be shown to be invalid for three reasons. First, the generalization is based on a biased sample which omits almost entirely the behavior of white-collar criminals. The criminologists have restricted their data, for reasons of convenience and ignorance rather than principle, largely to cases dealt with in criminal courts and juvenile courts, and these agencies are used principally for criminals from the lower economic strata. Consequently, their data are grossly biased from the point of view of the economic status of criminals and their generalizations that criminality is closely associated with poverty is not justified....

The hypothesis which is here suggested as a substitute for the conventional theories is that white-collar criminality, just as other systematic criminality is learned; that it is learned in direct or indirect association with those who already practice the behavior; and that those who learn this behavior are segregated from frequent and intimate contacts with law-abiding behavior. Whether a person becomes a criminal or not is determined largely by the comparative frequency and intimacy of his contracts with the two types of behavior. This may be called the process of differential association....

* Reprinted from Edwin H. Sutherland. (February 1940). "White-collar criminality." *American Sociological Review*. Vol. 5. No. 1. Pages 10–12.

Social Theories

Generally, in a class on criminology or a similar course in crime causation, a significant amount of time is expended in discussing social theories. The sociological theories are very popular in the United States when examining street crime. In this section, we will explore social theories as causations or justifications for white-collar criminal behavior.

Social theories tend to focus on the collective behavior of individuals as groups rather than on individual behavior. Sociologists tend to view delinquent behavior as learned social behavior. A person learns social behavior norms, values, etc., as a result of that person's socialization process.

The concept of socialization refers to the process by which a person learns and internalizes the ways of society. The mechanisms of socialization include family, friends, peers, and schools. Many social theorists contend that many types of deviancy and criminality are the result of inadequate or inappropriate socialization experiences during childhood.*

Does the white-collar criminal cheat, steal, or commit his or her criminal behavior because of his or her socialization process, because everyone else is doing it, or because of a defective value system? Each of these justifications could be considered as caused by sociological factors.

David Emile Durkheim (1858–1917)

Emile Durkheim was a French sociologist credited with teaching the first sociology course in a university. Durkheim also edited the first journal of sociology. His theory of anomie was originally developed to explain suicide. Durkheim was concerned primarily with the transformation of villages into modern societies and the attendant problems including social disorganization resulting from that transformation. He defined "anomie" [a Greek term meaning "lawlessness"] as a state or a condition that exists within people when a society evolves or changes from primitive to modern. Anomie is a condition in which norms of behavior have lost their meaning and become inoperative for large numbers of people. Anomie includes the feeling of social isolation, social loneliness, collective sadness, aimlessness, frustration, and hopelessness.†

Structural Approaches

Emile Durkheim was one of the first researchers to examine the effects that particular social structures have on social deviancy. He disagreed with those who blamed the causes of crime on external characteristics such as economic conditions, population densities, climate, or ecological circumstances. For Durkheim, crime was normal. A society exempt from crime would be a society with no room for individual differences. People in such a society would suffer an even greater crime—boredom. Does this concept apply to white-collar criminals? Is white-collar crime a necessary by-product of a complex commercial society? It does provide some excitement to our society as evidenced by movie actor Michael Douglas and his portrayal of a white-collar criminal in the "Wall Street" movies.

As Durkheim noted, crime has a functional purpose. Presently, it is one of our largest industries in the United States. More money is spent on crime

---

* Cliff Roberson. (2010). *Juvenile Justice: Theory and Practice.* Boca Raton, FL: Taylor & Francis.
† Emil Durkheim. (2008). *Encyclopedia Britannica* [online]. [Accessed on November 16, 2010.]

prevention, courts, and corrections than on education. If the crime problem were eliminated, many people, including this author, would be unemployed.

Strain Theories

Strain theories assume that excessive pressures or strain on the individual often result in criminal conduct. According to strain theorists, people are basically good. Excessive pressures placed on us by society cause some people to commit criminal acts. Strain theory is associated with the works of Robert Merton. Merton contended that there are institutionalized paths to success in society and that crime is caused by the difficulty that individuals have in achieving socially valued goals by legitimate means. As those who do not have the opportunity to achieve success, for example, individuals who cannot afford to attend college, have difficulty achieving wealth and status by securing well-paid employment. Accordingly, they are more likely to use criminal means to obtain these goals. Can we logically apply these concepts to white-collar criminals? Kenneth Lay of Enron fame, a college classmate of author Cliff Roberson at the University of Missouri, was certainly not from the lower class. Apparently, Lay's goals were not to achieve socially valued goals but to exceed all others in obtaining wealth.

Merton sets forth five adaptations to this dilemma:

- **Conformity:** In this mode, the individual accepts both the goals and the means to achieve those goals that are accepted by society at large. For example, financial security is a socially accepted goal. The accepted means of achieving this goal is by obtaining a good education. Conformity usually does not lead to deviance and is often considered society's middle-class response.
- **Innovation:** In this mode, the individual accepts the goals but not the means to achieve them. Innovation is likened to taking a short-cut. Merton believed that this mode of adaption was greater among the lower-socioeconomic-status groups but felt that it could also apply to white-collar crime. For example, in the goal of achieving financial security, the individual may use innovative rather than traditionally accepted means of achieving the goal (i.e., fraudulently obtaining money or property to achieve financial security). Another example would be where the goal is to make good grades in college; the student, rather than applying the acceptable means of attaining that goal—studying—cheats to obtain good grades.
- **Ritualism:** In this mode, the individual rejects the accepted goal but accepts the approved means for achieving that goal. Merton believed that this response, like conformity, does not seem to be a deviant

response. For example, parents who want their children to be college educated force their children to go to college. The children go through the ritual of attending classes but do not apply themselves because they have not accepted the goal of attaining a college education.

- **Retreatism:** This is when the individual rejects both the accepted goals and the means to achieve the goals. Retreatism is an escape response. Addicts, alcoholics, vagrants, and people who are mentally ill could be viewed as retreating.
- **Rebellion:** In this mode, the individual rebels against the accepted goals and defines his or her own goals and means to achieve them. Rebellion is an angry, revolutionary response. It differs from retreatism in that rebels generally have strong feelings about their goals. An example would be the outlaw motorcycle gang that has replaced accepted societal goals with their own goals.

There could be a good argument that the first three modes of adaption may explain some types and some forms of white-collar crime. The latter two modes of adoption, retreatism and rebellion, do not appear to explain white-collar crime. They seem inconsistent with white-collar crime.

Durkheim saw anomie as a temporary state. Merton, in contrast, saw anomie as a permanent feature of all modern societies. According to Merton, as long as society elevates goals and there are limited means to attain them, anomie will exist.

When studying street crime, a difficulty with the strain theory as the causation is that it does not explain why children of low-income families may have poor educational attainment in the first place. Another major difficulty is that very often, youth crime does not have an economic motivation. The strain theory may, however, explain white-collar crime based on the assumption that most white-collar crimes are economically motivated.

The strain theories are based on the assumption that

- If an individual fails to conform to social norms and laws, it is because there are excessive pressures or strain that propels the individual to commit criminal behavior.
- Lawbreaking and deviance are not normal.
- Misconduct or deviance is caused by immense pressures on the individual.
- Individuals are basically moral and innately desire to conform to society's rules of conduct.

The critical question for strain theorists is what are the pressures that cause a person to commit delinquent behavior?

PAPERS OF GENERAL INTEREST: LOW SELF-CONTROL, ORGANIZATIONAL THEORY, AND CORPORATE CRIME

[Adapted from a Sally Simpson (2002) article of the same name in *Law and Society Review*. Vol. 36. Pages 509–511.]

Corporate crime results when managers take organizational needs and pressures into account when solving business problems or when managers act in accordance with the dominant culture of the firm, subunit, or team in which they work. Theorists uniformly hold that structures, processes, and tasks are opportunity structures for misconduct because they provide the following:

- Normative support for misconduct
- The means for carrying out violations
- Concealment that minimizes detection and sanctioning

While some degree of self-interest may underlie offending decisions, corporate crime is not reducible to individuals and their characteristics because the individual and the organization are symbiotic. Managers are affected by, and in turn, contribute to the culture and structure of the organization. In short, corporate criminologists expect organizational characteristics as manifested in the behavior of individuals, not low self-control, to explain corporate illegality.

Social Control Theories

Social control theorists contend that individuals are by nature amoral and will commit deviant acts if they have the chance. The control theorists contend that people are by nature inclined to break the law, but if societal controls are present, the controls will restrain their unlawful behavior. Thus, the effectiveness of social controls determines whether or not individuals will become criminals. These theorists contend that social controls tend to be more effective in small, homogeneous communities than in groups of larger, heterogeneous communities. Social controls that restrain persons from committing criminal behavior include controls that are both external (i.e., police, peers, family, etc.) to the person and those that are internal (i.e., attachment, commitment, involvement, and belief). Since the social control theorists based the causation of crime on factors beyond the control of the individual, they fit into the positivist school.

Travis Hirschi believes that individuals will break the law and are only refrained from breaking it if special circumstances are present.* The special circumstances exist only when a person's bonds to mainstream society are strong. A person's bonds to mainstream society are based on four elements:

- **Attachment:** Attachment refers to the person's ability to be sensitive to the thoughts, feelings, and desires of others.
- **Commitment:** Commitment is the rational component in conformity. If a person is committed to society, that person is less likely to commit criminal behavior.
- **Involvement:** The more a person is involved in the community and conventional things, the less likely a person is to commit a crime.
- **Belief:** When a person's belief in the values of society or group is strong, the person will be less likely to commit criminal acts.

Drift

David Matza and Gresham Sykes, two leading control theorists, contended that individuals who have no commitment either to societal norms or to criminal norms will drift in and out of delinquency. Matza states that most criminals will spend the majority of their time in law-abiding activities and that the majority of them are drifters who drift into and out of crime. In essence, most criminals are not committed to criminal behavior but rather experimenting in it. There is a plausible argument that most white-collar criminals are law-abiding citizens a vast majority of the time. Even Charles Manson, the cult murderer, is reportedly to have stated that he did not like to drive in Los Angeles because the other drivers do not obey the traffic laws.

According to Matza and Sykes, people do not commit crimes when they are controlled by morals.† When morals are neutralized, people are more apt to commit crimes. Some "techniques of neutralization" are as follows:

- **Denial of Responsibility:** The delinquent contends that he or she is not responsible for his or her conduct. Bad acts are the result of unloving parents, bad companions, etc.
- **Denial of Injury:** There was no injury or harm to the victim. For example, embezzling from a large business does not hurt anyone because the business is insured. The criminal feels that that particular behavior does not create any great societal harm.

---

* Travis Hirschi. (1969). *Causes of Delinquency.* New Brunswick, NJ: Transaction Publishers.
† David Matza. (1964). *Delinquency and Drift.* New York: Wiley.

- **Denial of Victim:** The victim, a business or greedy investor, deserved to have something bad happen to it. This technique transforms the victim into the wrongdoer and the offender becomes Robin Hood. Thefts are justified because the store owner sells his products at an outrageous price. The same logic applies to street crime when the criminal contends that the rape was justified because the woman dressed provocatively.
- **Condemnation of the Condemners:** The offender contends that the business is corrupt. This is the "who-are-they-to-accuse-me" syndrome.
- **Appeal to Higher Loyalties:** The norms of the gangs or peer group are more important than society's norms. This is the I-did-it-for-the-benefit-of-the-gang syndrome or I did it to save Enron.

Later, Matza refined his theory of "drift," which originally had contended that people used neutralization to drift in and out of conventional behavior. He based his refined theory upon four observations:

- Criminals express guilt over their criminal acts.
- Criminals often respect law-abiding individuals.
- A line is drawn between those they can victimize and those they cannot.
- Criminals are not immune to the demands of conforming.

For the most part, the drift theory has not been widely supported by empirical tests, but it is considered as a key idea in explaining the causes of juvenile delinquency. Does it help explain white-collar criminal behavior? A major shortcoming of the drift theory is that it does not explain why some people in the same situation conform to law-abiding behaviors and others do not.

Neutralization

Early in his teaching career, Cliff Roberson agreed to teach a course in criminology in a federal prison. At the time, he thought that he was agreeing to teach a continuing education course to the correctional staff. It was only later that he learned that his students were all federal prisoners. As we discussed each of the theories on the causes of crime, he would ask the prisoners which criminological theory they considered as the most relevant theory. After receiving their answers and rationale, he would then ask the prisoners if it applied to their case. In each case, the prisoner would answer that it did not apply to them because… and then the prisoner would rationalize why his case was different.

Containment

Walter Reckless developed the containment theory by focusing on an individual's self-conception or self-image of being a good person as an insulator against peer pressure to engage in criminal behavior.[*] The theory holds that people have a number of social controls, containments, or protective barriers that help them in resisting the pressures that draw them toward crime. There are also similar containments that push individuals toward crime. Reckless indicated that there were two types of containment:

- Inner containment = positive sense of self
- Outer containment = supervision and discipline

The inner containment through self-images is developed within the family and is essentially formed by about the age of 12 years. Outer containment was a reflection of strong social relationships with teachers and other sources of conventional socialization within the neighborhood. The basic proposition is that there are "pushes" and "pulls" that will produce delinquent behavior unless they are counteracted by containment. The motivations to deviate as pushes are as follows:

- Discontent with living conditions and family conflicts.
- Aggressiveness and hostility, perhaps due to biological factors.
- Frustration and boredom, say, arising from membership of a minority group or through lack of opportunities to advance in school or find employment.

The pulls toward delinquency are as follows:

- Delinquent peers
- Delinquent subcultures

Reckless was of the belief that the internal containments provided the most effective controls on the person. Together, the internal and external containments prevent individuals from becoming criminals. The pulls to deviate include such factors as greed, poverty, poor family life, and deprived education.

[*] Walter Reckless. (1970). "Containment Theory." In: Marvin Wolfgang (Ed.). *The Sociology of Crime and Delinquency*. New York: Wiley.

Cultural Deviance Theories

Cultural deviance theories assume that individuals are not capable of committing criminal acts, and what are considered deviant acts are deviant only by mainstream standards, not by the offender's standards. According to cultural deviance theories, when a person's cultural values and norms conflict with those of mainstream society, cultural conflict occurs. Cultural deviance theorists accept that lower-class youths have separate identifiable cultural values and norms that are distinct from those of the middle class and contend that the lower-class youths have a value system that emphasizes aggression and violence in resolving problems.

Social Disorganization Theories

Social disorganization theories hold that there is a relationship between increasing crime and the increasing complexity of our society. They also contend that social disorganization is a causal factor in crime. Social disorganization is defined as a breakdown in the bonds of society, especially those involving relationships, teamwork, and morale. In addition, they hold that in communities where the traditional clubs, groups, etc., are no longer in existence, the community is disrupted and there is a lack of consensus of values and norms. Subsequently, this lack of consensus causes higher incidences of criminal behavior.

Differential Association

The two leading symbolic interactionist (SI) theories of delinquency causation are DA and labeling. The SI theories examine the process of becoming a criminal. Both SI theories hold that criminal behavior is a learned activity. Both theories also place the causes of our behavior in our interpretation of reality. As noted earlier, Sutherland is considered as the developer of the DA theory, and he considered it as the only theory that explained white-collar crime.

DA is generally considered as the most popular and influential social–psychological theory of crime causation over the past 60 years. The DA theory is the most talked about of the interactionist theory of deviance. This theory focuses on how individuals learn how to become criminals but does not concern itself with why they become criminals. They learn how to commit criminal acts; they learn motives, drives, rationalizations, and attitudes.*

According to DA, a person learns to commit criminal acts the same way we learn to play basketball, baseball, and other childhood games. The

---

* Edwin H. Sutherland. (1934). *Principles of Criminology.* 2nd ed. Philadelphia: Lippincott.

learning also includes the manner and techniques of committing the crime. Criminal behavior is learned from the message we receive from the people with whom we associate. Some associations, however, have a greater effect on us than others. For example, the messages we receive from our close friends or family have more impact on us than those we receive from the media.

Differential Association Propositions

- Criminal behavior is learned, not inherited; hence, anyone can learn to be a criminal.
- Criminal behavior is learned with other persons in the process of communication. According to Edwin Sutherland, founder of the DA theory, both criminal and noncriminal behaviors are learned through our associations with others.
- The principal part of learning criminal behavior occurs within intimate personal groups. We identify with our reference groups and they, in turn, guide our values. The contacts that a juvenile has with his or her peers, family, and friends have the greatest influence on the juvenile's behavior.
- When criminal behavior is learned, the learning includes the following:
  (1) Techniques of committing the crime, which can be very complicated or very simple.
  (2) The specific direction of motives, drives, rationalizations, and attitudes. Our associations with others influence not only whether or not we commit criminal acts, but also the methods we use to commit crimes.
- The specific direction of motives and drives is learned from definitions of the legal codes as favorable or unfavorable to the violation of the law.
- A person becomes delinquent because of an excess of definitions favorable to the violation of the law over definitions unfavorable to the violation of the law.
- DAs vary in frequency, duration, priority, and intensity.
- The process of learning criminal behavior by association with criminal and noncriminal patterns involves all of the mechanisms that are commonly involved in any other learning.
- Although criminal behavior is an expression of general needs and values, it is not explained by those general needs and values since noncriminal behavior is an expression of the same needs and values.

Labeling

Labeling theorists contend that society labels certain people as deviant. The selected persons accept the label and thus becomes deviant. For example, if we consider a youth bad and the youth subconsciously accepts that label, he will become delinquent. As Frank Tannenbaum, in his book *Crime and the Community*, states,

> The process of making the criminal... is a process of tagging, defining, identifying, segregating, describing, emphasizing, making, conscious, and self-conscious: it becomes a way of stimulating, suggesting, emphasizing, and evoking the very traits complained of.... The person becomes the thing he is described as being.*

When a person commits a crime, there is no automatic process that labels the person a criminal. Accordingly, the labeling theory focuses not on why a person commits a criminal act but rather on how the individual becomes labeled as a criminal or juvenile delinquent. The labeling theory of juvenile delinquency deals not with crime causation but with the effects of labels, or stigmas, on juvenile behavior. The theorists contend that society, by placing labels on juvenile delinquents, stigmatizes them, leading to a negative label for a youth to develop into a negative self-image. A court of law, some other agency, a youth's family and supervisors, and/or the youth's peers give a name—or a "label"—to the youth, often in "degradation ceremonies." These ceremonies may be a suspension hearing with the principal or dean of a school, a court trial, or a home punishment, among others.

Biological Theories

Biological theories are rarely considered when studying white-collar crime. They are reserved generally for street crimes and therefore will not be discussed in depth in this text. Biological theories are more popular in Europe than in the United States. The biological theories are based on the concept that the juvenile delinquent is biologically inferior to the nondelinquent youth. The biological process may be the result of our genetic makeup or brought on by the things we eat. Biological theories are concrete, simple, cause-and-effect answers to the complicated crime problem.

Psychological Theories

The psychological theories were developed from the fields of psychiatry and psychology in the early twentieth century. They are based primarily on the works

* Frank Tannenbaum. (1938). *Crime and the Community*. New York: Columbia University Press. Page 13.

of Sigmund Freud. Freud believed that aggression and violence have their roots in instinct. According to Freud, violence is a response to thwarting the pleasure principle. He developed the concept that each of us has a "death wish" that is a constant source of aggressive impulses and that this death wish tries to reduce the organism to an inanimate state. The death wish may be expressed directly, manifested indirectly as in hunting, or sublimated into sadomasochism.

Sigmund Freud (1856–1939)

Sigmund Freud was born in Freiberg, Moravia, of Jewish parents. In his youth, he was interested in philosophy and humanities. He was a distinguished graduate of the medical college at the University of Vienna. From 1881 to 1902, Freud was in private practice with an emphasis in neurology. In 1902, he was appointed a professor of neuropathology at the University of Vienna. Freud remained there until 1923, when he was forced to retire due to cancer. In 1938, he fled Vienna to escape the Nazis and moved to London. He was one of the most controversial and influential persons of the twentieth century. Freud was a person of great industry, learning, and extraordinary eloquence. He was also witty and expansive. Until 1902, however, he primarily worked in isolation and shrank from those who opposed him. After 1902, he worked with other famous scholars, including Carl Jung and Alfred Adler. However, later in his life, Freud considered them bitter enemies.*

Psychoanalytic and Personality Theories

The psychoanalytic and personality theories concentrate on the causes of crime as arising within the individual. The causes are not, however, seen as inherited or biologically determined. Generally, they are seen as the result of a dysfunctional or abnormal emotional adjustment or of deviant personality traits that were formed in early socialization or childhood development.

Sociopathy

Some theorists contend that delinquent behavior is the result of a particular personality structure known as the "sociopathic personality." The terms "sociopathy," "psychopathy," and "antisocial personality" are interchangeable and tend to refer to the same personality disorder. These terms refer to a pattern of behavior exhibited by many juvenile delinquents and nonjuvenile delinquents. Some researchers contend that the sociopath is mentally ill; others do not. Many people who are identified as sociopaths do not

---

* Louis Breger. (2000). *Freud: Darkness in the Midst of Vision.* New York: Wiley.

commit criminal behavior. As James Q. Wilson and Richard J. Herrnstein stated, "Psychopathy only overlaps with criminality; it is not identical with it. If for no other reason than the vagaries of the criminal justice system, there would be many non-psychopathic offenders and many psychopathic non-offenders."[*]

There are several theories regarding the causes of sociopathy. Some researchers believe that the personality disorder is biological, physical, and/or genetically based. Others contend that it is the result of the person's emotional development caused by poor relationships and faulty child–parent relationships in the person's early years. A third group sees the personality disorder as the result of the person's social environment (i.e., poverty, racism, disrupted family life, poor housing, and/or limited education).

Thinking Pattern Theories

The thinking pattern theorists study the offender's cognitive processes. These theorists contend that the delinquent juvenile has different thinking patterns from the nondelinquent juvenile. They focus on the offender's intellect, logic, mental processes, rationality, and language usage. The mind of the delinquent is affected by his or her cognitive processes, and it is, in turn, the cognitive processes that influence behavior. Accordingly, the way that delinquents think and what they tell themselves in their minds will determine the offender's behavioral choices.

The most detailed study regarding the thinking patterns of criminals was by Samuel Yochelson and Stanton E. Samenow. Their longitudinal study took place over a 15-year period and involved intensive interviews and therapy of criminals. Yochelson and Samenow concluded that criminals think differently from noncriminals.[†]

Moral Theory

If a young teenager spends her evening smoking marijuana, and upon returning home a bit wobbly is confronted by her parents who ask: "Are you drunk?" Is the teenager lying when she responds: "No?"[‡]

---

[*] James Q. Wilson and Richard J. Herrnstein. (1985). *Crime and Human Nature: The Definitive Study of the Causes of Crime.* New York: Simon and Schuster. Page 38.

[†] Samuel Yochelson and Stanton Samenow. (1977). *The Criminal Personality Vol. 2. The Change Process.* New York: Simon and Schuster. Page 28.

[‡] For a discussion on this scenario, see Peter J. Henning. (Spring 2008). "Book review: Lying, cheating, and stealing: A moral theory of white-collar crime." *New Criminal Law Review.* Vol. 11. Pages 323–333.

JUSTICE ROBERT H. JACKSON, FORMER
ASSOCIATE JUSTICE, U.S. SUPREME COURT

When he was the U.S. Attorney General, Justice Jackson in a speech noted that a "prosecutor has more control over life, liberty, and reputation than any other person in America." Justice Jackson also stated the following later in the speech:[*]

> If the prosecutor is obliged to choose his cases, it follows that he can choose his defendants. Therein is the most dangerous power of the prosecutor: that he will pick people that he thinks he should get, rather than pick cases that need to be prosecuted. With the law books filled with a great assortment of crimes, a prosecutor stands a fair chance of finding at least a technical violation of some act on the part of almost anyone.[†]

[*] Henning (2008), p. 354.
[†] Robert H. Jackson. (1940). "The federal prosecutor." *Journal of American Judicature Society*. Vol. 18. Pages 18–22.

Stuart Green, in his book *Lying, Cheating, and Stealing: A Moral Theory of White-Collar Crime*,[*] notes that "white-collar crime" is a term that is powerfully evocative and ultimately indispensable and is beyond definition. Green paints a picture of crime that dominates the popular imagination as one of unambiguous wrongdoing—manifestly harmful acts that are clearly worthy of condemnation. He notes that this picture of the criminal—the thief, the murderer—is a picture of society's failures—to be cast out and reintegrated through a process of punishment and penance. He contends, however, that our understanding of white-collar crime is pervaded by moral and imaginative ambiguity. Green wonders how it is possible to distinguish criminal fraud from mere lawful "puffing," tax evasion from "tax avoidance," insider trading from "savvy investing," obstruction of justice from "zealous advocacy," bribery from "log rolling," and extortion from "hard bargaining." Green also asks how we should distinguish the lawful from the unlawful, the civil from the criminal.

Green describes the ambiguities and uncertainties that pervade the white-collar crimes. He contends that a study of our criminal law reveals a complex and fascinating web of moral insights into the nature of guilt and innocence, and what fundamentally constitutes conduct worthy of punishment by criminal sanction.

[*] Stuart P. Green. (2006). *Lying, Cheating, and Stealing: A Moral Theory of White-Collar Crime*. New York: Oxford University Press.

Green presents eight moral norms that are associated with white-collar crime: cheating, deception, stealing, coercion, exploitation, disloyalty, promise-breaking, and disobedience. A white-collar criminal violates at least one and probably many of the eight moral norms. Green notes that often the line between criminality and acceptable conduct is unclear and that the use of the criminal justice system is inappropriate.

If the prosecutor is obliged to choose his cases, it follows that he can choose his defendants. Therein is the most dangerous power of the prosecutor: that he will pick people that he thinks he should get, rather than pick cases that need to be prosecuted. With the law books filled with a great assortment of crimes, a prosecutor stands a fair chance of finding at least a technical violation of some act on the part of almost anyone.*

Case Study

Richest Man Ever to Go to Prison?

The *Financial Times* in reporting on the Raj Rajaratnam case headlined one article on May 12, 2011, as follows: "Inside-trading trial was a drama worthy of Hollywood."† Raj Rajaratnam was convicted of insider trading. Rajaratnam, a hedge fund billionaire, was convicted on the previous day on insider trading charges. The trial featured friends who turned as government witnesses, a blonde trader fluent in locker room language, and the disclosure of the highest corporate world inside secrets. Rajaratnam was convicted on 14 counts by a jury who had heard candid real-time conversations through phone calls covertly recorded by government agents and had watched dramatic courtroom drama that would have been appropriate for one of television's *Law and Order* shows. Even an expert witness who was called to discuss statistical movements of stock prices verbally sparred with prosecutors seeking to discredit his analysis and testimony.

The principal government witness was a former classmate of Mr. Rajaratnam at the University of Pennsylvania's Wharton Business School. The witness testified that the alleged trading scheme began after he met Rajaratnam at a New York gala. Rajaratnam allegedly pulled him aside and offered to pay him for his insights. The prosecutors played 48 taped telephone conversations and called 18 witnesses in presenting the government's case. The trial lasted seven weeks.

---

* Robert H. Jackson. (1940). "The federal prosecutor." *Journal of American Judicature Society.* Vol. 18. Pages 18–22.
† Kara Scannell. (May 12, 2011). "Insider-trading trial was a drama worthy of Hollywood." *Financial Times.* Page 14.

The Federal Bureau of Investigation's (FBI) surveillance of the defendant involved many tactics commonly used in drug trafficking cases such as wiretaps and undercover agents. The defendant, a Sri Lankan-born American, started as a semiconductor analyst and rose to form Galleon hedge funds. His hedge fund grew to more than one billion dollars. Preet Bharaa, the Manhattan U.S. Attorney, is reported to have stated the following after the trial:

> The message today is clear—there are rules and there are laws, and they apply to everyone, no matter who you are or how much money you have...*

In late 2011, Rajaratnam was sentenced to 11 years in prison and required to forfeit $53.8 million in illegal gains. He was also fined $10 million dollars. This is the longest sentence to date (2011) for an insider trading case. The prosecution had asked for at least 19 years since at least 19 companies were victims of his scheme. The prosecutors also claimed that he had corrupted at least 20 fellow traders and at least 16 insiders with a lust for the millions of dollars that can flow to anyone who gets an edge in the securities markets. The judge in announcing the sentence cited the defendant's need for a kidney transplant and his advanced diabetes. The judge also noted that the defendant had been involved in helping multiple charities.

The sentencing culminated a series of convictions and sentencing that followed Rajaratnam's arrest in October 2009. More than 20 people were arrested and sentenced to serve prison terms from a few months to 10 years. The investigations relied heavily on extensive use of wiretaps.

Bernard Madoff, who was discussed in Chapter 1, and who had admitted to a fraud that cheated thousands of people out of billions, was sentenced to 150 years.[†]

Questions

1. What would you assign as the most likely reason that a billionaire would become involved in an insider trading scheme?
2. One crime watcher stated that, "The Rajaratnam conviction will and should encourage regulators and law enforcement officials to pursue other hedge funds and financial institutions involved in similar behavior." Do you agree? Why?

---

[*] Kara Scannell. (May 12, 2011). "Rajaratnam found guilty." *Financial Times*. Page 1.
[†] *Wall Street Journal*. (October 4, 2011). "Inside trader get 11 years in prison." Page B3.

Summary

Sutherland coined the phrase "white-collar crime" in 1939; however, the first reported American case in which the term was used was in 1955 in a New York State court discussing the Sherman Anti-Trust Act of 1890. The traditional concept that crime is caused by poverty or the psychopathic and sociopathic conditions associated with poverty is discredited because that concept omits almost entirely the behavior of white-collar criminals.

Is white-collar crime caused by societal or organizational pressures? Is the crime caused by organizational-specific pressures? Executives are prone to overstate the earnings and understate the liabilities of their companies because they are judged by the profit margin during their stewardship. Are certain personality characteristics more associated with white-collar criminals? For example, is an individual with a competitive personality more likely to commit white-collar criminality than an individual who does not have that personality?

The sociological theories are very popular in the United States when examining street crime. In this chapter, we explored social theories as causations or justifications for white-collar criminal behavior. Social theories tend to focus on the collective behavior of individuals as groups rather than on individual behavior. Sociologists tend to view delinquent behavior as learned social behavior.

Strain theories assume that excessive pressures or strain on the individual often result in criminal conduct. According to strain theorists, people are basically good. Excessive pressures placed on us by society cause some people to commit criminal acts. Social control theorists contend that individuals are by nature amoral and will commit deviant acts if they have the chance. The control theorists contend that people are by nature inclined to break the law, but if societal controls are present, the controls will restrain their unlawful behavior. David Matza and Gresham Sykes, two leading control theorists, contended that individuals who have no commitment to either societal norms or to criminal norms will drift in and out of delinquency. Matza states that most criminals will spend the majority of their time in law-abiding activities and that the majority of them are drifters who drift into and out of crime.

Walter Reckless developed the containment theory by focusing on an individual's self-conception or self-image of being a good person as an insulator against peer pressure to engage in criminal behavior. Cultural deviance theories assume that individuals are not capable of committing criminal acts, and what are considered deviant acts are deviant only by mainstream standards, not by the offender's standards. According to cultural deviance theories, when a person's cultural values and norms conflict with those of mainstream society, cultural conflict occurs.

Social disorganization theories hold that there is a relationship between increasing crime and the increasing complexity of our society. They also contend that social disorganization is a causal factor in crime. Social disorganization is defined as a breakdown in the bonds of society, especially those involving relationships, teamwork, and morale. The two leading SI theories of delinquency causation are DA and labeling. The SI theories examine the process of becoming a criminal. Both SI theories hold that criminal behavior is a learned activity. Both theories also place the causes of our behavior in our interpretation of reality.

DA is generally considered as the most popular and influential social–psychological theory of crime causation over the past 60 years. The DA theory is the most talked about of the interactionist theory of deviance. This theory focuses on how individuals learn how to become criminals but does not concern itself with why they become criminals. Green describes the ambiguities and uncertainties that pervade the white-collar crimes. He contends that a study of our criminal law reveals a complex and fascinating web of moral insights into the nature of guilt and innocence and what fundamentally constitutes conduct worthy of punishment by criminal sanction.

QUESTIONS IN REVIEW

1. How does Sutherland explain white-collar crime?
2. In your opinion, why do successful business persons commit white-collar crime?
3. Why does Justice Jackson contend that a prosecutor has more control over life, liberty, and reputation than any other person in America?
4. Explain using the "moral theory" why individuals commit white-collar crime.
5. Why are biological theories infrequently used when explaining white-collar crime?
6. How would Sigmund Freud explain white-collar crime?

Opportunity Structure of White-Collar Crime

3

Chapter Objectives

After studying this chapter, you should know the following:

- How to explain the routine activity theory
- How to explain the crime pattern theory
- Differences between situational crime prevention theory and crime pattern theory
- Meaning of the phrase "normalization of deviance"
- Distinction between the cognitive dimensions of opportunity and the structural dimensions of opportunity

Introduction

As noted by Michael Benson, Tamara Madensen, and John Eck in their article on white-collar crime from an opportunity perspective, it is not necessary to argue the importance of white-collar crime's devastating financial and physical effects.* They see the task now as one to develop better ways to control and prevent white-collar crimes. They argue that in order to reduce white-collar crime, we must first identify the specific opportunity structures associated with the offenses we wish to prevent and we must identify the features of the settings that allow the crime to occur. The authors in their article identify three major theories to accomplish this task: routine activity theory, crime pattern theory, and situational crime prevention theory. According to Benson et al. (2009), the three theories address how crime opportunities are formed by immediate environments and then discovered and evaluated by potential offenders.

Using Benson's approach, in this chapter, we will examine the three theories in detail, starting with the routine activity theory, followed by the crime

---

* Michael L. Benson, Tamara D. Madensen, and John E. Eck. (2009). "White-collar crime from an opportunity perspective". In: Sally S. Simpson and David Weisburd (Eds.). *The Criminology of White-Collar Crime*. New York: Springer.

pattern theory, and then the situational crime prevention theory. When examining the opportunity structure of white-collar crime, it is helpful, as noted by Benson et al. (2009), to distinguish between crime and criminality. The authors see crime as an event, something that happens in time and space. Criminality is used to refer to a behavioral disposition, a disposition that is manifested by behaving in ways that are labeled by society as criminal. Whether criminality is expressed as crime depends on situational factors external to the individual, most notably the opportunity structures that a potential offender confronts in daily life.

WOULD PUBLIC SHAMING DETER WHITE-COLLAR CRIMINALS?

Douglas Berman, a professor of Law at the Ohio State University, wonders whether our legal system might better deter white-collar crime by imposing extensive shaming sanctions rather than extensive prison terms. What if, after perhaps a couple of years in prison, a convicted inside trader was required every business day to ring the opening bell at the stock exchange while wearing a prison jumpsuit? What if Martha Stewart's magazines and televisions shows had to include an image of Stewart eating in the federal prison's cafeteria along with other convicted felons when she was imprisoned? What if all people convicted of a white-collar offense were required for decades to post a large sign on their lawns that highlighted to all that the resident inside did not always play by the rules?

Berman notes that a variety of shaming sanctions were widely used during the eighteenth century in America, in part because prisons did not then exist, and in part because shaming was viewed as a humane alternative to the death penalty, banishment, or brutal physical punishments. More recently, according to Berman, academics have debated the potential virtues and vices of modern shaming sanctions—often after a judge has ordered a shoplifter to wear publicly a sign saying, "I am a thief" or a police department has published drunk drivers' names on billboards. Because we have never tried to make white-collar offenders "pay" for their crimes through extensive and prominent use of shaming sanctions, Berman notes that deterrence research suggests very long prison terms for white-collar offenders may greatly extend their suffering (and taxpayer-funded imprisonment costs) with no corresponding benefit to society.*

---

* http://ideas.time.com/2011/10/18/what-will-deter-insider-trading/#ixzz1edtZF1YS [Accessed on November 26, 2011].

In this chapter, we will address white-collar crime as a crime, not a criminality. It is important to remember that white-collar crime differs greatly from the techniques used in committing ordinary street crime. In addition, the opportunity structures are different and important when developing a strategy to combat it. As with any type of crime, the opportunity structure must be present before a crime can be committed. For example, a bank robber needs a bank to rob before he or she can be a bank robber. Parking facilities provide opportunities for theft from vehicles. If these opportunities are foreclosed, it should reduce street crime. Likewise, the white-collar criminal needs an opportunity structure before he or she can commit a white-collar crime. It is unlikely that a homeless person has the opportunity structure to commit a white-collar crime.

Another important issue in trying to prevent white-collar crime is that it is often difficult to determine the temporal and geographic specificity of the crime. In other words, it is often impossible to determine when and where the crime started. Another critical issue is that with street criminals, research indicates that a significant proportion of them suffer from psychological and cognitive difficulties. The psychological and cognitive health of white-collar criminals is an area in which there has been little research. As noted by Benson et al. (2009), there is evidence that white-collar offenders are unwilling to define their behavior as criminal and many have a sense of superiority over their victims.[*]

Routine Activity Theory

> Criminal opportunities are now recognized as an important cause of all crime. Without an opportunity, there cannot be a crime.[†]

The routine activity theory was developed by Cohen and Felson in 1979, when they were trying to find a reason for high urban crime rates. The basic theory stated that criminal events originate in the routines of everyday life. The researchers stated that there must be three elements involved in order for a crime to be committed: a motivated offender, a suitable target, and the lack of guardianship. The principal assumption of the theory is that three elements must be in place to create the necessary conditions for crime: a target, a motivated offender, and a common place where the offender can gain access to the target. If these three elements are present, a crime will occur in the

---

[*] Benson et al. (2009), p. 177.
[†] Michael L. Benson and Sally S. Simpson. (2009). *White-Collar Crime: An Opportunity Perspective*. New York: Routledge. Page 76.

absence of an effective controller.* Benson and Simpson, in discussing the routine activity theory, use only two elements in defining a criminal opportunity. To them, criminal opportunity consists of the elements of suitable target and lack of capable guardianship. A target may be a person or some kind of property. From an offender's point of view, according to Benson and Simpson, the attractiveness or suitability of a person as a target depends on their vulnerability and in some cases their symbolic or emotional values to the offender. As noted by the researcher, big people hit little people. Property is more valuable to an offender if it is moveable, valuable, and fungible.†

The theory seeks to explain criminal violations and give the parameters in which the violations will occur. Cohen and Felson give a wide range in which the theory can be applied. A major advantage of this theory is that it can be applied to many different types of studies and crimes, including homicides, hot spots of crime, property and violent crimes, natural disasters, and even Internet crimes.

The routine activity theory is controversial among sociologists who believe in the social causes of crime. The theory is based on the classical school of criminology, in that criminals decide that to commit the crime or not commit it is based on whether it will be beneficial to them.

What do the routine activity theorists mean when they use the phrase "lack of a capable guardianship?" While it includes the presence of a big strong person to guard you, the term is used in a broader sense by these theorists. It means anything or any person that can keep the offender from getting to a target. Thus, locks on an automobile door may or may not be a capable guardian depending on the type of locks and the skill of the offender. The phrase is used to mean anything that may discourage or prevent the offender from accomplishing his or her mission. It could also mean a police-person passing by. In addition to blocking the offender, a capable guardianship may make the target too risky in the eyes of the offender. For example, if the offender notices that the piece of property may easily be traced, that may make it too risky for the offender to take.

Consider the example of a medical doctor who defrauds Medicare. The fact that the doctor can easily perform this action within the safety of the doctor's office increases the likelihood that the doctor may attempt to commit this type of fraud. If, however, the doctor had to break into the offices of the federal Medicare to commit the crime, he or she would probably find that the risks involved are too great to attempt this type of fraud. The primary technique used by almost all white-collar criminals is deception; rarely is there a need to resort to violence that is generally present in the commission of street crimes.

---

* Lawrence E. Cohen and Marcus Felson. (1979). "Social change and crime rate trends: A routine activity approach." *American Sociological Review*. Vol. 44. Pages 588–608.
† Benson and Simpson (2009), p. 77.

ROUTINE ACTIVITY THEORY AND JAIL ESCAPES*

USING THE BELOW DATA, RICHARD CULP CONCLUDED THAT THE ROUTINE ACTIVITY THEORY COULD BE USED TO EXPLAIN MOST JAIL ESCAPES. DO YOU AGREE WITH HIM?

In 2001, six inmates slipped out of the unlocked housing unit door of an 18-year-old, 1,300-bed maximum-security prison. Bright lights bathed the exterior grounds, but the nearest watch tower was unmanned and an intervening building blocked the view from the closest occupied tower. All six inmates were serving sentences of 25 years or more and three members of the group were serving life without parole for murder. Perimeter security included inner and outer 12-foot-high fences topped with razor wire, and a third, electrified fence between them. The electric fence was designed to deliver a 600-volt shock to anyone who touched it, followed by a lethal dose of 5,000 volts if someone continued to hold on or touched it again. As a final safeguard, a roving correctional officer circled the exterior perimeter in a vehicle.

The six inmates had drawn cards to determine who would be the one to initially breach the electric fence. They snipped a hole in the first fence with a pair of wire cutters stolen from a prison maintenance shop. Next, they propped up the electric fence using an insulating device constructed from contraband materials: two broom handles, covered in cloth and wrapped with duct tape. After sliding under the deadly fence, they lifted an unsecured bottom section of the third perimeter fence, shimmied underneath and stole a car parked near the prison.

A total of 127 inmates were involved in the 96 prison escape incidents reported by the media news in 2001. The escapes occurred in 37 different states. The escapees do not differ from the general prison population by either age or gender. Prison escapes are not more likely to occur during any particular month of the year or day of the week. Although there is slight variation, the differences are not statistically significant. The time of day of escapes charts a more uneven pattern. Escapes are most likely to occur in the busy morning or evening hours. During 2001, there were only three incidents involving inmates overpowering staff in the course of an escape from secure custody—4.3 percent of the escapes—and none of the incidents resulted in serious staff injury.

---

* Richard F. Culp. (May 2005). "Examining prison escapes and the routine activities theory." *Corrections Compendium.*

Escapes involving sophisticated planning and deception are the exception rather than the rule. The most common contributing factor involved improper accounting for tools, which inmates were able to steal and use to cut through chain-link fencing. Routine activities theory provides a useful perspective for examining and explaining escapes from secure custody. Escapes occur when a "perfect storm" of events—a motivated offender, a suitable target, and the absence of capable guardians—converge in time and place. Newer formulations of routine activities theory, particularly the tripartite specification of guardianship, are well tailored for the study of inmate misconduct. Escape appears to be a largely impulsive act and, though it is used in many prison classification instruments, "time left to serve" does not appear to be a reliable predictor of escape risk. The most common scenarios of prison escape involved escapes from nonsecure areas of prisons, scaling or cutting of perimeter fences, and escapes while being transported outside of the facility. For escapes from within secure facilities, the most common contributing factors included shoddy tool control, poor maintenance, leaving items that could be used as ladders unsecured, and laxity in checking staff and inmate identification.

DOES THE ROUTINE ACTIVITY THEORY PROVIDE AN EXPLANATION THAT CAN BE USED WHEN STUDYING WHITE-COLLAR CRIME?

One of the most often repeated maxims that is used in embezzlement prevention classes is that, "No one can embezzle from you unless you trust them." This maxim is based on the premise that unless you trust someone with access or information on your financial accounts, the person does not have the opportunity to embezzle from the accounts. If in a small retail business only one person opens the mail, that person is probably the only one who has an opportunity to steal from the incoming mail.

Crime Pattern Theory

The crime pattern theory was developed by Canadian environmental criminologists Pat and Paul Brantingham. The theory exerts the strongest influence in geographic profiling. It suggests that crime sites and opportunities are not random.* Using the principles of the routine activity theory, the crime pattern theory (also labeled as the offender search theory) contends that offenders become aware of criminal opportunities as they engage in their

* P.J. Brantingham and P.L. Brantingham. (1984). *Patterns in Crime*. New York: Macmillan.

A NEW WHITE-COLLAR CRIME TREND—
REVENGE BY COMPUTER

James O'Brien, fired by a travel agency, hacked into his former employer's computer system and canceled 60 customers' airline tickets, federal prosecutors in Boston charge. The move cost the agency $96,000 and left dozens of would-be holiday vacationers stranded at airports. The Boston Globe stated that O'Brien's alleged crime is the new face of hacking: irate workers who in low-tech days might have simmered or spread slander about their ex-bosses now are wreaking havoc on their former workplaces by infiltrating their computer systems.

The U.S. Attorney's office in Boston, in November 2011, was working on 10 other cases involving fired employees who allegedly struck back at their former bosses by hacking company computers. The phenomenon poses a costly threat to corporations, which can lose millions of dollars to hacker attacks by former insiders who know their systems' vulnerabilities.

Robert Boule, a 29-year-old Framingham man, pleaded guilty in February 2011 to breaking into his former company's computer system to monitor its product lines so he could undercut its bids.*

* http://www.boston.com/dailyglobe2/142/metro/Workers_vengeance_makes_its_way_on_Web+.shtml [Accessed on November 26, 2011].

normal legitimate activities. Under this theory, offenders tend to find their targets in familiar places. Therefore, criminal opportunities that are close to the "areas" that an offender moves through during their everyday activities are more likely to be taken advantage of by the offender than opportunities in areas less familiar to the offender.*

According to Benson and his research group, the crime pattern theory can be adapted to detect and explain the distribution of white-collar crimes across targets. The researchers note that in the case of white-collar offenders, they do not discover their opportunities by walking down familiar streets. Rather, their awareness of white-collar crime opportunities arises out of their employment or occupation. White-collar offenders take advantage of criminal opportunities that arise out of the patterns and activities associated with their occupational positions.

The crime pattern theorists opine that opportunity structure for any particular white-collar crime is dependent on the "nodes" and "paths" used by the offender. The nodes of a white-collar criminal refers to the business

* Benson et al. (2009), p. 181.

or organization they work within and other outside agency, organization, groups of clientele served, or other departments within their own organization that they interact with to accomplish their objectives. The paths used to navigate between these nodes include the procedures and networks used to establish communication or conduct business with others.

Look at the routine activities of a bank clerk and those of a day laborer. It is almost impossible for the day laborer to commit a white-collar crime, whereas the bank clerk in his or her routine activities has numerous nodes and paths to commit a white-collar crime like embezzlement.

Situational Crime Prevention Theory

The situational crime prevention theory is based on the concepts that to prevent crime, we need to reduce the opportunities for criminals to commit crime, change the criminals' ideas about whether they can get away with the crime, and make it harder and more risky for them to commit crime. Some examples are making changes to building and streets to make them safer, using common sense to stop criminals, using neighborhood watch associations, and getting across the idea that it is everybody's job to prevent crime.

Situational crime prevention is focused on the settings for crime, rather than upon those committing criminal acts. It seeks to forestall the occurrence of crime, rather than to detect and sanction offenders. As noted by Clarke, it seeks not to eliminate criminal or delinquent tendencies through improvement of society or its institutions, but merely to make criminal action less attractive to offenders. Central to this concept is not the law enforcement, but a host of public and private organizations and agencies—schools, hospitals, transit systems, shops and malls, manufacturing businesses, and phone companies that should work to prevent crime.* At a recent seminar, it was explained to co-author Cliff Roberson that no one can embezzle from you unless you trust him or her. In other words, to prevent an employee from embezzling from your business, trust no one.

Clarke contends that the problem of explaining crime has been confused with the problem of explaining the criminal. He correctly notes that most criminological theories have been concerned with explaining why certain individuals or groups, exposed to particular psychological or social influences, or with particular inherited traits, are more likely to become involved in delinquency or crime. However, according to Clarke, this is not the same as explaining why crime occurs. The commission of a crime requires not

---

* Ronald Clarke. (1997). *Situational Crime Prevention Successful Case Studies.* Guilderland, NY: Harrow and Hester.

merely the existence of a motivated offender but, as he points out that every detective story reader knows, also the opportunity for crime.*

Clarke also contends that modern criminology tends to confuse the problem of controlling crime with that of dealing with the criminal. Clarke opines that the surest route to reducing crime is not to focus on the offender or potential offender but on the opportunity. He points out that every day, we all do such things as lock our doors, secure our valuables, counsel our children, and guard our purses to reduce the risk of crime. To this end, we also buy houses in safe neighborhoods, we invest in burglar alarms, and we avoid dangerous places and people. Similarly, schools, factories, offices, shops, and many other organizations and agencies routinely take a host of precautions to safeguard themselves, their employees, and their clients from crime. According to Clarke, it is into this group of crime control measures that situational crime prevention fits.†

Clarke states that situational prevention consists of opportunity-reducing measures that‡

- Are directed at highly specific forms of crime.
- Involve the management, design, or manipulation of the immediate environment in as systematic and permanent way as possible.
- Make crime more difficult and risky, or less rewarding and excusable as judged by a wide range of offenders.

As Roberson notes in his book *Preventing Employment Misconduct*,§ embezzlement is a crime that may be prevented using situational crime prevention techniques. Embezzlement is theft by a person in a position of financial trust. Although it is a form of employee theft, because of its unique nature, a separate chapter has been devoted to it. For example, most employee thefts are spur-of-the-moment actions as opportunities present themselves, whereas the embezzler carefully plans the crime and at the same time plans the scheme for hiding it.

Roberson notes that one embezzling employee can quickly bankrupt a company. In one three-month period, three major U.S. banks discovered that they had been the victims of embezzlements by senior executives of $21.3 million, $20 million, and $17 million. In one case, the bank executive was known for his flamboyant lifestyle. Instead of suspecting him of embezzlement, his employers assumed that he had a secret partner that was financing his business ventures. Each year, employers, especially banks, lose

* Clarke (1997), p. 6.
† Clarke (1997), pp. 6–7.
‡ Clarke (1997), p. 10.
§ Cliff Roberson. (2010). *Preventing Employee Misconduct*. Houston: Booklocker.

three times as much from employee embezzlement as they do from robberies and burglaries. The average robbery nets the robber under $4,000, the average burglary under $500.00, whereas the average embezzlement loss exceeds $50,000. In addition, most employers who would not hesitate to prosecute a robber or burglar are reluctant to prosecute an embezzler. Roberson discusses a study of 339 embezzlement cases by IBM executives where it was noted that 85% of the 339 embezzlers were never involved in criminal proceedings and less than 2% of them went to prison. Roberson concludes from this scenario that it is apparent that in most cases, embezzlement does pay.*

Roberson also examined the question of who embezzles. He concluded that to be able to embezzle, the employee must be in a position of financial trust and sufficiently familiar with company procedures to steal and to cover up his or her wrongdoing. Because of these facts, most embezzlers appear to be law-abiding citizens until they are discovered. Most are usually middle- to upper-class citizens of middle age. Accordingly, they do not fit the accepted mold of most criminals. Recently, one criminologist described embezzlement as the crime that takes place when there is a meeting of desire and opportunity. Roberson concludes that most embezzlers would not steal if it were not so easy for them to do so.†

Noted criminologist Donald Cressey in his research work on embezzlement states that most embezzlers are normally straight employees and that there are four events that cause them to steal from their employers and violate the financial trust placed in them.‡

1. The embezzler-to-be is placed in a position of financial trust and he or she accepts this position with no intention of using it to steal.
2. The embezzler-to-be develops a personal problem that he or she is too embarrassed to share with anyone and that appears to be solvable by obtaining extra money.
3. The embezzler-to-be develops the technical skills regarding his or her position and in that learning process discovers the method to violate the trust placed in him or her.
4. The embezzler-to-be acquires the mind set that justifies the embezzlement. The employee often considers the embezzlement as a form of borrowing or temporary taking of the money. Most embezzlers fully intend to return the money "someday."

---

* Roberson (2010), p. 11.
† Roberson (2010), p. 12.
‡ Donald Cressey. (1973). *Other People's Money: A Study in the Social Psychology of Embezzlement.* Montclair, NJ: Patterson Smith.

Cressey also states that, since embezzlers must be in positions of trust in order to steal, their positions insulate them from suspicion, often making them feel protected from detection. He also indicates that embezzlers must rationalize their conduct in order to maintain their self-image of being a trusted person.*

One criticism of Cressey's explanation of the embezzlement causative process is that the personal problem referred to in paragraph 2 is very general and that everyone has problems. According to Cressey's critics, the problem that is cited as triggering the embezzlement is often used by the employee after he or she is caught to justify his or her actions. Many critics contend that an embezzler will always find a problem to justify his or her actions when caught, that is, that people have a natural ability to rationalize their bad actions.[†]

Some criminologists contend that embezzlement results from a combination of desire and opportunity. Employees, who desire to enrich themselves, if provided the opportunity, will. According to this school of thought, the sum of the two factors determines if employees will violate the financial trust placed in them by their employers. If the desire is strong enough, employees will find a method to embezzle. However, if an employee has little desire to steal but the opportunity is readily apparent; he or she may still embezzle.

According to Roberson, research of embezzlement cases indicates that employees who embezzle tend to have higher indebtedness, change jobs more frequently, and have lower incomes than employees in similar positions with other companies. Contract employees and those working on commission also are frequent embezzlers. He noted that a study of 97 embezzlers indicated that 75 of them were in financial difficulty at the time of their embezzlement. The next highest numbers of embezzlers were employees who perceived their income to be inadequate. One such employee who perceived his income to be inadequate had recently purchased a Lear Jet and a $600,000 home.[‡]

As noted earlier, since embezzlement is a violation of financial trust, an employee cannot embezzle from you if you do not trust him or her. Many credit unions learned this fact only after they became victims of embezzlement. Some of the classic cases involving embezzlement were accomplished by key senior executives. In most of the cases, the embezzlement continued for a relatively long period of time because of the lack of controls and checks on these key executives.

Roberson opines that to prevent embezzlement, the employer needs to establish a system of checks and balances that ensures that all financial

---

* Cressey (1973), p. 123.
† Lawrence M. Salinger. (2004). *Encyclopedia of White-Collar and Corporate Crime.* Thousand Oaks, CA: Sage.
‡ Roberson (2010), p. 14.

transactions are checked by more than one employee and that no one is entrusted with a fiduciary duty that is not subject to verification by someone else. Never allow one employee to handle all aspects of any financial transaction. Establish procedures that create the expectation that all financial transactions will be audited. He concludes that inadequate attention to detail by managers provides the opportunity for persons under their supervision to embezzle. Managers, therefore, should not continually leave all details to subordinates without occasionally checking. A system of random checks will create the general feeling that all aspects of every financial transaction are subject to verification.[*]

According to Roberson, in addition to reducing the opportunity to embezzle, you should be alerted by employees who are living above their apparent income and who have a record of financial problems. As a rule, persons who embezzle do not hide the money in a secret account; they tend to spend the money as soon as they embezzle it. In only less than 1% of the cases examined did the embezzler save the money or invest it wisely. They normally use it to support a living standard beyond their apparent means or to solve present financial problems.[†]

Requiring key employees to submit full financial disclosure statements to detect sudden changes in a person's net worth would be a situational crime prevention technique. A negative change in the personal estate of a key employee would then be treated as a danger flag. Generally, employees who adequately manage their financial affairs do not embezzle.

Situational Crime Prevention Theory in Action

Consider this scenario: You are a successful businessperson operating a business that generates a lot of cash. The business has been operated by you and your spouse but has grown too large and you need additional help. The decision is made to hire an assistant to handle incoming mail. Using the situational crime prevention techniques and being a prudent businessperson, what would you look for in hiring an assistant?

- If permitted by state and local law, would you conduct a credit check on the final applicants?
- If an applicant meets all the qualifications but has a poor credit history, would you hire him or her?
- Would you hire someone who has been convicted of a theft-related crime?

[*] Roberson (2010), p. 15.
[†] Roberson (2010), p. 15.

- Would you hire someone who has been convicted of a nontheft-related felony?
- After you have hired the applicant who best meets your requirements, what steps would you take to make sure that the new employee does not embezzle from you?
- Suppose an employee had worked for you for about 10 years, should you trust that employee to open mail that may contain cash?
- One mail order company requires that two people must always be present when the mail is opened. How does this practice fit with the situational crime prevention theory techniques?

Clarke opines that the need to tailor measures to particular offenses should not be taken to imply that offenders are specialists—only that the commission of specific kinds of crime depends crucially on a constellation of particular environmental opportunities and that these opportunities may

SWISS BANK CONSPIRACY

In August 2007, federal prosecutors in New York City allege that a Swiss banker entered a local restaurant for a meeting with two U.S. citizens. One of the citizens carried an envelope containing $16,000 in cash. The cash was to be delivered to the banker for deposit in the Swiss bank. The federal prosecutors claim that secret rendezvous such as this allow wealthy Americans to evade federal taxes on at least $1.2 billion in assets by hiding them in foreign bank accounts. According to the federal prosecutors, it is standard procedure for private bankers to go to extreme lengths to conceal these types of transactions.

The prosecutors announced that an indictment had been issued against one of the oldest Swiss banks, the bank's client advisor, and two fellow bankers in the bank's Zurich branch. This was apparently the first time that a foreign bank had been indicted on charges of facilitating U.S. tax fraud. Later, the indictments were expanded to include 10 additional Swiss banks. In addition, the prosecutors used a civil forfeiture statute to seize more than $16 million of the Swiss banks that was being held in a correspondent account at a U.S. bank located in Stamford, CT.

Later, the U.S. bank disclosed to the prosecutors the names and account data of more than 4,500 clients of the Swiss banks. The disclosures resulted in dozens of tax-related indictments and convictions.*

* Kevin McCoy. (February 6, 2012). "Secret meetings and cash drops." *USA Today*. Page 10B.

need to be blocked in highly specific ways. To him, an important feature of the definition of situational prevention is the implicit recognition that a wide range of offenders, attempting to satisfy a variety of motives and employing a variety of methods, may be involved in even highly specific offenses. He further recognizes that all people have some probability of committing crime depending on the circumstances in which they find themselves. Thus, situational prevention does not draw hard distinctions between criminals and others.[*]

White-Collar Crime by Government Officials

In 1994, Orange County, CA, was considered by most individuals as one of the most affluent and fiscally conservative counties in the United States. In December 1994, the county declared bankruptcy. At the time, it was the largest government failure in U.S. history. Prior to the declaration, Orange County was considered as a "county investment pool" which was run by county treasurer Robert Citron. Citron had been the treasurer for over 20 years. He eventually pleaded guilty to fraud charges. Investors' losses were estimated to be between $1.5 billion and $2 billion.[†]

The situation started with the passage of Proposition 13 by the California voters in 1978. The proposition was an antitax measure that restricted the ability of government units to impose or raise taxes. In addition, Orange County voters imposed requirements on the county, which mandated specific levels of spending on education without providing resources to pay for the mandated services. Citron had indicated that he could guarantee profit for the county without using any county money and that he would be investing funds borrowed from institutional investors who buy the county's interest-paying taxable notes. However, the apparently safe investments did not return the level of income necessary to pay the guarantee returns to the investors and leave sufficient operating funds for the county.[‡]

In discussing the bankruptcy, then California State Senator Lucy Kallea characterized the process by which the county attempted to raise money as a casino where billions of dollars of public funds were wagered on risky bets and side bets that were touted as safe ones; one table in particular—the Orange County investment pool—was paying out record winnings.[§]

---

[*] Clarke (1997), p. 8.
[†] Susan Wells, Henry Pontell, and Richard Cheung. (1998). "Risky business revisited: White-collar crime and the Orange County bankruptcy." *Crime and Delinquency*. Vol. 44. Issue 3. Pages 367–378.
[‡] Wells et al. (1998), p. 372.
[§] Wells et al. (1998), p. 369.

Occupational Opportunities

Before you can commit a successful crime, you must have the opportunity. For example, according to David Wolman in his 2011 book *The End of Money*, Wolman contends that if we had an electronic system to substitute the use of cash, there would be significantly fewer robberies.* The fact that individuals carry money creates the opportunity for criminals to rob them. If the criminal knew that an individual had no money, it is unlikely that the criminal would rob that individual. In examining white-collar crimes, it is noted that the crimes occur when there are occupational opportunities.

In 2012, a Texas medical doctor was indicted for bilking Medicare of nearly $375 million by recruiting homeless and other fake patients to sign for care that was never provided. This is an example of an occupational opportunity. It is unlikely that the average person will ever be in a position to bilk Medicare out of millions of dollars. During the year 2011, the U.S. Attorneys' offices recovered nearly $4.1 billion in funds that were "stolen or taken improperly" from federal healthcare programs by professions in the healthcare field. In addition, more than 700 healthcare providers were convicted of fraud during 2011. While the number of convictions and moneys recovered are enormous, you cannot help but wonder why it took the federal government over five years to indict the Texas doctor. According to one researcher, to be able to bilk the federal government out of $375 million, you would need to treat over a million patients.†

Sense of Identity

"Identity" may be defined as the distinctive characteristic belonging to any given individual, or shared by all members of a particular social category or group. The term is thus essentially comparative in nature, as it emphasizes the sharing of a degree of sameness or oneness with others in a particular area or on a given point. Identity is best construed as being both relational and contextual.

In the area of white-collar crime, when we refer to an individual's sense of identity, generally, we are referring to the fact that most white-collar criminals do not identify themselves with criminal activity and that they do not see themselves as criminals. They sense that the conduct may be in violation of regulations or laws, but it is not criminal. For example, Gilbert Geis reported that during a congressional hearing on an antitrust case in 1961,

---

* David Wolman. (2011). *The End of Money.* New York: Da Capo Press.
† Richard Serrano. (February 29, 2012). "Doctor charged in nation's largest healthcare fraud scam." *The Los Angeles Times.* Page A-1.

OVERVIEW OF THE LAW ENFORCEMENT STRATEGY
TO COMBAT INTERNATIONAL ORGANIZED CRIME

(U.S. DEPARTMENT OF JUSTICE, 2008)

In recent years, international organized crime has expanded considerably in presence, sophistication and significance—and it now threatens many aspects of how Americans live, work and do business. International organized crime promotes corruption, violence, and other illegal activities, jeopardizes our border security, and causes human misery. It undermines the integrity of our banking and financial systems, commodities and securities markets, and our cyberspace. In short, international organized crime is a national security problem that demands a strategic, targeted, and concerted U.S. Government response.

The Law Enforcement Strategy to Combat International Organized Crime establishes an investigation and prosecution framework that emphasizes four priority areas of action against international organized crime:

- MARSHAL INFORMATION AND INTELLIGENCE: Collect, synthesize and timely disseminate the best available information and intelligence from multiple sources—including law enforcement, the intelligence community, foreign partners and the private sector—to optimize law enforcement's ability to identify, assess and draw connections among nationally-significant IOC threats;
- PRIORITIZE AND TARGET THE MOST SIGNIFICANT IOC THREATS: Select and target for high-impact law enforcement action the international organized crime figures and organizations that pose the greatest threat to the United States, and ensure the national coordination of investigations and prosecutions involving these targets;
- ATTACK FROM ALL ANGLES: Employ all available law enforcement and nonlaw enforcement tools—including drawing upon the unique expertise of every participating U.S. law enforcement agency in domestic operations, partnering with foreign counterparts to pursue cases at home and abroad, and employing U.S. government sanctions and advisories—all in a crosscutting effort to disrupt IOC activity; and
- ENTERPRISE THEORY: Develop aggressive strategies for dismantling entire criminal organizations, especially their leadership, by using proactive investigative techniques and multilayered prosecutions.

This strategy is itself the product of sustained cooperation among: the Organized Crime and Racketeering Section of DOJ's Criminal Division, in collaboration with other sections of the Criminal Division; the Federal Bureau of Investigation (FBI); U.S. Immigration and Customs Enforcement (ICE); the Internal Revenue Service; the Postal Inspection Service; the Secret Service; the Drug Enforcement Administration; the Bureau of Alcohol, Tobacco, Firearms, and Explosives; the Bureau of Diplomatic Security; the Department of Labor/Office of the Inspector General; components of the State Department, the Treasury Department, and the intelligence community.

INTERNATIONAL ORGANIZED CRIME DEFINED

For purposes of the strategy, "international organized crime" refers to those self-perpetuating associations of individuals who operate internationally for the purpose of obtaining power, influence, monetary and/or commercial gains, wholly or in part by illegal means, while protecting their activities through a pattern of corruption and/or violence. There is no single structure under which international organized criminals operate; they vary from hierarchies to clans, networks and cells, and may evolve to other structures. The crimes they commit also vary. International organized criminals act conspiratorially in their criminal activities and possess certain characteristics which may include, but are not limited to:

A. In at least part of their activities they commit violence or other acts which are likely to intimidate, or make actual or implicit threats to do so;
B. They exploit differences between countries to further their objectives, enriching their organization, expanding its power, and/or avoiding detection and apprehension;
C. They attempt to gain influence in government, politics, and commerce through corrupt as well as legitimate means;
D. They have economic gain as their primary goal, not only from patently illegal activities but also from investment in legitimate business; and
E. They attempt to insulate both their leadership and membership from detection, sanction, and/or prosecution through their organizational structure.

While this definition may be read broadly to include international drug trafficking organizations and international street gangs engaged in criminal activity, those groups are not the focus of the strategy. The strategy places its highest priority on those IOC groups that threaten the national security of the United States, the stability of the U.S. economy, and/or the integrity of government institutions, infrastructure, or systems in the United States.

THE STRATEGIC THREATS POSED BY INTERNATIONAL ORGANIZED CRIME

International organized crime poses eight strategic threats. For the purposes of this summary, examples of these threats are set out below, drawn from published reports, publicly indicted cases and publicly available information from law enforcement partners. Due to the necessity of referencing only public, nonsensitive information, this summary contains historical information (albeit some quite recent), since most of the evidence of ongoing threats—and our law enforcement response—is law enforcement sensitive or classified for operational and/or national security reasons.

THREAT 1: International organized criminals have penetrated the energy and other strategic sectors of the economy. International organized criminals and their associates control significant positions in the global energy and strategic materials markets that are vital to U.S. national security interests. They are now expanding their holdings in the U.S. strategic materials sector. Their activities tend to corrupt the normal workings of these markets and have a destabilizing effect on U.S. geopolitical interests.

One of the most frequently reported examples involves Semion Mogilevich and several members of his criminal organization who were charged in 2003 in the Eastern District of Pennsylvania in a 45-count racketeering indictment for their involvement in a sophisticated securities fraud and money laundering scheme. Published reports state that since that indictment and being placed on the FBI most-wanted list, Mogilevich has continued to expand his criminal empire, to the point where he is said to exert influence over large portions of the natural gas industry in parts of the former Soviet Union. Many commentators have noted the significant role that area of the world plays in global energy markets. Mogilevich was arrested by Russian police on tax charges in January 2008. Other members of his organization remain at large.

THREAT 2: International organized criminals provide logistical and other support to terrorists, foreign intelligence services and governments. Each of these groups is either targeting the United States or otherwise acting in a manner adverse to U.S. interests.

International organized criminals have repeatedly demonstrated their willingness to provide logistical support to terrorists.

Viktor Bout, an international arms trafficker, was charged in March 2008 with conspiring to sell millions of dollars worth of weapons to the Revolutionary Armed Forces of Colombia (FARC), a U.S. State Department-designated foreign terrorist organization. Along with an accomplice, Bout allegedly agreed to sell 100 surface-to-air missiles to the FARC, as well as launchers for armor-piercing rockets. Unbeknownst to Bout, the people he believed to be FARC members were actually confidential sources working with the Department of Justice. Viktor Bout is being held in Thailand on a provisional arrest warrant and complaint issued out of the Southern District of New York. The Department of Justice is currently seeking Bout's extradition from Thailand, where he is being held, to face trial in the United States.

Likewise, an ICE undercover investigation revealed an Indonesian smuggling ring that, in 2006, conspired to export state-of-the-art firearms, machine guns and ammunition, surface-to-air missiles, night vision goggles, and other military weapons from the United States to the Liberation Tigers of Tamil Eelam (Tamil Tigers) operating within Sri Lanka, to be used to fight against Sri Lankan government forces. The Tamil Tigers, a U.S. State Department-designated foreign terrorist organization, has advocated the violent overthrow of the Sri Lankan government, employing acts of violence, including suicide bombings, against both civilian and military targets. In this case, the conspirators contacted an undercover business located in Maryland about the sale of military weapons. Six members of the international smuggling ring, Thirunavukarasu Varatharasa, Haji Subandi, Haniffa Osman, Erick Wotulo, Reinhard Rusli, and Helmi Soedirdja have pleaded guilty in the United States District Court in the District of Maryland.

A number of published works on organized crime point out that, historically, governments and their intelligence and security services have used organized criminals to further their ends. It is not surprising then that such relationships continue today, particularly in locations where lines between organized crime and the intelligence/security services are often blurred.

THREAT 3: International organized criminals smuggle/traffic people and contraband goods into the United States. Smuggling/trafficking activities seriously compromise U.S. border security and at times national security. Smuggling of contraband/counterfeit goods costs U.S. businesses billions of dollars annually, and the smuggling/

trafficking of people leads to exploitation that threatens the health and lives of human beings.

Whether smuggling people or goods, international organized crime groups view borders as profit-making opportunities rather than obstacles. Whether they are transporting human beings, narcotics, pharmaceuticals, cigarettes or weaponry, sophisticated criminal networks are adept at exploiting gaps and weaknesses in border controls and finding opportunities for corruption.

In February 2008, five members of an alien smuggling organization were sentenced for their roles in a conspiracy to smuggle purported terrorists to the United States from Colombia. Victor Daniel Salamanca, Jalal Sadat Moheisena and Carmen Maria Ponton Caro were sentenced to 70 months in prison after pleading guilty to conspiracy to provide material support or resources to the FARC. Their co-conspirators Nicolas Ricardo Tapasco Romero and Edizon Ramirez Gamboa were sentenced to three years' incarceration after pleading guilty to conspiracy to commit alien smuggling and bringing aliens to the United States for private financial gain. The international smugglers obtained fraudulent Colombian and Spanish passports and other identity documents for people they believed to be terrorists seeking illicit travel to Miami for the purposes of laundering FARC money from the United States to Colombia. In fact, the purported terrorists were informants working in an ICE sting operation.

In March 2006, one of the most successful alien smugglers of all time, Cheng Chui Ping, better known as "Sister Ping," was sentenced to 35 years in prison for her role in leading an international alien smuggling organization. She smuggled more than 1000 aliens into the United States during the course of her career, sometimes hundreds at a time, and her actions exemplify the threats to health and life inherent to the trade. The trial revealed one incident in which 14 aliens died when one of her smuggling boats capsized. In another notorious incident, 10 aliens drowned when the Golden Venture, a smuggling ship Sister Ping helped finance for several other alien smugglers, intentionally grounded off the coast of Queens, N.Y., in June 1993 because the offloading vessel failed to meet it at sea. Sister Ping also hired armed thugs from the Fuk Ching, a vicious gang in New York's Chinatown, to transport her customers and ensure they paid their smuggling fees.

A pair of companion cases—Operation Royal Charm in New Jersey and Operation Smoking Dragon in Los Angeles—exemplifies the economic and public health costs of contraband smuggling. These investigations uncovered an Asian criminal organization that was smuggling nearly every form of contraband imaginable, providing a one-stop-shopping point to its customers. The investigations resulted in the indictment of 87 individuals who were involved in smuggling goods into the ports of Newark, N.J., Los Angeles, and Long Beach, Calif., by using shipping containers with bills of lading that falsely identified the contents as toys and furniture from China. Instead, the smugglers brought in high quality counterfeit U.S. currency that had reportedly been produced in North Korea, as well as contraband from China. The contraband included counterfeit cigarettes, ecstasy, methamphetamine and counterfeit pharmaceuticals. Two of the defendants, in a conversation with federal undercover agents, entered into a deal to provide various weapons, including silenced pistols, rocket launchers, silenced submachine guns, and automatic rifles.

The Camorra, an Italian organized crime group based in the Campania region of Italy, manufactures designer clothing knock-offs in Italy, then transports some of their material to the United States, where Camorra members retail these wares to U.S. customers. Proceeds filter back to Italian-based Camorra clans. Camorra clans are primarily involved in extortion, infiltration of legitimate businesses, labor racketeering, document forgery, alien smuggling, and the sale of counterfeit goods. Press reports indicate that these enterprises earn the Camorra clans roughly $25 billion annually, with counterfeit goods sales representing more than 10 percent of this total. In July 2004, Italian authorities issued approximately 70 arrest warrants targeting a Camorra ring that trafficked in tens of millions of dollars in counterfeit goods, including designer clothing, electronic camera equipment, and power tools. The ring operated in many countries outside Italy, including the United States. With assistance from U.S. law enforcement, approximately 300 million Euros worth of real property, bank accounts, and businesses were seized at the time of the arrests.

THREAT 4: International organized criminals exploit the U.S. and international financial system to move illicit funds. International organized criminals transfer billions of dollars of illicit funds annually through the U.S. financial system. To continue this practice, they seek to corrupt financial and nonfinancial intermediaries globally.

Eurasian organized crime groups are a particular concern because of their systemic use of sophisticated schemes to move and conceal their criminal proceeds using U.S. banking institutions and U.S. incorporated shell companies. These groups have mastered techniques to overcome robust antimoney laundering controls and are able to move illicit funds through the formal banking system while disguising the source and ownership of the funds. They offer their illegal financial services for a fee to others who are similarly interested in disguising the sources and ownership of their funds.

The Bank of New York (BNY) case was an early example of such a scheme. In 2000, Peter Berlin, a Russian émigré, and his wife, Lucy Edwards, also a Russian émigré, who was a BNY vice president, pleaded guilty in the U.S. District Court for the Southern District of New York to conspiracy to commit money laundering and to operate an unlawful banking and money transmitting business, and to aid and abet Russian banks in conducting unlawful and unlicensed banking activities in the United States. Berlin and Edwards teamed in their illegal scheme with two Moscow-based banks that offered to move money for "clients" without regard to the source or ownership of the funds. During the three and half years Edwards and Berlin were involved in the illegal operation, approximately $7 billion flowed through the BNY accounts they had established to third-party transferees around the world. BNY admitted its antimoney laundering control lapses, entering into a non-prosecution agreement with the U.S. Attorneys' Offices for the Southern and Eastern Districts of New York in November 2005 to resolve two separate criminal investigations. BNY agreed to forfeit $26 million to the United States, and to pay $12 million in restitution to victims of a fraud scheme in the Eastern District case.

Another example is the case of Garri Grigorian, a Russian national living in the United States who helped launder more than $130 million on behalf of the Moscow-based Intellect Bank and its customers, through bank accounts in Sandy, Utah. Grigorian and his co-conspirators set up two U.S. shell companies and then set up multiple bank accounts for those companies in Utah. The companies never did any business; they existed only to create the illusion that transactions to and from their bank accounts were legitimate trade. Once those accounts were set up, Intellect Bank could use them to conduct U.S. dollar wire transfers on behalf of their clients. In total there were more than 5,000 of these wire transfers in a little more than two years. In August 2005, Grigorian was sentenced to 51 months in prison and ordered to pay $17.42 million in restitution to the Russian government.

Criminals have learned from the Bank of New York and Grigorian prosecutions and devised a more complicated version of the same scheme to evade law enforcement. Criminals who establish shell corporations in the United States are now increasingly opening bank accounts for those corporations in offshore jurisdictions where customer identification requirements may be less rigorous. However, these corporations are still able to gain access to the U.S. financial system if the foreign bank has a correspondent account at a U.S. financial institution. On the surface, it appears as though wire transfers are being made to further foreign trade with a U.S. company that has a bank account in New York. In actuality, the criminals are running a sophisticated money laundering scheme in which it is nearly impossible to determine the source, nature or destination of the money moving through it (which by all estimations amounts to billions of dollars annually).

THREAT 5: International organized criminals use cyberspace to target U.S. victims and infrastructure. International organized criminals use an endless variety of cyberspace schemes to steal hundreds of millions of dollars at a cost to consumers and the U.S. economy. These schemes also jeopardize the security of personal information, the stability of business and government infrastructures, and the security and solvency of financial investment markets.

One example of the intersection between organized crime and cybercrime is found in Romania. There, traditional Romanian organized crime figures, previously arrested for crimes such as extortion, drug trafficking and human smuggling, are collaborating with other criminals to bring segments of the young hacker community under their control. They organize these new recruits into cells based on their cybercrime specialty and they routinely target U.S. businesses and citizens in a variety of fraud schemes.

One of the most lucrative schemes involves online auction fraud, where U.S. citizens are tricked into buying or selling goods, and never receive the funds or merchandise. One particular online criminal, using the online nickname "Vladuz" engaged in multiple fraud schemes, including hacking into the computers of eBay, the largest online auction retailer. On April 17, 2008, Vlad Duiculescu, a/k/a "Vladuz" was arrested in Romania by Romanian police officials and charged with crimes related to these schemes. It is believed that Vladuz is a participant in a ring of Romanian hackers who work together to develop joint U.S. targets for online frauds, share hacking techniques and launder proceeds from multiple crimes committed in the United States. U.S. prosecutors and law enforcement agents worked in Romania with Romanian officials to ensure that a case could be successfully prosecuted in Romania.

THREAT 6: International organized criminals are manipulating securities exchanges and perpetrating sophisticated frauds. International organized criminals use fraud to steal from U.S. investors and rob U.S. consumers and government agencies of billions of dollars.

Increasingly, domestic and international securities markets have become ripe sectors for abuse by international organized criminals who seek to enrich themselves from the pockets of unsuspecting investors. Using the fast-paced securities markets, the Internet and the wire services—where money, communications and inducements can be exchanged in milliseconds—international organized criminals manipulate international borders and the limitations in law enforcement's detection capability to their advantage without the need to set up a base of operations in any one location. International organized criminals are also adept at using the Internet, wire services, and the mails for sophisticated fraud schemes.

Highly organized groups of overseas scam artists have been preying on North American consumers via the mail or over the Internet, attempting to pass authentic-looking counterfeit business checks or money orders. Victims have been approached after posting items for sale or rent on the Internet, meeting a supposed companion on a social dating website, or via "spam" e-mails sent by the West African criminal groups based in Nigeria, the Netherlands, or Canada, announcing the victim has won a prize or can share in a business opportunity. In all the scams, the victim is sent a check for an advance payment of the item being offered, or to pay taxes or fees on the sudden riches. The criminal instructs the victim to wire all or part of the check back overseas. However, it often takes weeks for counterfeits to be discovered and the victim is responsible for what has been wired away. U.S. Postal Inspectors have been working with law enforcement in Nigeria, Canada, the Netherlands, and the United Kingdom to stop the counterfeit checks from reaching their victims. Since the global counterfeit initiative targeting these international criminal organizations began in January 2007, 77 arrests have been made and more than 600,000 fake checks valued at over $2.5 billion have been seized.

Telemarketing fraud is yet another means by which international organized criminals fraudulently obtain funding. For example, in Canada, the Royal Canadian Mounted Police have linked the leaders of telemarketing fraud rings operating out of boiler rooms with traditional organized crime groups in Canada. The Canadian antifraud call center estimates that 500 to 1,000 criminal telemarketing boiler room operations are conducted on any given day in Canada, grossing about $1 billion a year.

One Montreal-based telemarketing ring, broken up in a U.S.-Canadian joint operation in December 2006, victimized as many as

500 people per week, many of them U.S. citizens. Investigators targeted boiler rooms from which the ring would contact its victims and arrested 40 Canadian citizens on the suspicion of fraud. The criminals used two different telemarketing schemes to swindle unsuspecting victims, netting $8 to $13 million annually. In the first, a lottery scheme, victims were persuaded they had won the lottery, but needed to send check payments ranging from $1,500 to $60,000 to cover various costs. Approximately 90 percent of the victims in this case were more than 60 years old. The second scheme, a mass telemarketing fraud, used several approaches including telling victims they were eligible to receive a $7,000 grant, selling victims healthcare kits or billing victims for services never rendered. In each instance, victims were told to send money via certified check or money order.

THREAT 7: International organized criminals corrupt and seek to corrupt public officials in the United States and abroad. International organized criminals must corrupt public officials to operate and protect their illegal operations, and to increase their sphere of influence. They have been successful in systematically corrupting public officials around the world, including countries of vital strategic importance to the United States, and they are increasingly seeking to influence U.S. officials by legal and illegal means.

In March 2008, the Bulgarian chief directorate for combating organized crime (CDCOC), a branch of the Ministry of Interior, reportedly revealed that several officials from the ministry had had contacts with controversial businessmen, linked to international organized crime, who were currently under investigation. As part of the scandal, Ivan Ivanov, deputy head of CDCOC, was charged with leaking confidential information. Ilia Iliev, chief secretary of the Ministry of Interior, was arrested for his responsibility in granting documents to travel within the European Union to a Serbian national with ties to organized crimes.

In some countries, corrupt public figures and organized criminals have attained status, power, and wealth far outweighing those of legitimate authorities. In others, corruption occurs as an accepted means of doing business. Corrupt foreign leaders who aid, support and are beholden to organized crime cause substantial harm to their own people and often to U.S. strategic interests. In the most serious instances, the corrupt official him or herself, is for all practical purposes, the leader of an organized criminal group.

For example, former Ukrainian Prime Minister Pavel Lazarenko defrauded and extorted millions of dollars from his countrymen and ultimately laundered his illicit fortune through U.S. financial institutions. Specifically, in the 1990s, Prime Minister Lazarenko defrauded and extorted $44 million dollars from Ukrainian citizens and proceeded to launder $20 million of these funds through U.S. banks. After fleeing to the United States, Lazarenko was arrested in 2004 and tried in a federal court in San Francisco on money laundering, wire fraud, and fraudulent interstate transportation charges. He is currently serving a nine-year prison sentence and was fined $10 million by the court.

Similarly, Arnoldo Aleman, his family and other related officials embezzled several million dollars from Nicaragua during his time as president (1997–2002). Nicaragua convicted Aleman of money laundering and theft of government funds. In a related investigation to recover assets at the request of the Nicaraguan government, ICE initiated an investigation into the embezzlement of Nicaraguan government funds. The ensuing investigation led to the seizure of approximately $6 million in assets in the United States, approximately $2.7 million of which was forfeited in U.S. courts and transferred back to Nicaragua during the Bolaños administration to be used for an education program and anticorruption expenses. Additional funds remain pending in U.S. proceedings.

THREAT 8: International organized criminals use violence and the threat of violence as a basis for power. International organized criminals who use violence are a threat to the physical security of the U.S. public, as well as the economic wellbeing of people and neighborhoods and the ability of law enforcement to investigate their crimes when the threat of violence is used as a tool of coercion. Violent tactics used by international organized criminals outside the United States also threaten U.S. interests when their violence sustains and increases their power to operate globally.

International organized crime and violence are fundamentally connected, such that there is no shortage of examples demonstrating this inherent connection. For example, the August 2007 killing of six Italian men as they left a pizzeria in Duisburg, Germany, has been attributed to the 'Ndrangheta crime syndicate. The killers fired at least 70 shots at the six victims with automatic weapons and then proceeded to shoot each victim once in the head. Published reports claimed the killings were the product of a dispute between two rival 'Ndrangheta clans. According to the FBI, the 'Ndrangheta, based in Calabria, Italy, has about 160 cells with roughly 6,000 members. They have a presence in the United States, primarily in the Northeast. 'Ndrangheta specializes in kidnapping and political corruption, but also engages in drug traf-ficking, murder, bombings, counterfeiting, gambling, frauds, thefts, labor racketeering, loan-sharking, and alien smuggling. According to published reports, Italian prosecutors estimate 'Ndrangheta operations at home and abroad are worth approximately $50 billion. Prosecutors say the 'Ndrangheta has set up a network of pizzerias, restaurants, and hotels for laundering the group's money.

On March 12, 2007, a federal court in Los Angeles sentenced Iouri Mikhel and Jurijus Kadamovas to death for their role in leading an international criminal organization that abducted and murdered five victims in the United States. Between the summer of 2001 until their arrests on February 19, 2001, Mikhel and Kadamovas targeted wealthy Los Angeles residents who they could abduct and hold hostage for ran-som in order to fund their lavish lifestyle. Regardless of whether the ransom money was paid or not, once they confirmed payment of the ransom, Mikhel and Kadamovas brutally murdered each one of their victims by either asphyxiating or strangling them. Then, with the help of their criminal partners, Mikhel and Kadamovas transported the bodies of their victims to the New Melones Reservoir, approximately 400 miles from their base of operations in Los Angeles. Once there, Mikhel and Kadamovas attached weights to their victims' bodies and threw them from one of two bridges spanning the reservoir.

The evidence offered at trial confirmed Mikhel and Kadamovas intended to kill more than the initial five victims. After they killed their last two victims, Mikhel and Kadamovas flew to Colorado to ski and look for new potential victims. They also began planning to send a member of their criminal organization to the east coast to scout potential victims and planned a trip to a yacht show in Florida to search for wealthy Russians who they could kidnap. Kadamovas directly informed one of his co-conspirators that he and Mikhel planned to commit as many additional kidnappings in the future as necessary to amass a fortune of $50 million dollars, intending to kid-nap and kill their victims until the bodies they dropped into the New Melones Reservoir were "stacked on top of each other" to the surface of the reservoir. Evidence presented at trial also established Mikhel and Kadamovas' involvement in previous similar homicides commit-ted in Cyprus and Turkey in 2000 and 2001. Adding to the interna-tional scope of the group's activities, the money they received from victims moved around the globe in its laundering process, including the United Arab Emirates, Latvia, Barbados, Jamaica, Switzerland, and England.

KEYS TO UNDERSTANDING AND RESPONDING TO INTERNATIONAL ORGANIZED CRIME

Several critical factors provide essential context for understanding the threats international organized crime poses to the United States and for developing effective responses to these threats. These key factors include:

- International organized criminals do not need to reside in the United States to engage in criminal activities targeting the United States, its interests and its people. With the advent of globalization, the Internet, international banking and modern technologies, international organized criminals can remain in countries that provide them with a safe haven from arrest while perpetrating criminal activities targeting the United States and its people.
- The most powerful international organized crime groups benefit from the symbiotic relationship that their leaders have developed with corrupt public officials and business tycoons. The three elements combine forces to form strategic alliances.
- International organized crime in its highest form is far removed from the streets. These groups are highly sophisticated, have billions of dollars at their disposal, are highly educated, and employ some of the world's best accountants, lawyers, bankers, and lobbyists. They go to great lengths to portray themselves as legitimate businessmen and even advocates/benefactors for the local populace and others.
- International organized criminals have evolved toward loose network structures and away from traditional hierarchical structures.
- There are large gaps in our intelligence on various aspects of international organized crime. These gaps jeopardize our ability to keep pace with international organized crime threats as they emerge and develop.

The IOC threats and key factors summarized above provided the factual foundation for the strategy and served as a catalyst for discussion among federal law enforcement agencies as well as across the broader interagency community on what is needed to combat the IOC problem and how we may effectively integrate law enforcement and nonlaw enforcement efforts to maximize success.

STRATEGIC GOALS

The strategy consists of nine strategic goals that emphasize programmatic areas cutting across all international organized crime threats. Some goals propose new tools and capabilities needed to combat IOC, while others enhance or improve existing tools and capabilities. Each strategic goal encompasses specific objectives and actions that will enable the Department of Justice and its law enforcement partners to achieve measurable results in combating the threats posed by international organized crime. The strategic goals are summarized below.

GOAL 1: Prioritize and Target International Organized Crime Figures and Organizations for Concerted, High-Impact Law Enforcement Action

In order to most effectively utilize resources, it is essential to formally identify the international organized crime figures and organizations that pose the greatest and most immediate threats to our national interests. Other law enforcement segments within the U.S. government—particularly those combating drug trafficking—have effectively marshalled intelligence and strategically targeted major offenders. Those combating organized crime have experienced similar success over the last half-century in strategically targeting La Cosa Nostra, the Italian–American mafia. Each of these targeting programs has clearly identified the threats emanating from their targets and focused law enforcement and prosecutorial resources on the most notorious individuals and organizations. Selecting high-priority IOC targets will be a crucial step toward disrupting their activities and dismantling their organizations.

KEY RESULTS: Establish and lead an interagency committee to select and target the international organized crime figures and organizations that pose the greatest threat to the United States, and ensure the national coordination of investigations and prosecutions involving these targets. This will focus law enforcement, intelligence and other resources on disrupting and dismantling significant IOC operations and lead to the apprehension of high value IOC figures worldwide.

GOAL 2: Pursue Concerted, High-Impact Domestic Law Enforcement Operations against International Organized Crime Targets

U.S. law enforcement is constantly challenged by highly sophisticated international organized criminals and groups that operate across borders, exploit our economy from within as well as from abroad, and which are always evolving to elude and thwart our efforts to bring them to justice. U.S. law enforcement agencies must therefore work together in cross-cutting, concerted domestic law enforcement operations to attack international organized crime from multiple angles and on a nationwide basis. This will require every participating U.S. law enforcement agency, from headquarters to the field, to systematically exchange information on IOC targets and emerging threats; combine their unique skills and expertise; and coordinate their resources and capabilities to disrupt and dismantle international criminal organizations. The effect will be to bring the collective weight of U.S. law enforcement to bear against the serious threats international organized crime poses to U.S. national security.

KEY RESULTS: Assemble teams of prosecutors, investigators, and analysts to pursue each IOC target; develop meaningful measures to reward action against IOC and ensure account-ability; and undertake initiatives to identify new IOC targets. This will enable U.S. law enforcement to organize and coor-dinate resources to minimize bureaucratic barriers and maxi-mize impact against IOC targets, and to properly account for the use of resources devoted to international organized crime.

GOAL 3: Team with Foreign Counterparts to Pursue Domestic, Foreign, and Joint Law Enforcement Operations against International Organized Crime Threats

Every day, law enforcement authorities in the United States and worldwide are engaged in parallel campaigns against international organized crime. Globalization has created a vast new battleground for organized crime that extends beyond national and jurisdictional boundaries. This presents unprec-edented challenges to the international law enforcement com-munity. IOC groups increase the scope and depth of their activities exponentially while authorities attempt to navigate international laws and protocols to conduct long-distance investigations. Nations throughout the world recognize the need to cooperate with one another to combat the common threats of IOC. Presently, 137 countries, including the United States, are parties to the United Nations Convention against Transnational Organized Crime. The United States has led efforts with foreign authorities to share information, develop strategies, and conduct joint investigations on IOC matters of mutual interest. Yet, there remains much more to be accomplished. To effectively carry-out cross cutting operations to disrupt and dismantle IOC groups, U.S. law enforcement must capitalize on established relationships with vetted foreign officials and build international partnerships to collaborate in the domestic and foreign prosecution of IOC cases.

KEY RESULTS: Establish operational task forces with foreign counterparts in key locations worldwide to target IOC threats; deploy experienced U.S. prosecutors abroad to coordinate IOC investigations and prosecutions with foreign counterparts; and build the capacity for U.S. law enforcement to collect, translate, and analyze criminal intelligence information on international organized crime from foreign counterparts. This will result in more productive relationships with foreign counterparts and will improve our knowledge and understanding of IOC operations abroad.

GOAL 4: Employ Non–Law Enforcement Measures to Prevent International Organized Criminals from Operating in the United States

In today's global economy, international organized criminals enjoy seemingly endless opportunities for moving, concealing, and investing their ill-gotten wealth through the world's major financial centers. Their market of choice is often the United States, whose banking system, securities and commodities markets, and industrial/commercial assets offer stability, prestige, and global influence. The movement of criminal assets into the U.S. financial system and the investment of these assets in U.S. businesses pose a serious threat to the U.S. economy. There are several nonlaw enforcement tools the U.S. Government can aggressively utilize to target international organized criminals, freeze their illicit assets, and thwart their ability to use the U.S. banking system and commercial and industrial sectors to advance their criminal purposes. In order for these powerful tools to be employed as a component of U.S. law enforcement's cross-cutting efforts to disrupt and dismantle international criminal organizations, however, the law enforcement community must effectively provide their nonlaw enforcement counterparts with critical information that can be considered and acted upon.

KEY RESULTS: Utilize all available U.S. Government programs, capabilities, and resources to their greatest possible effect to protect the U.S. financial, commercial, and industrial sectors from international organized crime and its illicit assets, and to prevent international organized criminals from entering and operating in the United States. This will ensure that the U.S. Government assertively employs its arsenal of powerful economic, consular, and other nonlaw enforcement means to target IOC figures and organizations, freeze or seize their assets, and disrupt their ability to exploit U.S. banks, businesses, and strategic assets.

GOAL 5: Collect and Synthesize Critical Information on International Organized Crime Targets for Law Enforcement Action

The ability of U.S. law enforcement to successfully investigate and prosecute targeted international organized crime figures or organizations will depend heavily on the quality of information that is available on the targets and the capability of law enforcement personnel to systematically collect, synthesize, and analyze that information. As international organized criminals cross borders to conduct their illicit operations, U.S. law enforcement must closely coordinate and communicate across agencies and jurisdictions to identify and exchange the best information available on IOC targets so that quick and decisive action can be taken against the targeted individuals or organizations.

KEY RESULTS: Convene an interagency analytical team that will systematically collect, synthesize, and disseminate to headquarters and the field law enforcement and intelligence information on selected IOC targets as well as emerging IOC threats and trends. This will result in a functioning intelligence mechanism that will facilitate critical information sharing among agencies and enable investigators and prosecutors to make connections across jurisdictions to uncover and take action against priority international criminal organizations.

GOAL 6: Develop and Retain Skilled and Knowledgeable Analysts, Investigators, and Prosecutors to Fight International Organized Crime

International organized crime has become increasingly sophisticated in penetrating financial systems, manipulating securities and commodities markets, harnessing cyberspace to perpetrate high-tech crimes, and carrying out numerous other schemes. As they have become more advanced in their criminal operations, international organized crime groups also have adapted to the realities and opportunities of globalization, evolving toward looser organizational structures that are flexible, mobile, and elusive. The U.S. law enforcement community must make every effort to keep pace with international organized crime, by ensuring that domestic law enforcement personnel as well as select foreign counterparts are fully equipped with the specialized skills and knowledge required to effectively investigate and prosecute international organized criminals and to dismantle their organizations.

KEY RESULTS: Hold regular criminal intelligence briefings for U.S. law enforcement to ensure that investigators, prosecutors, and analysts have sufficient and up-to-date knowledge of the most significant IOC threats; develop a training cadre to provide IOC training to domestic and foreign law enforcement personnel in the specialized skills required to combat IOC; promote measures to retain experienced personnel; and develop a reserve group of IOC experts to provide case-specific training and mentoring. This will provide U.S. law enforcement and selected foreign counterparts with specialized skills to combat international criminal organizations, and will ensure continuity in the IOC program.

GOAL 7: Provide Law Enforcement with Updated Legislation and Operational Procedures Needed to Combat International Organized Crime

In today's world of international crime fighting, the categories of "domestic" or "foreign" law enforcement cases are almost archaic. International organized criminals simply do not operate within the confines of national borders and geographic law enforcement jurisdictions. Yet, all too often, our criminal laws and operational procedures do not sufficiently equip us to address the modern realities and needs of international crime fighting. United States law enforcement and our foreign counterparts are joined in a global offensive against organized crime. We must consider this problem in that broad context and amend relevant laws to enable us to effectively fight international organized crime domestically and in cooperation with our foreign partners.

KEY RESULTS: Expand, update, or modify U.S. laws, regulations, and procedures in critical areas to enhance investigators' and prosecutors' abilities to take action against IOC figures domestically and abroad, and assist foreign countries in developing legislative frameworks for combating international organized crime. This will enhance the arsenal of tools available to federal law enforcement personnel and their foreign counterparts in their efforts to bring IOC organizations and figures to justice.

GOAL 8: Raise Awareness and Leverage Resources in Combating International Organized Crime through Outreach to Public and Private Institutions

The IOC Threat Assessment illustrates the pervasive nature and widespread impact of organized crime. On a daily basis, organized crime directly and collaterally affects individuals and entities in both the public and private sectors. All segments of American society risk being victimized by organized crime, and all share in the increased costs for goods and services. In response, many public and private institutions have acted unilaterally to minimize the impact of organized crime on their respective businesses. These institutions share interests and objectives parallel to those of law enforcement.

KEY RESULTS: Engage the private sector to raise awareness, form public–private alliances, and gather information on IOC threats, and engage other parts of the U.S. government, as well as state, local, and foreign governments, to promote understanding of international organized crime. This will provide U.S. law enforcement with new avenues for exchanging information and leveraging resources to target international organized crime.

GOAL 9: Reconvene the Attorney General's Organized Crime Council to Provide Direction on Policy and Resources and Ensure Accountability in the International Organized Crime Program

The Attorney General has been in charge of coordinating all federal law enforcement activity against organized crime since a 1968 executive order by President Lyndon Johnson established that authority. Similarly, the Organized Crime Council has existed in various forms since 1970 and has always been charged with establishing priorities and formulating a national unified strategy to combat organized crime. This will be the first time the Organized Crime Council has ever convened to focus on the threat from international organized crime and to develop a responsive strategy to that threat. The Organized

Crime Council consists of the Deputy Attorney General, the Assistant Attorney General for the Criminal Division, the Chair of the Attorney General's Advisory Committee, and the leaders of nine participating federal law enforcement agencies, which include: FBI; U.S. Drug Enforcement Agency; the Bureau of Alcohol, Tobacco, Firearms, and Explosives; U.S. Immigration and Customs Enforcement; U.S. Secret Service; Internal Revenue Service; U.S. Postal Inspection Service; Diplomatic Security and U.S. Department of Labor's Office of the Inspector General.

KEY RESULTS: Reconvene the Attorney General's Organized Crime Council to oversee implementation and dedication of resources dedicated to this strategy, review progress in combating international organized crime, examine options for how best to organize the IOC program, and provide recommendations to the National Security Council on new interagency efforts or capabilities to advance the fight against international organized crime. This will enable the Department to engage the broader federal law enforcement community at the policy level to provide oversight, guidance, and direction to the international organized crime program.

DOES WALL STREET CREATE CONVICTS?

In a September 5, 2012, article in the USA Today newspaper, Lynne Street and Jordan Thomas imply that Wall Street does in fact create convicts.* Street and Thomas state that it is time to admit that Wall Street has lost its moral compass. They noted that in a recent survey of financial professionals in the United States and the United Kingdom, that at least 25% of the professionals had observed or had personal knowledge of wrongdoings in the workplace. Forty percent believed that their competitors had engaged in wrongful conduct and 16% admitted that they would engage in insider trading if they thought that they would not get caught.

---

* Lynne Street and Jordan Thomas. (September 5, 2012). "How Wall Street creates convicts." USA Today. Page 9A.

The researchers contend that the financial industry has become a criminogenic environment that tempts otherwise ethical individuals into criminal conduct. The authors disagree with that statement and opine that the present industry only provides an opportunity for unethical people to engage in criminal behavior. The researchers fail to account for the fact that the majority of individuals involved in the financial industry do not commit crime. The authors contend that the individuals who commit the criminal behavior would commit a different type of criminal behavior if given different opportunities. Whether an unethical person becomes a white-collar criminal or a street criminal depends not on their ethics, but their economic position.

WHAT IS YOUR OPINION?

one executive was asked whether he knew that his conduct was illegal.* He replied, "Illegal, yes, but not criminal." Geis also reported that during the punishment phase of the trial, one attorney for an executive argued that his client should not be confined with criminals.

White-collar criminals do not see themselves as criminals. They continue to classify themselves as merely businesspersons. Thus, despite their criminal activity, they see themselves as noncriminals.

Cognitive Dimensions of Opportunity

According to Benson and Simpson, the world of business is imbued with a set of values and ideologies that are used to define illegal business activities in favorable terms. According to the two researchers, business people follow norms, customs, and precepts that are balanced between convention and crime, and businesspersons who help white-collar offenders symbolically construct activities in ways that make illegal behavior seem acceptable. The technique is similar to that used by juvenile delinquents denying

---

* Gilbert Geis. (1977). "The heavy electrical equipment antitrust cases of 1961." In: Gilbert Geis and Robert Meier (Eds.). *White Collar Crime: Offenses in Business, Politics, and the Professions.* New York: Free Press. Pages 117–132.

responsibility. White-collar criminals know that they are doing wrong but do not see themselves as directly responsible for the act or its consequences.*

Structural Dimensions of Opportunity

The structural dimensions of opportunity refer to the fact that in many white-collar crime situations, there is an excellent chance that the criminal conduct will not be detected. Unlike the street criminal who robs a local convenient store, the white-collar criminal's acts have a high probability of not being detected.

The opportunity to commit financial crimes is also available to the white-collar criminal. The average street criminal is never entrusted with other people's money, and therefore, he or she cannot commit embezzlement or other financial crimes. It is often stated that a person cannot embezzle from you unless you trust that person with your financial assets. When Cliff Roberson served as a board member of a federal credit union, this fact was emphasized constantly by security experts. Since no one trusts the street criminal, he or she cannot embezzle from others.

Normalization of Deviance

There is a difference between the normalization of deviance and the neutralization of deviance. When offenders use justifications that neutralize their criminal conduct, they understand that their behavior is not acceptable, except in their case, they neutralize it. For example, the businessperson cheats on his or her income taxes because everyone else is doing it. Cliff Roberson once taught a class in criminology in a federal prison. Most of the offenders were there for either drug or white-collar crimes. During the class, as we discussed the various theories of why people commit crimes, he would ask a student (who was a prisoner) what theory he accepted. After the student answered, he would then ask the student if it applied in his case. Every time, the students would explain why it did not apply in their case. In one example, one prisoner who was serving time for auto theft stated that he knew it was wrong to steal cars, but that he did it because none of the automobile dealers would give him a job as a mechanic.

When we talk about the normalization of deviance, we are referring to those situations where because of self-deception, the individuals do not feel that they are violating the law. A corporate executive in an investment firm may make risky and possible illegal investments in order to provide his investors with a higher rate of return on their money. Suppose that the executive had been taking these risks for a long time without any adverse effects; then it could be concluded that he had normalized his actions and therefore considered them to be normal.

---

* Michael Benson and Sally Simpson. (2009). *White-Collar Crime: An Opportunity Perspective*. New York: Routledge. Pages 43–45.

THE CHALLENGER DISASTER AND THE
PROCESS OF NORMALIZING DEVIANCE

According to researchers Michael Benson and Sally Simpson (2009), the Challenger Space Shuttle disaster is an example of the process of normalizing deviance.

In 1986, the Space Shuttle *Challenger* exploded shortly after take-off. The officials at the National Space and Aeronautics Administration knew that the launch was risky and they had been warned about the possibilities of a catastrophic event, but they launched the shuttle anyway because of the pressures to keep the space program on schedule. Because of faulty O-rings in the solid rocket booster, the rings failed in cold weather. The company that had manufactured the solid rocket boosters had argued against the launch. The initial investigation after the disaster concluded that the launch had violated safety rules.

EXCERPTS FROM OFFICIAL REPORT

The consensus of the Commission and participating investigative agencies is that the loss of the Space Shuttle Challenger was caused by a failure in the joint between the two lower segments of the right Solid Rocket Motor. The specific failure was the destruction of the seals that are intended to prevent hot gases from leaking through the joint during the propellant burn of the rocket motor. The evidence assembled by the Commission indicates that no other element of the Space Shuttle system contributed to this failure…

FINDINGS OF PRESIDENT'S COMMISSION

1. The Commission concluded that there was a serious flaw in the decision making process leading up to the launch of flight 51-L. A well structured and managed system emphasizing safety would have flagged the rising doubts about the Solid Rocket Booster joint seal. Had these matters been clearly stated and emphasized in the flight readiness process in terms reflecting the views of most of the Thiokol engineers and at least some of the Marshall engineers, it seems likely that the launch of 51-L might not have occurred when it did.
2. The waiving of launch constraints appears to have been at the expense of flight safety. There was no system which made

it imperative that launch constraints and waivers of launch constraints be considered by all levels of management.

3. The Commission is troubled by what appears to be a propensity of management at Marshall to contain potentially serious problems and to attempt to resolve them internally rather than communicate them forward. This tendency is altogether at odds with the need for Marshall to function as part of a system working toward successful flight missions, interfacing and communicating with the other parts of the system that work to the same end.

4. The Commission concluded that the Thiokol Management reversed its position and recommended the launch of 51-L, at the urging of Marshall and contrary to the views of its engineers in order to accommodate a major customer.

SOURCES:

The Presidential Commission on the Space Shuttle Challenger Accident Report. (June 6, 1986). Pages 40, 70–81. Available online at http://science.ksc.nasa.gov/shuttle/missions/51-l/docs/ rogers-commission [Accessed on October 1, 2012].

Michael L. Benson and Sally S. Simpson. (2009). *White-Collar Crime: An Opportunity Perspective.* New York: Routledge. Pages 147–149.

Bribery in Foreign Countries

In 2012, U.S. citizens were shocked to learn that a major retail store chain in the United States was accused of bribing officials in Mexico for favorable treatment to secure necessary permits in that country. The conduct of the chain's executives, as reported in the media, probably constituted violations of the Foreign Corrupt Practices Act (FCPA).

The FCPA prohibits the bribing of foreign officials. The act requires that publicly traded companies are to maintain accurate books and records, and to have a system of internal controls sufficient to prevent and provide reasonable assurances that transactions in foreign countries are in conformity with generally acceptable accounting principles.

The FCPA prohibits illegal conduct anywhere in the world by directors and officers of publicly traded companies. This prohibition extends to employees and stockholders and in certain circumstances to third parties.

The antibribery provisions of the act generally prohibit any offer, payment, or promise to pay or give anything of value to any foreign official, foreign political party, or candidate for public office that is intended to influence any act or decision or to assist in obtaining or retaining business. The term "anything of value" includes cash, property, medical supplies, or other items of value. The term "foreign official" is also broadly defined and can include any officer or employee of a foreign government or any department thereof.

The FCPA also prohibits the payment of bribes to any person while knowing that some or all of the payment will be used to directly or indirectly bribe foreign officials or other prohibited recipients. The act provides that the word "knowing" includes the willful blindness to the high probability of bribery.

There are three defenses provided under the FCPA. First is that the conduct falls within the "routine government action" exception to the FCPA. The FCPA routine government action does not apply to payments designed to expedite or secure the performance of an action. The second defense is when the payment is lawful under the laws of the foreign country. The third exception is when the payment is reasonable and a bona fide expenditure such as authorized travel or lawful lobbying.

The Securities and Exchange Commission is generally tasked with the duties of monitoring the requirements under the FCPA, and prosecution of violations are generally handled by the U.S. Department of Justice.

Summary

- It is not necessary to argue the importance of white-collar crime's devastating financial and physical effects. The task is seen now as one to develop better ways to control and prevent white-collar crimes.
- In order to reduce white-collar crime, we must first identify the specific opportunity structures associated with the offenses we wish to prevent and we must identify the features of the settings that allow the crime to occur.
- There are three major theories to accomplish this task: routine activity theory, crime pattern theory, and situational crime prevention theory. The three theories address how crime opportunities are formed by immediate environments and then discovered and evaluated by potential offenders.
- When examining the opportunity structure of white-collar crime, it is helpful to distinguish between crime and criminality. Crime is an event, something that happens in time and space, and criminality is used to refer to a behavioral disposition, a disposition that is manifested by behaving in ways that are labeled by society as criminal.

- Whether criminality is expressed as crime depends on situational factors external to the individual, most notably the opportunity structures that a potential offender confronts in daily life.
- The opportunity structures are different and important when developing a strategy to combat it. As with any type of crime, the opportunity structure must be present before a crime can be committed.
- It is unlikely that a homeless person has the opportunity structure to commit a white-collar crime.
- Another important issue in trying to prevent white-collar crime is that often it is difficult to determine the temporal and geographic specificity of the crime.
- The psychological and cognitive health of white-collar criminals is an area in which there has been little research. There is evidence that white-collar offenders are unwilling to define their behavior as criminal and that many have a sense of superiority over their victims.
- The routine activity theory was developed by Cohen and Felson in 1979 when they were trying to find a reason for high urban crime rates.
- The basic theory stated that criminal events originate in the routines of everyday life.
- The researchers stated that there must be three elements involved in order for a crime to be committed: a motivated offender, a suitable target, and the lack of guardianship.
- The principal assumption of the theory is that three elements must be in place to create the necessary conditions for crime: a target, a motivated offender, and a common place where the offender can gain access to the target.
- The routine activity theory is controversial among sociologists who believe in the social causes of crime. The theory is based in the classical school of criminology, in that criminals decide that to commit the crime or not commit it is based on whether it will be beneficial to them.
- The crime pattern theory was developed by Canadian environmental criminologists Pat and Paul Brantingham; the theory exerts the strongest influence on geographic profiling. It suggests that crime sites and opportunities are not random.
- Using the principles of routine activity theory, the crime pattern theory (also labeled as the offender search theory) contends that offenders become aware of criminal opportunities as they engage in their normal legitimate activities. Under this theory, offenders tend to find their targets in familiar places. Therefore, criminal opportunities that are close to the "areas" that an offender moves through during their everyday activities are more likely to be taken advantage of by the offender than opportunities in areas less familiar to the offender.

- Situational crime prevention theory is based on the concepts that to prevent crime, we need to reduce the opportunities for criminals to commit crime, change the criminal's ideas about whether they can get away with the crime, and make it harder and more risky for them to commit crime.
- Before you can commit a successful crime, you must have the opportunity. The fact that individuals carry money creates the opportunity for criminals to rob them. If the criminal knew that an individual had no money, it is unlikely that the criminal would rob that individual. In examining white-collar crimes, it is noted that the crimes occur when there are occupational opportunities.
- "Identity" may be defined as the distinctive characteristic belonging to any given individual, or shared by all members of a particular social category or group.
- In the area of white-collar crime, when we refer to an individual's sense of identity, generally, we are referring to the fact that most white-collar criminals do not identify themselves with criminal activity and that they do not see themselves as criminals.
- According to researchers, business people follow norms, customs, and precepts that are balanced between convention and crime.
- The structural dimensions of opportunity refer to the fact that in many white-collar crime situations, there is an excellent chance that the criminal conduct will not be detected. Unlike the street criminal who robs a local convenient store, the white-collar criminal's acts have a high probability of not being detected.
- There is a difference between the normalization of deviance and the neutralization of deviance. When offenders use justifications that neutralize their criminal conduct, they understand that their behavior is not acceptable, except in their case, they neutralize it.
- When we talk about the normalization of deviance, we are referring to those situations where because of self-deception, the individuals do not feel that they are violating the law.

QUESTIONS IN REVIEW

1. Explain why white-collar criminals do not see themselves as criminals.
2. Explain the concepts involved in the situational crime prevention theory.
3. Explain the crime pattern theory.
4. Explain the differences between the situational crime prevention theory and the crime pattern theory.
5. Explain the meaning of the phrase "normalization of deviance."
6. Distinguish between the cognitive dimensions of opportunity and the structural dimensions of opportunity.

Laws That Govern the Securities Industry

4

Chapter Objectives

After studying this chapter, the reader should be able to do the following:

- Explain the federal government's approach to securities fraud.
- Explain what constitutes securities fraud.
- Summarize the duties of the Securities and Exchange Commission.
- Describe the key federal statutes that attempt to prevent securities fraud.
- Discuss the relationship between securities fraud and organized crime.
- Discuss the importance of truthful disclosure in combating securities fraud.

Introduction

In this chapter, we will focus on securities related crime or securities fraud. Also known as stock fraud or investment fraud, securities fraud is the violation of the rules of investing and trading to cheat or take advantage of public investors. This is a serious white-collar crime in which a person or company, such as a stockbroker, brokerage firm, corporation, or investment bank, misrepresents information that investors use to make decisions. In almost all cases, the crimes involve securities fraud. It can also be committed by independent individuals (such as by engaging in insider trading). The types of misrepresentation involved in this crime include providing false information, withholding key information, offering bad advice, and offering or acting on inside information. The Securities and Exchange Commission (SEC) is the principal law enforcement agency that regulates securities fraud.

The SEC fraud prevention theory is based on the concept of truthful disclosure. According to the approach, if investors understand the facts and that all essential disclosures are provided to them, they will make their own decision as to the wisdom of investing in a selected security. Included in this chapter are excerpts from SEC officials' statements to the U.S. Congress. The selected excerpts should help the reader understand the issues involved in combating securities fraud as well as the involvement of organized crime in the area.

FBI'S FINANCIAL CRIME VICTIMS BROCHURE

[This is a copy of a brochure that the Federal Bureau of Investigation publishes on financial crime.]

THE IMPACT OF FINANCIAL CRIME

The impact of a financial crime may have serious and long-term consequences. Individuals who experience financial crimes report feeling isolated, hopeless, and betrayed, but there is help. The FBI realizes that you will most likely have questions about how your case will be handled and what services and information will be available to you.

HOW WILL I OBTAIN INFORMATION?

Federal crime victims have a number of rights during their participation in the criminal justice system, including the right to limited information about the status of the case. You may either receive periodic updates through our Victim Notification System or you may contact the case agent or agency's Victim Specialists on an ongoing basis.

It is very important that you report any address changes you have during the criminal investigation, prosecution, and incarceration of the defendant.

THE INVESTIGATION

Although the months or years ahead may be difficult for you and your family, cooperation is important to ensure that justice is fully achieved. The investigation of a possible financial crime can be lengthy and complex and often involves several law enforcement agencies. Some investigations may involve hundreds of victims in one case. During this process, your case agent or Victim Specialist will remain your [principal] contact. If you learn of or remember anything additional about the crime, contact the case agent. Due to the sensitive nature of an ongoing federal investigation, information available to you will be limited. For information on your rights during the investigation, please refer to the FBI Help for Victims of Crime brochure.

WHAT CAN I DO ABOUT MY FINANCIAL LOSSES?

Collect and save all documents and electronic transmissions that directly relate to your loss, including expenses incurred during your participation in the investigation or prosecution. If an arrest is made and a conviction is obtained, the judge may require the offender to pay restitution. This means the sentencing judge may order a convicted defendant to pay identified victims for certain losses suffered as a result of the crime. You may be asked to provide verification of your loss amount.

In addition, some losses may be tax-deductible. Tax laws are complicated, so consult a qualified tax adviser or the Internal Revenue Service to see if your losses qualify.

Finally, if you believe the fraud perpetrator had assets, you may be able to recover losses through a civil lawsuit. Contact your state or local bar association for the names of attorneys who specialize in this area of law to determine if your case is appropriate for civil action. Remedies may include, but are not limited to, compensation provided from reparations funds and forfeiture. Also, if small amounts of money are involved (the amount depends on local law), you may be able to bring a claim in small claims court in the county in which the crime occurred.

WILL I GET MY MONEY BACK?

Victims often want to know if they will get their money back through restitution. Many federal crimes require payment of restitution; however, the reality is that convicted defendants with no money or limited potential to make money may be unlikely to ever make meaningful restitution, particularly in financial crime cases with many victims.

Restitution may also be awarded to the victim's estate in the event of the victim's death.

Be assured that the federal government will work earnestly to ensure that any assets owned by a sentenced defendant can be considered for payment of court-ordered restitution. An order of restitution is enforceable for 20 years from the date a criminal judgment requiring restitution to be filed or for 20 years after the convicted defendant's release from prison.

To ensure the proper receipt of any ordered restitution, it is especially important that you notify your Victim Assistance Program or the Victim Notification System of any changes in contact information.

WHAT CAN I DO TO ADDRESS FINANCIAL AND CREDIT PROBLEMS?

Some victims have losses so severe that they are unable to meet current financial obligations. If personal information was stolen, credit may be affected which can impact your immediate financial situation. In both of these situations, consider these options:

Contact creditors and/or a nonprofit credit counseling service to help you to reduce or modify your payments or help you to limit access to your accounts.

Submit a written statement to local and national credit reporting agencies about your victimization. Provide supporting documentation such as a copy of the criminal judgment.

Be alert. Many fraud artists contact victims claiming they can help recover your losses for a fee or may sell your name to others committing financial scams. If called, contact the case agent or your state's Consumer Protection Agency to verify the company's legitimacy.

Many victims feel anger, resentment, frustration, shame, embarrassment, and guilt, as well as fear for financial security and personal safety. Some victims find it helpful to seek services from a counselor, clergy member, or advocacy program. Contact your Victim Specialist for resources in your area.

WEBLINKS AND PHONE NUMBERS

FTC, Federal Trade Commission: a noninvestigative agency, the FTC collects information about ongoing scams to share with law enforcement.

FTC Consumer Response Center | 1-877-382-4357 http://www.ftc.gov

FTC Identity Theft Hotline | 1-877-438-4338 http://www.consumer.gov/idtheft

FTC Do Not Call Registry | 1-800-275-8777 http://www.donotcall.gov

Source: FBI website http://www.fbi.gov/stats-services/victim_assistance/fincrime_vic.

Insider Trading

Insider trading is the buying or selling of a security by someone who has access to material, nonpublic information about the security. For example, the president of XYZ Company, a company that is traded on the New York Stock Exchange, realizes that his company is in serious financial trouble and will seek bankruptcy within the next few days. This information is not known to the public. The president sells all of his stock in his company before the public is aware that the company is in serious financial trouble. In this situation, the president of the company has committed the crime of insider trading. In a reverse situation, if the company has discovered a new process that will create a large profit for the company and thus increase the value of

MARTHA STEWART AND THE SEC

Martha Stewart was in the news for several months in 2011 because the U.S. Securities and Exchange Commission contended that she was informed by her friend Sam Waksal that his company ImClone's cancer drug had been rejected by the Food and Drug Administration before this information was made public. The rejection was a huge blow to the drug company, and the price of its stock declined significantly. Martha Stewart was not financially hurt because she had her broker sell her 4,000 shares before this news was made public. If the contentions of the SEC were correct, then Martha Stewart committed the crime of insider trading. However, Stewart was convicted in a federal court for obstructing justice and lying to the government about a superbly timed stock sale. Stewart, who averted more than $51,000 in losses by selling when she did, was not charged with insider trading; instead, she and her broker were accused of lying about the transaction and altering records to support the alleged cover story.

If Stewart was in fact guilty of insider trading, it makes you wonder why a woman of considerable wealth would risk so much to save only $51,000.

Insider trading is only illegal when a person bases their trade of stocks in a public company on information that the public does not know. It is illegal to trade your own stock in a company based on this information, but it is also illegal to give someone that information, a tip, so they can trade their stock.

the company's stock, the president should not, based on this inside information, purchase large numbers of his company's stock.

Insider trading can be illegal or legal depending on when the insider makes the trade: it is illegal when the material information is still nonpublic—trading while having special knowledge is unfair to other investors who do not have access to such knowledge. Illegal insider trading therefore includes tipping others when you have any sort of nonpublic information. Directors are not the only ones who have the potential to be convicted of insider trading. People such as brokers and even family members can be guilty.

Insider trading is legal once the material information has been made public, at which time the insider has no direct advantage over other investors. The SEC, however, still requires all insiders to report all their transactions. So, as insiders have an insight into the workings of their company, it may be wise for an investor to look at these reports to see how insiders are legally trading their stock.

Securities Act of 1933

The Securities Act of 1933* is often referred to as the "truth in securities" law; the Securities Act of 1933 has two basic objectives:

- Require that investors receive financial and other significant information concerning securities being offered for public sale.
- Prohibit deceit, misrepresentations, and other fraud in the sale of securities.

The primary methods to accomplish the goals are the requirements of the disclosure of important financial information through the registration of securities. This information enables investors to make informed judgments about whether or not to purchase a company's securities. While the SEC requires that the information provided be accurate, the act does not guarantee it. Investors who purchase securities and suffer losses have recovery rights if they can establish that there was incomplete or inaccurate disclosure of important or required information.

Securities that are regulated by the act must be registered before they can be sold in the United States. The registration process requires that companies' files provide essential facts while minimizing the burden and expense of complying with the law. In general, registration forms call for the following:

- A description of the company's properties and business
- A description of the security to be offered for sale
- Information about the management of the company
- Financial statements certified by independent accountants

Registration statements and prospectuses become public shortly after filing with the SEC. If filed by U.S. domestic companies, the statements are accessible at http://www.sec.gov. Registration statements are subject to examination for compliance with disclosure requirements.

Not all offerings of securities must be registered with the Commission. Some exemptions from the registration requirement include the following:

- Private offerings to a limited number of persons or institutions
- Offerings of limited size
- Intrastate offerings
- Securities of municipal, state, and federal governments

---

* The full text of this Act is available at http://www.sec.gov/about/laws/sa33.pdf.

By exempting many small offerings from the registration process, the SEC contends that it seeks to foster capital formation by lowering the cost of offering securities to the public.

Securities Exchange Act of 1934

By the Securities Exchange Act of 1934,* Congress created the SEC. The Act empowers the SEC with broad authority over all aspects of the securities industry. This includes the power to register, regulate, and oversee brokerage firms, transfer agents, and clearing agencies. The SEC also oversees the nation's securities self-regulatory organizations (SROs). The various stock exchanges, such as the New York Stock Exchange and the American Stock Exchange, are included in the designation of SROs. The National Association of Securities Dealers, which operates the NASDAQ system, is also considered as an SRO.

The Act also identifies and prohibits certain types of conduct in the markets and provides the SEC with disciplinary powers over regulated entities and persons associated with them. In addition, the SEC has the authority to and requires periodic reporting of information by companies with publicly traded securities.

Corporate Reporting

Companies with more than $10 million in assets whose securities are held by more than 500 owners must file annual and other periodic reports. These reports are available to anyone through the SEC's EDGAR database.

Proxy Solicitations

The Securities Exchange Act requires the disclosure in materials used to solicit shareholders' votes in annual or special meetings held for the election of directors and the approval of other corporate actions. The information, generally included in proxy materials, must be filed with the Commission in advance of any solicitation to ensure compliance with the disclosure rules. Solicitations, whether by management or shareholder groups, must disclose all important facts concerning the issues on which holders are asked to vote.

---

* The full text of this Act can be read at http://www.sec.gov/about/laws/sea34.pdf.

Tender Offers

The Securities Exchange Act requires disclosure of important information by anyone seeking to acquire more than 5% of a company's securities by direct purchase or by a tender offer. Such an offer is often extended in an effort to gain control of the company. This required information allows shareholders to make informed decisions on these critical corporate events.

Registration of Exchanges, Associations, and Others

The Act requires a variety of market participants to register with the SEC, including exchanges, brokers and dealers, transfer agents, and clearing agencies. Registration for these organizations involves filing disclosure documents. In addition, the documents must be updated on a regular basis.

Sarbanes–Oxley Act of 2002

The Sarbanes–Oxley Act of 2002 mandates a number of reforms to enhance corporate responsibility, enhance financial disclosures, and combat corporate and accounting fraud. The Act created the Public Company Accounting Oversight Board, also known as the PCAOB, to oversee the activities of the auditing profession. The full text of the Act is available at http://uscode.house.gov/download/pls/15C98.txt. Links to all SEC rulemaking and reports issued under the Sarbanes–Oxley Act may be obtained at http://www.sec.gov/spotlight/sarbanes-oxley.htm.

Dodd–Frank Wall Street Reform and Consumer Protection Act of 2010

The Dodd–Frank Wall Street Reform and Consumer Protection Act was designed to reshape the U.S. regulatory system in a number of areas, including but not limited to consumer protection, trading restrictions, credit ratings, regulation of financial products, corporate governance and disclosure, and transparency. The full text of the Act is available at http://www.sec.gov/about/laws/wallstreetreform-cpa.pdf.

Investment Company Act of 1940

The Investment Company Act of 1940 regulates the organization of companies, including mutual funds, that engage primarily in investing, reinvesting, and trading in securities and whose own securities are offered to the investing public. The regulation is designed to minimize conflicts of interest that arise in these complex operations. The Act requires these companies to disclose their financial condition and investment policies to investors when stock is initially sold and, subsequently, on a regular basis. The focus of this Act was on disclosure to the investing public of information about the fund and its investment objectives, as well as on investment company structure and operations. It is important to remember that the Act does not permit the SEC to directly supervise the investment decisions or activities of these companies or judge the merits of their investments. The full text of this Act is available at http://www.sec.gov/about/laws/ica40.pdf.

Investment Advisers Act of 1940

The Investment Advisers Act of 1940 regulates investment advisers. With certain exceptions, this Act requires that firms or sole practitioners compensated for advising others about securities investments must register with the SEC and conform to regulations designed to protect investors. Since the Act was amended in 1996 and 2010, generally, only advisers who have at least $100 million of assets under management or advise a registered investment company must register with the Commission. The full text of this Act is available at http://www.sec.gov/about/laws/iaa40.pdf.

Trust Indenture Act of 1939

The Trust Indenture Act of 1939 applies to debt securities such as bonds, debentures, and notes that are offered for public sale. Even though such securities may be registered under the Securities Act, they may not be offered for sale to the public unless a formal agreement between the issuer of bonds and the bondholder, known as the trust indenture, conforms to the standards of this Act. The full text of this Act is available at http://www.sec.gov/about/laws/tia39.pdf.

JOBS Act of 2012

The Jumpstart Our Business Startups Act (the JOBS Act) was enacted on April 5, 2012. Portions of the Act modified the disclosure requirements that were in place for the protection of investors. In this discussion, only those parts of the JOBS Act that modified the disclosure requirements are discussed. The primary provisions include the following:

- Increase the number of shareholders a company may have before being required to register its common stock with the SEC and become a publicly reporting company.
- Provide a new exemption from the requirement to register public offerings with the SEC, for certain types of small offerings, subject to several conditions. This exemption would allow use of the internet "funding portals" registered with the government, the use of which in private placements is currently extremely limited by current law.
- Relieve certain kinds of companies, which the bill calls "emerging growth companies," from certain regulatory and disclosure requirements in the registration statement they originally file when they go public, and for a period of five years after that. The most significant relief provided is from obligations imposed by Section 404 of the Sarbanes–Oxley Act and related rules and regulations. Currently, new public companies have a two-year phase-in, so this bill would extend that by an additional three years.
- Lift the current ban on "general solicitation" and advertising in specific kinds of private placements of securities.

The act was opposed by some securities regulators and consumer and investor advocates. Among the complaints were that the loosening of investment protections would expose small and inexperienced investors to fraud.

Does the government overregulate the sale of securities? Please read the comments of the SEC in its testimony before the U.S. Senate in 2012 regarding investor protection, which are included in the Crime Reporter Box.

Foreign Corrupt Practices Act

The Foreign Corrupt Practices Act (FCPA) generally prohibits the bribing of foreign officials. The FCPA also requires publicly traded companies to maintain accurate books and records, and to have a system of internal controls sufficient to provide reasonable assurances that transactions are executed and assets are accounted for in accordance with management's authorization, and recorded as necessary to permit the preparation of financial statements in conformity with generally accepted accounting principles (GAAP). The FCPA can apply to prohibited conduct anywhere in the world, even, in certain circumstances, where there is no U.S. territorial connection, and extends to publicly traded companies ("issuers") and their officers, directors,

INVESTOR PROTECTION IS NEEDED FOR
TRUE CAPITAL FORMATION

Does the SEC overregulate the securities industry? To provide information on this issue, consider the testimony of the SEC Commissioner
before the U.S. Senate.

Commissioner Luis A. Aguilar
U.S. Securities and Exchange Commission

[Excerpts from SEC Commissioner's testimony before the U.S. Senate
on March 16, 2012.]

At issue was the question as to whether the SEC overregulates the
securities industry. The Jumpstart Our Business Startups Act (the
"JOBS Act") was enacted on April 5, 2012. The act reduced the disclosure requirements of the SEC for certain disclosures before the advertising of securities for sale. A significant number of researchers contended
that the proposed changes would increase securities fraud. One of those
persons was then Commissioner Luis Aguilar.

Last week, the House of Representatives passed H.R. 3606, the
"Jumpstart Our Business Startups Act." It is clear to me that H.R. 3606
in its current form weakens or eliminates many regulations designed
to safeguard investors. I must voice my concerns because as an SEC
Commissioner, I cannot sit idly by when I see potential legislation that
could harm investors. This bill seems to impose tremendous costs and
potential harm on investors with little to no corresponding benefit.

H.R. 3606 concerns me for two important reasons. First, the bill
would seriously hurt investors by reducing transparency and investor
protection and, in turn, make securities law enforcement more difficult.
That is bad for ordinary Americans and bad for the American economy.
Investors are the source of capital needed to create jobs and expand
businesses. True capital formation and economic growth require investors to have both confidence in the capital markets and access to the
information needed to make good investment decisions.

Second, I share the concerns expressed by many others that the bill
rests on faulty premises. Supporters claim that the bill would improve
capital formation in the United States by reducing the regulatory burden on capital raising. However, there is significant research to support
the conclusion that disclosure requirements and other capital markets
regulations enhance, rather than impede, capital formation, and that
regulatory compliance costs are not a principal cause of the decline in
IPO activity over the past decade.

Moreover, nothing in the bill requires or even incentivizes issuers to use any capital that may be raised to expand their businesses or create jobs in the U.S.

Professor John Coates of Harvard Law School has testified that proposals of the type incorporated into H.R. 3606 could actually hurt job growth.

While [the proposals] have been characterized as promoting jobs and economic growth by reducing regulatory burdens and costs, it is better to understand them as changing…the balance that existing securities laws and regulations have struck between the transaction costs of raising capital, on the one hand, and the combined costs of fraud risk and asymmetric and unverifiable information, on the other hand. Importantly, fraud and asymmetric information not only have effects on fraud victims, but also on the cost of capital itself. Investors rationally increase the price they charge for capital if they anticipate fraud risk or do not have or cannot verify relevant information. Antifraud laws and disclosure and compliance obligations coupled with enforcement mechanisms reduce the cost of capital.

… Whether the proposals will in fact increase job growth depends on how intensively they will lower offer costs, how extensively new offerings will take advantage of the new means of raising capital, how much more often fraud can be expected to occur as a result of the changes, how serious the fraud will be, and how much the reduction in information verifiability will be as a result of the changes.

Thus, the proposals could not only generate front-page scandals, but reduce the very thing they are being promoted to increase: job growth.

Similarly, Professor Jay Ritter of the University of Florida has testified before the Senate banking committee that such proposals could in fact reduce capital formation:

In thinking about the bills, one should keep in mind that the law of unintended consequences will never be repealed. It is possible that, by making it easier to raise money privately, creating some liquidity without being public, restricting the information that stockholders have access to, restricting the ability of public market shareholders to constrain managers after investors contribute capital, and driving out independent research, the net effects of these bills might be to reduce capital formation and/or the number of small [emerging growth company] IPOs.

As drafted, H.R. 3606 would have significant detrimental impacts on the U.S. securities regulatory regime, including the following:

First, the bill will reduce publicly available information by exempting "emerging growth companies" from certain disclosure and other requirements currently required under the Federal securities laws. The bill's definition of "emerging growth company" would include every issuer with less than $1 billion in annual revenues (other than large accelerated filers and companies that have issued over $1 billion in debt over a three-year period) for five years after the company's first registered public offering.

It is estimated that this threshold would pick up 98% of IPOs and a large majority of U.S. public companies for that five-year period.

An emerging growth company would only have to provide two years (rather than three years) of audited financial statements, and would not have to provide selected financial data for any period prior to the earliest audited period presented in connection with its initial public offering. It would also be exempt from the requirements for "Say-on-Pay" voting and certain compensation-related disclosure. Such reduced financial disclosure may make it harder for investors to evaluate companies in this category by obscuring the issuer's track record and material trends.

"Emerging growth companies" would also be exempt from complying with any new or revised financial accounting standards (other than accounting standards that apply equally to private companies), and from some new standards that may be adopted by the PCAOB. Such wholesale exemptions may result in inconsistent accounting rules that could damage financial transparency, making it difficult for investors to compare emerging companies with other companies in their industry. This could harm investors and, arguably, impede access to capital for emerging companies, as capital providers may not be confident that they have access to all the information they need to make good investment decisions about such companies.

Second, the bill would greatly increase the number of record holders a company may have before it is required to publish annual and quarterly reports. Currently, companies with more than 500 shareholders of record are required to register with the SEC pursuant to Section 12(g) of the Securities Exchange Act and provide investors with regular financial reports. H.R. 3606 would expand that threshold to 2000 record holders (provided that, in the case of any issuer other than a community bank, the threshold would also be triggered by 500 nonaccredited investors). Moreover, the bill would exclude from such counts any shareholders that acquire securities through crowd funding initiatives and those that acquire securities as eligible employee compensation. Thus, a company could have a virtually unlimited number of record stockholders, without being subject to the disclosure rules applicable to public companies. This effect is magnified by the fact that the reporting threshold only counts record holders, excluding the potentially unlimited number of beneficial owners who hold their shares in "street name" with banks and brokerage companies and thus are not considered record holders.

This provision of the bill raises concerns because it could significantly reduce the number of companies required to file financial and other information. Such information is critical to investors in determining how to value securities in our markets. Regular financial reporting enhances the allocation of capital to productive companies in our economy.

Third, the bill would exempt "emerging growth companies" from Section 404(b) of the Sarbanes–Oxley Act, which requires the independent audit of a company's internal financial controls. Section 404(b) currently applies only to companies with a market capitalization above $75 million; companies below that threshold have never been subject to the internal controls audit requirement and were exempted from such requirement in the Dodd–Frank Act. The internal controls audit was established following the accounting scandals at Enron, WorldCom, and other companies, and is intended to make financial reporting more reliable. Indeed, a report last year by Audit Analytics noted that the larger public companies, known as accelerated filers, that are subject to Section 404(b), experienced a 5.1% decline in financial statement restatements from 2009 to 2010; while nonaccelerated filers, that are not subject to Section 404(b), experienced a 13.8% increase in such restatements.

A study by the SEC's Office of the Chief Accountant recommended that existing investor protections within Section 404(b) be retained for issuers with a market capitalization above $75 million. With the passage of H.R. 3606, an important mechanism for enhancing the reliability of financial statements would be lost for most public companies during the first five years of public trading.

Fourth, the bill would benefit Wall Street, at the expense of Main Street, by overriding protections that currently require a separation between research analysts and investment bankers who work in the same firm and impose a quiet period on analyst reports by the underwriters of an IPO. These rules are designed to protect investors from potential conflicts of interests. The research scandals of the dot-com era and the collapse of the dot-com bubble buried the IPO market for years. Investors won't return to the IPO market, if they don't believe they can trust it.

Fifth, H.R. 3606 would fundamentally change U.S. securities law, by permitting unlimited offers and sales of securities under Rule 506 of

Regulation D (which exempts certain nonpublic offerings from registration under the Securities Act), provided only that all purchasers are "accredited investors." The bill would specifically permit general solicitation and general advertising in connection with such offerings, obliterating the distinction between public and private offerings.

This provision may be unnecessary. A recent report by the SEC's Division of Risk, Strategy and Financial Innovation confirms that Regulation D has been effective in meeting the capital formation needs of small businesses, with a median offering size of $1,000,000 and at least 37,000 unique offerings since 2009. Regulation D offerings surpassed $900 billion in 2010. The data does not indicate that users of Regulation D have been seriously hampered by the prohibition on general solicitation and advertising.

I share the concerns expressed by many that this provision of H.R. 3606 would be a boon to boiler room operators, Ponzi schemers, bucket shops, and garden variety fraudsters, by enabling them to cast a wider net, and making securities law enforcement much more difficult. Currently, the SEC and other regulators may be put on notice of potential frauds by advertisements and Internet sites promoting "investment opportunities." H.R. 3606 would put an end to that tool. Moreover, since it is easier to establish a violation of the registration and prospectus requirements of the Securities Act than it is to prove fraud, such scams can often be shut down relatively quickly. H.R. 3606 would make it almost impossible to do so before the damage has been done and the money lost.

In addition, others have noted that the current definition of "accredited investor" may not be adequate and that the requirement that purchasers be accredited investors would provide limited protection. For example, an "accredited investor" retiree with $1 million in savings, who depends on that money for income in retirement, may easily fall prey for a "hot" offering that is continually hyped via the Internet or late night commercials.

These are just a few observations regarding H.R. 3606. It also includes other provisions that require substantial further analysis and review, including among other things the so-called crowd funding provisions.

The removal of investor protections in this bill are among the factors that have prompted serious concerns from the Council of Institutional Investors, AARP, the North American Securities Administrators Association, the Consumer Federation of America, and Americans for Financial Reform, among others.

employees, agents, and stockholders. Agents can include third-party agents, consultants, distributors, joint-venture partners, and others.

Antibribery Provisions

The antibribery provisions of the FCPA generally prohibit any offer, payment, promise, or authorization to pay money or anything of value to any foreign official, foreign political party, or candidate for public office that is intended to influence any act or decision in order to assist in obtaining or retaining business.

The term "anything of value" may include, among other things, cash, computer equipment, medical supplies, and vehicles.

The term "foreign official" is defined broadly and can include any officer or employee of a foreign government or any department, agency, or instrumentality thereof, or of a public international organization, or anyone acting on behalf of such government or department. For example, foreign officials would include foreign military officers in charge of procurement contracts, ministry-level officials, and officers and employees of government-owned or government-controlled entities.

The FCPA also prohibits bribes made to any person ("indirect bribes") while "knowing" that some or all of the payments will be used by the person, directly or indirectly, to bribe foreign officials or other prohibited recipients. In this context, "knowing" includes willful blindness to the high probability of bribery.

Enforcement of SEC Regulations

When there is a question as to the violation of a regulatory requirement, the SEC may issue an Order Instituting Proceedings. In the order, the Commission directs that an Administrative Law Judge conduct a public administrative proceeding to determine whether the allegations in the Order are true and to issue an Initial Decision in a specified period of time. Administrative Law Judges are independent judicial officers who in most cases conduct hearings and rule on allegations of securities law violations initiated by the Commission's Division of Enforcement. They conduct public hearings at locations throughout the United States in a manner similar to nonjury trials in the federal district courts. Among other actions, they issue subpoenas, conduct prehearing conferences, issue defaults, and rule on motions and the admissibility of evidence. At the conclusion of the public hearing, the parties submit proposed findings of fact and conclusions of law. The Administrative Law Judge prepares an Initial Decision that includes factual findings and legal conclusions, and, where appropriate, orders relief.

Robert S. Khuzami, Director, Division of Enforcement, U.S. Securities and Exchange Commission, in a public speech in New York City on June 1, 2011; discussed why it was difficult to prosecute financial crimes. Excerpts of his speech are as follows:

DEFINING THE PROBLEM

I just finished reading James Stewart's new book, *Tangled Web*. He details high-profile cases of lying, including those of Martha Stewart and Bernie Madoff. His conclusion?

There is an "epidemic of perjury and false statements occurring at the highest levels of business, politics, sports, and culture." Our own Jim Comey, former Deputy Attorney General, describes perjury and obstruction as "nearing crisis [levels]."

Stewart's book caused me to think about some of the episodes of questionable tactics by defense counsel in SEC investigations that have crossed my desk, and whether they are on the rise as well.

I'm not sure if there has been an increase, but too frequently we see defense counsel behavior that is questionable, or worse.

This includes, in no particular order:

- Multiple representations of witnesses with what appear to be adverse interests;
- Multiple witnesses represented by the same counsel who all adopt the same implausible explanation of events;
- Witnesses who answer "I don't recall" dozens and dozens of times in testimony, sometimes hundreds of times, including in response to questions about basic and uncontroverted facts documented in their own writings;
- Counsel signaling to clients during testimony; and
- Questionable tactics in document productions and internal investigations.

Now, this might be a more serious topic than I would otherwise choose, given the number of familiar faces in the audience and the kind words directed my way. But because you represent some of the best and brightest of the white-collar and securities enforcement defense bar, this is perhaps exactly the right audience for this issue.

None of you, I'm sure, would engage in the types of questionable conduct that I'll describe tonight. But, as knowledgeable and experienced members of the white-collar bar, I'd like to suggest that you carefully consider these issues so that you can, in the words of the immortal Obi Wan Kenobi, "use your powers for good, not evil."

I am most decidedly not dismissive of the crucial role played by defense counsel. Counsel are obligated to zealously defend and promote the interests of their clients, particularly when faced with the life-altering consequences of an SEC enforcement proceeding.

The fact that there are many defense lawyers who are zealous and aggressive, yet also successful with the SEC on behalf of their clients, demonstrates that we value effective counsel. Indeed, the opposing narrative provided to us by good defense lawyers helps us to make fair and informed enforcement decisions.

There also is the view that, as sovereign, the SEC should not be distracted by questionable defense practices, even those perilously close to the line, but rather should focus only on the objective evidence regardless of the externalities like the conduct of counsel.

That we should, in short, stay above the fray. That may be true, up to a point.

But the Enforcement Division cannot remain passive when confronted with conduct that frustrates our investigations.

It's difficult, and often impossible, for government to timely detect frauds perpetrated with management collusion, particularly in the early stages, and dilatory or obstructive conduct only increases that difficulty.

Such tactics also cause substantial delay and increased expense as our investigative plans must be altered or extended, and we have to seek other, more costly alternative ways to secure the evidence improperly denied to us.

More broadly, when the truth-seeking function of the investigative process is corrupted, the wrongdoers may not be held fully accountable for their unlawful conduct, and injustice results. Law-abiding citizens reconsider their own decisions to live within the law, or at a minimum become increasingly cynical and skeptical about the government's ability to deliver on its obligations under the social compact.

And clearly the last thing anyone needs, especially now, is more cynicism about any of our institutions, be they business, legal, or the SEC.

MULTIPLE REPRESENTATIONS

So what do we see in the Enforcement Division that concerns us?

Multiple representations remain fairly common, both involving the company and individual employees, as well as among groups of individuals.

In many cases, there is no problem presented by multiple representations—such as when one lawyer or one firm represents employees who are purely witnesses with no conflicting interests or material risk of legal exposure.

But we have seen cases where the same counsel represented both the company and over 30 employees, in another the company and over 20 individuals, all where there was a real potential that some of those persons faced material legal exposure.

There also are numerous examples of defense counsel representing multiple individuals with seemingly divergent interests.

We have seen counsel represent both the supervisor and the person he supervised in a "failure to supervise" case.

In another case, a lawyer represented himself, the alleged wrongdoer and the principal investor, who testified that he was not concerned that he had invested almost his whole net worth with an individual who had multiple felony convictions.

It is worth noting that the SEC's new Cooperation Program raises the stakes in multiple representation situations. The Program, announced by the Commission in January 2010, provides for reduced sanctions, or even no sanctions, in exchange for truthful and substantial assistance in an SEC investigation.

This increases the likelihood that one counsel cannot serve the interests of multiple clients, given the real benefits that could result from cooperation, such as one client testifying against another client represented by the same counsel.

In light of the potential for cooperation, we are taking a closer look at such multiple, seemingly adverse, representations. You will likely see an increase in concerns expressed by SEC staff in those situations.

LACK OF RECOLLECTION

The lack of recollection by witnesses in SEC testimony also is a significant issue. To be sure, a lawyer should discourage their clients from guessing in testimony, given the risk that a misstatement or speculation could be viewed as an admission.

Memories do fade over time, and sometimes the "I don't recall" response may be an appropriate response to staff questions about a document or event about which the witness has no knowledge or involvement.

But sometimes, witnesses display an apparent lack of recollection about nearly everything of any substance, including even the most basic facts, such as their own job responsibilities, that the failure of recollection lacks credibility.

For example, a former vice president of a company in an FCPA investigation, who approved and processed at least two of a subsidiary's requests for payments alleged to be bribes, had no recollection of his role or any of his responsibilities—to the point where he seemed unable to provide a credible description of the job he allegedly performed.

It is not unreasonable to draw the most negative inferences from the evidence when faced with this kind of implausible testimony.

In these situations, one is left to wonder whether witnesses are under instructions only to testify about those events that they recall with near certainty, even in response to questions inviting the witness to qualify the answer with whatever level of recollection the witness possesses. Under these circumstances, if the witness continues to insist that he or she has little or no recollection as to recent, significant events, the testimony is likely to be viewed with much skepticism.

Another fact pattern that makes us skeptical is when no amount of contemporaneous documents can refresh a witness's absence of recollection on seemingly inculpatory points, but that same witness offers specific, detailed and consistent memories on most every point potentially helpful to his defenses, often down to minute details.

Other times, the skepticism arises from a failure to acknowledge what is clear from the plain language of documents, the significance of the events under scrutiny, or the uniqueness of the circumstances under which the event occurred.

For example, in one case the witness refused to confirm that a particular person performed certain audit procedures even where their initials appear on the audit work papers, and where the events surrounding the audit were surely memorable, since they resulted in significant accounting issues that prompted a restatement, internal investigations and litigation.

In another case, an intelligent, highly educated, and accomplished executive claimed more than 500 times over two days of SEC testimony not to remember significant, high-intensity events in which he played a key role. He persisted in claiming a lack of recollection despite reviewing and being questioned about over 50 contemporaneous documents that he either authored or received. He similarly claimed that his recollection was not refreshed by approximately 15 hours of preparation with his counsel.

SIGNALING DURING TESTIMONY

Another source of concern is conduct during investigative testimony.

A witness who backtracks on a previous answer after her counsel's long speaking objection, or who returns to the testimony room after a break and repudiates her earlier testimony on an important point, could suggest inappropriate conduct by counsel.

I will recount one troubling episode. During the testimony of a former Assistant Controller at a Fortune 100 company, the SEC staff noticed that the witness's left foot was touching his counsel's right foot, and that defense counsel would subtly tap his client's foot with his own after certain questions were asked.

When that happened, the witness would invariably and immediately answer "I don't remember."

When confronted during the break, defense counsel unequivocally denied any impropriety.

When testimony resumed, counsel placed both of his feet under his chair. The witness—who had no idea what transpired during the break—returned his foot to the same place.

Following a question, the witness noticed that his counsel's foot wasn't next to his, so the witness moved his foot further towards counsel by a couple of inches.

Finding nothing, he moved it further still. Still finding nothing, he then began sliding it over in the obvious hope of eventually finding his counsel's guiding foot.

After extending his leg completely, he realized the guiding foot wasn't there to help him.

At this point, with his foot extended so far that he was almost doing a split—I may be admitting my age, but it reminds me of those pictures offered by President Nixon, which showed his assistant, Rosemary Woods, sprawled out like a contortionist, in a failed attempt by him to suggest how she could have mistakenly erased 18 and one-half minutes from one of the Watergate tapes.

Several weeks later, with another witness—this time, the Vice Chairman of a Fortune 100 company—and with a different, but just as well-known, defense attorney, we saw the same foot-tapping strategy.

PROBLEMS WITH DOCUMENTS

Other suspicions derive from the handling and production of documents. Let me emphasize that we understand the burden and cost of responding to one of our subpoenas. And we have encouraged the use of targeted subpoenas with narrower categories of requests where appropriate.

But there are certain practices that cause us concern.

There are productions that are not made until the eve of the witness's testimony, thus making full preparation for the testimony extremely difficult.

In addition, there seems to be an increasing phenomenon where lower-level associates or contract document reviewers are setting aside as potentially privileged an extremely large and overinclusive group of documents, including anything that is sensitive, for review by senior reviewers. Those senior reviewers then apparently fail to review them in a timely fashion or defer producing them for a long time as they search for some slender basis for claiming privilege—resulting in a last-minute supplemental production long after many witnesses have already testified.

This practice has the effect of depriving us of documents when we need them and requiring us to make a decision about whether to recall a witness.

In my view, fear of waiving privilege does not entirely explain this practice.

We have similar concerns about extended delays in the production of a privilege log, which thwarts our ability to assess the validity of privilege claims in a timely fashion, as well as long delays in sending preservation notices, such that relevant documents and back-up tapes are destroyed in the interim.

INTERNAL INVESTIGATIONS

Similar concerns arise in internal investigations.

Most defense counsels take seriously the role for which they are hired and perform thorough, deliberate, and wide-ranging independent investigations.

But we are seeing some that engage in questionable investigative tactics, including interviewing multiple witnesses at once, aggressively promoting exculpatory evidence while dismissing clear and identifiable red flags, scape-goating lower-level employees, and/or protecting senior management who have longstanding relationships with the counsel in question, and failing to acknowledge constraints placed on the scope of their inquiry.

In one investigation, counsel interviewed together the two senior executives with exposure in the investigation, and let one serve as document custodian with full and unsupervised access to all documents related to the investigation and the ability to destroy them. The company dismissed the senior executives on the eve of the report being made public, giving them large severance payments with unenforceable cooperation agreements, making documents in their possession unobtainable without lengthy MLAT procedures.

SEC RESPONSE—EXISTING TOOLS

What is the appropriate response for the SEC to situations where counsel appears to cross the line from aggressive practice to unethical or obstructive behavior?

Regardless of one's view of the frequency of this behavior, there is good reason for us to use fully the tools we have, in situations where the misconduct is clear.

Where we view multiple representations of adverse witnesses as creating an incurable conflict, and counsel does not take these concerns seriously, we can and will request that witnesses specifically confirm that they have been informed of the counsel's potential conflict of interest, and have willingly chosen to proceed with the engagement.

Where conflicts we raised later come to pass, we can and will decline to extend courtesies—for example, if counsel chooses to wait until the Wells notice to secure independent counsel for a client whose interests diverged from those of other clients, requests for extensions of time to respond may be cut back or denied.

We can and will do more to get senior supervisors involved when obstructive practices in testimony cannot be resolved by counsel and the examining SEC staff attorney.

We can and will increase the number of referrals under Rule 7(e) of the SEC Rules Relating to Investigations (17 CFR Sect. 203.7(e)) where appropriate. That section authorizes the Enforcement staff to report dilatory, obstructionist or contumacious conduct to the Commission, which in practice means a referral to the SEC's Office of General Counsel, who conducts an investigation.

If the Commission finds unethical or improper professional conduct, as was found in at least one recent case, *SEC v. Altman*, counsel may be suspended or barred from practice before the Commission, excluded from participation in the particular investigation, or censured.

We can and will increase referrals to the Department of Justice for witnesses who engage in obstruction and perjury, including false claims of a lack of recollection. We can and will also increase referrals to state bar associations, and to the Department of Justice where appropriate, of attorneys who participate or assist in such misconduct.

And to be fair, we recognize our own obligations—where defense counsel behavior is a reaction to shortcomings in the taking of testimony or the conduct of investigations, we can and will improve training and take other steps to insure that Enforcement Division staff is acting appropriately.

CONCLUSION

But beyond these "hard" responses, there is a larger and more important lesson here—less stick and more carrot—that is my true purpose in raising this issue today.

Our enforcement recommendations to the Commission are based not only on testimony and documents gathered in the investigation, but also on staff's view of the credibility of counsel.

Counsel serves as a kind of prism through which the staff invariably assesses certain evidence developed in the investigation, including that based on representations of counsel.

If counsel has chosen to be obstructive, to disregard the fundamental tenets of professionalism, ethics and integrity, the evidence could be viewed in a harsher light.

For that reason, counsel should consider whether having witness after witness come in and profess, "I have no specific recollection" in response to many, many questions from the staff, regardless of the documents placed before them, is a good tactic.

Similarly, defense counsel should ask themselves whether it really constitutes good lawyering to have one's client testify to objectively farfetched and implausible explanations of incriminating documents.

Conceding nothing may appear to be a "win," but that may prove to be short-lived if others in the Enforcement Division, as well as any reasonable trier of fact, would find it transparently self-serving and unbelievable.

Obstructive tactics are also a higher-risk proposition these days.

Our new Whistleblower Program, which rewards persons who voluntarily provide original information that leads to a successful enforcement action, together with our new Cooperation Program, only increases the chances that an insider with intimate knowledge of the wrongdoing may well emerge, and reveal the client's testimony to be implausible or worse.

We also encourage open communications within the Enforcement Division.

The staff shares with each other their experiences with certain lawyers or firms. Senior managers also listen closely to staff who bear the brunt of the tactics I've described. Lawyers contemplating sharp practices should ask themselves what kind of reputation, and what level of credibility, they want to have with the staff, and whether that matters to them—and to their clients.

My purpose in talking about this topic tonight is not to chill a vigorous defense, or to retaliate against "disobedient" defense counsel. Indeed, we think the process only benefits from strong and zealous representation.

But taken too far, to get caught up in the kind of tactics and gamesmanship I've discussed will only diminish credibility of counsel and damage your client's interests. And that is in no one's interest, not yours, not ours.

Thank you.*

---

* Complete speech may be read at http://www.sec.gov/news/speech/2011/spch 060111rk.htm.

The Commission may seek a variety of sanctions through the administrative proceeding process. An Administrative Law Judge may order sanctions that include suspending or revoking the registrations of registered securities, as well as the registrations of brokers, dealers, investment companies, investment advisers, municipal securities dealers, municipal advisers, transfer agents, and nationally recognized statistical rating organizations. In addition, Commission Administrative Law Judges can order disgorgement of ill-gotten gains, civil penalties, censures, and cease-and-desist orders against these entities, as well as individuals, and can suspend or bar persons from association with these entities or from participating in an offering of a penny stock.

Initial Decisions and significant orders are posted on the Commission's Web site under Administrative Law Judges and appear in legal research forums. Parties may appeal an Initial Decision to the Commission, which performs a *de novo* review and can affirm, reverse, modify, set aside, or remand for further proceedings. Appeals from Commission action are to a United States Court of Appeals.

Investor Alerts

The SEC's Office of Investor Education and Advocacy issues Investor Alerts to warn investors about investment scams. For example, in July 2012, the SEC issued an alert that one company was offering investors the opportunity to buy pre-IPO shares of companies, including social media and technology companies such as Facebook and Twitter.* SEC stated in the alert that its staff was aware of a number of complaints and inquiries about these types of frauds, which may be promoted on social media and Internet sites, by telephone, email, in person, or by other means.

The alert warned that the Commission's Division of Enforcement continues to take action in this area. The alert noted that on April 4, 2012, the U.S. District Court for the Southern District of Florida in Miami issued an Order to Show Cause and Other Emergency Relief to halt a defendant's fraudulent sale of securities of an investment vehicle that he falsely represented to be owned pre-IPO shares of Facebook, Inc. In that matter, the Commission's motion for an Order to Show Cause alleges that Allen Weintraub, using entities with names such as "Private Stock Transfer, Inc.," "PST Investments III, Inc.," and "World Financial Solutions" falsely represented that he would sell the investors pre-IPO shares of Facebook, Inc., and that PST Investments had an ownership interest in Facebook stock. The Commission's motion also alleges that Weintraub utilized the Web site privatestocktransfer.com to perpetrate his scheme. The Division of Enforcement urges anyone who believes that Allen Weintraub may have recently defrauded them to contact John Rossetti, Senior Counsel, at 202-551-4819.[†]

Summary

- Also known as stock fraud or investment fraud, securities fraud is the violation of the rules of investing and trading to cheat or take advantage of public investors.
- The Securities and Exchange Commission (SEC) is the principal law enforcement agency that regulates securities fraud.
- The SEC fraud prevention theory is based on the concept of truthful disclosure. According to the approach, if investors understand the facts and that all essential disclosures are provided to them, they will make their own decision as to the wisdom of investing in a selected

---

* http://www.sec.gov/index.htm [Accessed August 10, 2012].
† *SEC v. Allen E. Weintraub and AWMS Acquisitions, Inc., d/b/a Sterling Global Holdings,* Case No. 11-21549-CIV-HUCK/BANDSTRA (S.D. FL).

security. Included in this chapter are excerpts of statements from SEC officials to the U.S. Congress.

- The impact of a financial crime may have serious and long-term consequences. Individuals who experience financial crimes report feeling isolated, hopeless, and betrayed, but there is help.
- Insider trading is the buying or selling of a security by someone who has access to material, nonpublic information about the security.
- Insider trading can be illegal or legal depending on when the insider makes the trade: it is illegal when the material information is still nonpublic—trading while having special knowledge is unfair to other investors who do not have access to such knowledge.
- Illegal insider trading therefore includes tipping others when you have any sort of nonpublic information. Directors are not the only ones who have the potential to be convicted of insider trading. People such as brokers and even family members can be guilty.
- The Securities Act of 1933 is often referred to as the "truth in securities" law; the Securities Act of 1933 has two basic objectives: require that investors receive financial and other significant information concerning securities being offered for public sale, and prohibit deceit, misrepresentations, and other fraud in the sale of securities.
- The primary methods to accomplish the goals are the requirements of the disclosure of important financial information through the registration of securities.
- Registration statements and prospectuses become public shortly after filing with the SEC.
- By the Securities Exchange Act of 1934,* Congress created the SEC. The Act empowers the SEC with broad authority over all aspects of the securities industry.
- The Sarbanes–Oxley Act of 2002 mandates a number of reforms to enhance corporate responsibility, enhance financial disclosures, and combat corporate and accounting fraud; it created the Public Company Accounting Oversight Board.
- The Dodd–Frank Wall Street Reform and Consumer Protection Act was designed to reshape the U.S. regulatory system in a number of areas, including but not limited to, consumer protection.
- The Investment Company Act of 1940 regulates the organization of companies, including mutual funds, that engage primarily in investing, reinvesting, and trading in securities, and whose own securities are offered to the investing public.

* The full text of this Act can be read at http://www.sec.gov/about/laws/sea34.pdf.

- The Foreign Corrupt Practices Act (FCPA) generally prohibits the bribing of foreign officials.
- When there is a question as to the violation of a regulatory requirement, the SEC may issue an Order Instituting Proceedings.
- In the order, the Commission directs that an Administrative Law Judge conduct a public administrative proceeding to determine whether the allegations in the Order are true and to issue an Initial Decision in a specified period of time.
- Administrative Law Judges are independent judicial officers who in most cases conduct hearings and rule on allegations of securities law violations initiated by the Commission's Division of Enforcement.

QUESTIONS IN REVIEW

1. Explain why the SEC is demanding full disclosure on investment programs.
2. Does the SEC have too much power in controlling financial transactions?
3. Explain why the SEC considers insider trading as an unfair advantage to the public.
4. When and why was the SEC established?
5. If Joe, the owner of a local gas station, wants to invite 10 people to invest in his business, would he be subject to SEC regulations? Explain your answer.

Banking and Currency Related Crimes

5

Chapter Objectives

After studying this chapter, you should be able to

- Describe the bank fraud crimes and their elements.
- Explain the reporting requirements imposed on financial institutions.
- Explain why the efforts to combat money laundering are critical to reduce organized crime.
- Explain the process of money laundering.
- Discuss the requirement elements of money laundering.

Introduction

As noted by the chapter title, banking and currency related crimes are discussed in this chapter. In recent years, money laundering offenses have been the government's primary weapon in its fight against organized crime. The accumulation of large sums of legal currency is a problem with white-collar criminals, drug cartels, and other organized crime groups. Currency is of no value unless it can be used, and before it can be used, it must be cleaned or "laundered." In addition, large sums of currency are bulky and often alert law enforcement to criminal activity. It is often stated that to investigate organized or white-collar crime—follow the money.

In this chapter, bank fraud crimes are discussed, followed by a discussion on the reporting requirements of banks. Requiring banks to maintain and report certain money transactions is an additional method of trying to detect and prevent criminal organizations from profiting from illegal activities.

Bank Fraud

The purpose of the Bank Fraud Statute is to protect the interests of the federal government as an insurer of financial institutions.*

* Dan Fasanello, Lisa Umans, and Tom White. (Spring 2011). "Financial institutions fraud." *American Criminal Law Review.* Vol. 48. Issue 2. Page 697.

Title 18, Section 1344 of the U.S. Code is commonly referred to as the Bank Fraud Statute (BFS). The statute was the result of a U.S. Supreme Court decision in *Williams v. United States*,* in which the Court held that the crime of making false statements to financial institutions did not include check-kiting schemes. Section 1344 was passed because of Congress's reaction to this decision and to give the government the ability to prosecute check kiting. The BFS also criminalized other conduct that was intended to defraud federally insured financial institutions.

The BFS established a variety of offenses that could be committed against federally insured financial institutions. Because of constitutional restrictions on federal jurisdiction, generally, the crimes are limited to transactions involving federally insured institutions. Most states have enacted similar crimes where the victim is a state bank or institution that is not federally insured.

The statutory federal offenses include the following:

- Check kiting
- Check forging
- False statements and nondisclosures on loan applications
- Stolen checks
- Unauthorized use of automated teller machines
- Credit card fraud
- Student loan fraud
- Bogus transactions between offshore "shell" banks and domestic banks
- Automobile title frauds
- Diversion of funds by bank employees
- Submission of fraudulent credit card receipts
- False statements intended to induce check cashing
- Mortgage fraud

18 U.S. Code 1344 was enhanced by the Financial Institutions Reform, Recovery, and Enforcement Act of 1989 (FIRREA) and the Crime Control Act of 1990. Today, these legislative enactments along with Section 1344 have become the basic tools used to prosecute bank fraud offenses committed against federally insured financial institutions. The crimes established by the previously cited legislation do not, however, include the crimes of money laundering, bribery of bank officials, fraud committed by a bank on its customers, and schemes to pass bad checks.

* 458 U.S. 279 (1982).

The elements of an offense under 18 U.S. Code 1344 are that the defendant

- Knowingly
- Executed or attempted to execute
- A scheme or artifice to either
- Defraud, or
- Through false or fraudulent pretenses, representations, or promises
- Obtain the monies or other property of
- A financial institution

Intent Requirement

The BFS crimes are specific intent crimes in that the knowledge element of the BFS requires the government to establish that the defendant had the intent to defraud a financial institution. This intent cannot be inferred from the mere presence of a defendant at the scene of the crime or association with members of a criminal conspiracy.* The intent may be established by circumstantial evidence, which is often based on the totality of the evidence or evidence of similar acts. There is no requirement that the defendant concealed his or her actions from bank employees to satisfy the intent element. If the government establishes the required intent, the government does not need to prove that the defendant received benefits or meant to do harm to the bank.[†]

The specific intent element of Section 1344 does not require the government to prove that the defendant knowingly made direct misrepresentations to the financial institution or whether the defendant knew that the financial institution was federally insured. The knowledge element depends on what the defendant actually knew about the status of the accounts in question. A showing of reckless indifference or conscious avoidance of the truth of a scheme to defraud is sufficient to support a conviction.[‡]

Execution of a Scheme

Section 1344 does not define the "execute a scheme" requirement. Generally, the courts have looked at a number of factors to determine whether a scheme has been executed or attempted to be executed. The factors include the following:

- The objective of the scheme
- The nature of the scheme

---

* *United States v. McCarrick*, 294 F.3d 1286, 1294 (11th Cir. 2002).
† *United States v. Stathakis*, 320 F. App'x 74, 76 (2nd Cir. 2009).
‡ *United States v. Key*, 76 F.3d 350, 353 (11th Cir. 1996).

- The benefits intended
- The interdependence of the acts
- The number of parties involved

Section 1344 requires a scheme or artifice to defraud a financial institution. The courts have interpreted this language to include any plan, pattern, or course of action intended to deceive others to obtain something of value.[*] In some cases, the courts need to determine if the separate acts constitute the execution of the same scheme or if the acts constitute separate schemes. The test is that an act constitutes a separate execution if it is intended to put the financial institution at a separate, distinguishable financial risk from the risk it has already undertaken.[†]

Under Section 1344, the government must prove that the defendant either executed or attempted to execute a scheme to defraud a financial institution. An indictment may include both the "execute" and "attempt to execute" language. In which case, a jury must unanimously find only that the defendant either executed or attempted to execute a scheme to defraud a financial institution in order to find the defendant guilty.

Materiality is required under Section 1344, but reliance is not. A scheme need not have exerted actual influence so long as it was intended to do so and had the capacity to do so. A false representation is material if it has a natural tendency to influence, or is capable of influencing, the decision of the decision-making body to which it was addressed, but it need not induce actual reliance. The Supreme Court noted that under Section 1344, Congress intended to incorporate the well-settled meaning of the common-law terms it uses, and the Court cannot infer from the absence of an express reference to materiality that Congress intended to drop that element from the fraud statutes.[‡]

The false or fraudulent pretenses element of Section 1344 covers a wide variety of actions, including forging sale documents, falsifying appraisals, and failing to repay bank loans. The false or misrepresentations may be either explicit or implicit. They do not need to be made prior to the transaction. However, since a check is not a factual statement, merely presenting checks that were knowingly drawn on insufficient funds is not covered by Section 1344.

Financial Institution under Section 1344

Section 1344 requires that the victim or intended victim be a federally insured financial institution. Note: The bank need not be the immediate victim of the

---

[*] *United States v. Colon-Munoz*, 192 F.3d 210 (1st Cir. 1999).
[†] *United States v. Anderson*, 188 F.3d 886 (7th Cir. 1999).
[‡] *Neder v. United States*, 527 U.S. 1 (1999).

fraud. Generally, if a bank or institution has custody or control of the funds in question, it is considered as a victim.*

In *United States v. Everett*,[†] a court held that BFS does not require the defendant to put the bank at risk of loss in the "usual sense" but merely for someone to cause the bank to transfer funds under its possession and control. In *United States v. Colton*,[‡] the court stated that Section 1344 requires only that financial institution be exposed to actual or potential risk of loss. In *United States v. Hoglund*,[§] the appellate court noted that the defendant need only have intended to put the bank at risk of loss while rejecting the defendant's argument that the element of bank fraud is exposing the bank to risk of loss.

The prosecution must establish that the institution is federally insured for Section 1344 to apply. A financial institution is defined by 18 U.S. Code 20(1) and includes mortgage lending institutions, credit unions, and national banks.

False or Fraudulent Pretenses

Section 1344 also requires as a statutory element the defrauding or obtaining of monies by false or fraudulent pretenses. There are two methods to violate this element: either implementing a scheme or artifice to defraud, or employing false pretenses or promises to obtain property owned, held, or controlled by a financial institution. An indictment under Section 1344 may refer to either method.[¶]

A scheme to defraud a third party of money held in a bank account by a federally insured institution is a violation of Section 1344. A conviction under Section 1344 does require that the defendant's scheme also intended to defraud a federally insured financial institution. Fraudulent ATM transactions that simultaneously defraud the legal account holder and the financial institution from which the funds are withdrawn may be prosecuted under Section 1344.**

Currency Reporting Requirements

In 1970, the United States enacted the Currency and Foreign Transaction Reporting Act, which is commonly referred to as the Bank Secrecy Act

---

* *United States v. Moran*, 312 F.3d 480, 489 (1st Cir. 2002).
[†] 270 F.3d 986, 991 (6th Cir. 2001).
[‡] 231 F.3d 890, 908 (4th Cir. 2000).
[§] 178 F.3d 410, 413 (6th Cir. 1999).
[¶] *United States v. Crisci*, 273 F.3d 235, 239 (2nd Cir. 2001).
** *Lavin v. United States*, 299 F.3d 123, 128–29 (2nd Cir. 2002).

(BSA). The BSA was designed to address tax evasion and organized crime use of financial institutions to launder money.* The act requires banks (financial institutions) to keep certain records and make certain reports. Under BSA, financial institutions are required to report currency transaction over $10,000.† The BSA was amended by the U.S.A. Patriot Act in 2002. The amendment broadened the definition of financial institutions and expanded the requirements for financial and business transactions record keeping. The amendment also increased the civil and criminal penalties for certain BSA violations involving foreign financial institutions.

The BSA, as amended, authorizes the Secretary of the U.S. Treasury to issue regulations requiring banks, securities brokers and dealers, and certain uninsured financial institutions to maintain adequate records of customer transactions that may be used in criminal tax or regulatory investigations and proceedings. The required records must be retained for a period of not less than five years. In addition, every bank is required to obtain a taxpayer identification number of any customer involved or of a person having a financial interest in an account.

Presently, a bank must maintain records covering a wide range of business transactions, including checks, money orders drawn, or deposits in amounts in excess of $100 and foreign financial transactions in excess of $10,000. In addition, a bank must retain signatory cards for each account-holding customer. The documentation requirements are designed to facilitate the identification of customers and the transactions in which they engage in an effort to decrease the incidence of fraudulent banking activity.

Brokers and any dealers in securities are required to secure and maintain the taxpayer identification numbers of customers within 30 days of the date a brokerage account is opened. The broker or dealer in securities is also required to retain the original copies of the following:

- A signature card or grant of trading authority.
- Each record required by the Securities Exchange Commission under 17 C.F.R. 240.17a-3(a)(1)–(3), (5)–(9).‡
- A record of each remittance or transfer of funds, or of currency, checks, other monetary instruments, investment securities, or credit of more than $10,000 to a person, place, or account outside the United States.
- A record of each receipt of currency, checks, other monetary instruments, investment securities, or credit of more than $10,000 received on any one occasion directly from any person, place, or account outside the United States.

---

* *Cal. Bankers Ass'n v. Shultz,* 416 U.S. 21 (1974).
† 12 U.S. Code 1829b and 31 U.S. Code 5311.
‡ Code of Federal Regulations (CFR).

A broker or dealer violates the above listed requirements unless he or she within 30 days does the following:

- Make reasonable efforts to secure the customer's identification and maintains.
- Make available to the Secretary a list of names, addresses, and account numbers of persons from whom it has been unable to secure such identification.

Currency dealers and currency exchangers must secure within 30 days the names, addresses, and taxpayer identification numbers of all persons opening an account, receiving a line of credit, or presenting a certificate of deposit for payment into an account.

All money service businesses must provide the government with a list of its agents, including their addresses and telephone numbers, and the types of service each agent provides. This must be provided and updated on a yearly basis. In addition, the businesses must report each agent who has a gross transaction amount that exceeds $100,000. This list of agents must be available on demand to any law enforcement officer.

Money Laundering

> Money laundering is the process by which one conceals the existence, illegal source, or illegal application of income, and disguises that income to make it appear legitimate.*

The current efforts of the government in its antimoney laundering efforts are designed to target a wide range of profitable criminal activities, including narcotics trafficking, terrorism activities, illegal sales of weapons, human trafficking, fraud, political corruption, and child pornography.

According to the United Nations Office on Drugs and Crime (UNODC), money laundering fuels corruption and organized crime. Corrupt public officials need to be able to launder bribes, kickbacks, public funds and, on occasion, even development loans from international financial institutions. Organized criminal groups need to be able to launder the proceeds of drug trafficking and commodity smuggling. As noted by the UNODC, terrorist groups use money laundering channels to get cash to buy arms. The social consequences of allowing these groups to launder money can be disastrous. The unit contends that taking the proceeds of crimes from corrupt public

---

* Anna Driggers. (Spring 2011). "Money laundering." *American Criminal Law Review.* Vol. 48. No. 2. Page 929.

officials, traffickers, and organized crime groups is one way to deter this type of criminal activity.*

As noted by Teresa Adams,[†] regardless of the crime, money launderers typically resort to a three-step process when converting illicit proceeds into apparently legal monies or goods:

- **Placement:** The criminally derived money is placed into a legitimate enterprise.
- **Layering:** The funds are layered through various transactions to obscure the original source.
- **Integration:** The newly laundered funds are integrated into the legitimate financial world in the form of bank notes, loans, letters of credit, or other recognizable financial instruments.

The primary statute used by the federal government in its antimoney laundering efforts is the Money Laundering Control Act of 1986 (MLCA).[‡] Earlier efforts to curb money laundering were to require financial institutions to comply with certain reporting requirements, some of which were discussed under the BSA. The MLCA targets the conversion of illegally derived funds into clean or useable form and created criminal liability for any individual who conducts a monetary transaction knowing that the funds were derived through unlawful activity.[§]

The MLCA was incorporated into 18 U.S. Code 1956 and 1957. Section 1956 covers prohibited financial transactions and prohibited financial transportation, and authorizes government sting operations. Section 1957 regulates transactions involving property exceeding $10,000 derived from the specified unlawful activities.

Section 1956 addresses the following:

- Domestic money laundering and participation in transactions involving criminal proceeds
- International money laundering and transportation of criminally derived monetary instruments in foreign commerce
- The use of government sting operations to expose criminal activity

---

*International Money Laundering Information Network. (2007). *Model Provisions for Common Law Legal Systems on Money Laundering, Terrorist Financing, Preventive Measures and Proceeds of Crime Finalised*. Geneva, United Nations. Available at http://www.imolin.org/imolin/en/common-law-model-provisions [Accessed on September 12, 2012].

[†] Teresa E. Adams. (2000). "Tacking on money laundering charges to white collar crimes: What did congress intend, and what are the courts doing?" *Georgia State University Law Review*. Vol. 17. Pages 531, 535–538.

[‡] 18 U.S. Code 1956–1957.

[§] Driggers (2011), p. 929.

The crimes established by 1956(a)(1) are known as "transaction money laundering" offenses because the prohibited act is the financial transaction itself. The four prohibited financial transactions are as follows:

- Transactions conducted with the intent to promote specified unlawful activity.
- Transactions conducted with the intent to engage in tax evasion violations.
- Transactions designed to conceal or disguise the nature, location, source, ownership, or control of the proceeds of specified unlawful activity.
- Transactions designed to avoid a state or federal reporting requirement.

The transportation money laundering crimes are established by Section 1956(a)(2). This subsection creates three separate offenses that are associated with the transportation, transmission, or transfer of criminally derived proceeds into or out of the United States. The three transportation money laundering offenses are as follows:

- The intent to promote the carrying on of specified unlawful activity.
- The transportation of a monetary instrument that represents the proceeds of some form of unlawful activity designed to conceal or disguise that instrument.
- Transportation of the monetary instrument that represents the proceeds of some form of unlawful activity designed to avoid a state or federal transaction reporting requirement.

The U.S. Supreme Court* holds that it is not necessary for the government to prove that the defendant attempted to make illegal funds appear legitimate to satisfy the designed to conceal element; instead, the government must establish that the defendant did more than merely hide the funds during transport. To obtain a conviction, the government must prove that a defendant knew that a purpose of the transportation was to conceal or disguise the nature, the location, the source, the ownership, or the control of funds.

The crimes established by the MLCA have four elements:

- Knowledge
- Existence of proceeds derived from a specified unlawful activity
- Existence of a financial transaction
- Intent

---

* *Cuellar v. United States,* 553 U.S. 550 (2008).

Transactions

For purposes of the MLCA, 18 U.S. Code 1956(c)(4) defines "financial transaction" as a transaction which in any way or degree affects interstate or foreign commerce

- Involving the movement of funds by wire or other means, or
- Involving one or more monetary instruments, or
- Involving the transfer of title to any real property, vehicle, vessel, or aircraft, or
- Involving the use of a financial institution that is engaged in, or the activities of which affect interstate or foreign commerce in any way or degree

In 2001, the 1956(c) was amended to include foreign banks within the definition of a financial institution, thus making it clear that the Government could rely on the use of a foreign bank to satisfy the requirements of Section 1956(c)(4)(B).

The term "transaction" in Section 1956 includes the purchase, sale, loan, pledge, gift, transfer, delivery, or other disposition and, with respect to a financial institution, includes a deposit; withdrawal; transfer between accounts; exchange of currency; loan; extension of credit; purchase or sale of any stock, bond, certificate of deposit, or other monetary instrument; use of a safe deposit box; or any other payment, transfer, or delivery by, through, or to a financial institution, by whatever means effected.

Section 1957 requires also that a "monetary transaction" occur but defines this term to exclude any transaction necessary to preserve a person's right to representation as guaranteed by the sixth amendment to the U.S. Constitution. Under this definition, payment to your attorney for legal advice or presentation is not considered as a "money laundering" offense.

The appellate court in *United States v. Baker* [*] decided that the depositing of the proceeds of prostitution sufficed as a financial transaction.

In *United States v. Burgos*,[†] an appellate court stated that Section 1956 covers attempted transactions as well as completed transactions. However, to constitute an attempted transaction, a substantial step toward completing the activity must be taken.

Knowledge Requirement

Section 1957, by contrast, only requires knowledge that a transaction is occurring and that the transaction involves criminally derived property; it requires

---

[*] 227 E3d 955, 962 (7th Cir. 2000).
[†] 254 F.3d 8, 12 (1st Cir. 2001).

no intent or design to conceal. In *United States v. Bierd*,[*] an appellate court found that an undercover officer's statement to the defendant that the money being transferred came from drug sales was sufficient to show that the defendant knew he was transacting in criminally derived property. The appellate court in *United States v. Hill*[†] concluded that the government is not required to show that the defendant knew the precise nature of the unlawful activity as long as he knew that it was an illegal activity. In *United States v. Pizano*,[‡] the court held that circumstantial evidence of the defendant's relationship with her drug dealer brother and her lies regarding the source of her money was sufficient to show that she knew she was conducting transactions with drug proceeds.

Is evidence that a person received $50,000 in cash in brown paper bag in exchange for a cashier's check sufficient to establish that the defendant knew that it came from an unlawful source? One appellate court held that it was.[§]

The court in *United States v. Sayakhom* stated that a defendant may not be convicted solely on what he "should have known."[¶] In *United States v. Flores*, the court stated that an attorney who was "willfully blind" to the illegal source of a client's money may be convicted of conspiring with the client to commit money laundering by opening bank accounts and conducting financial transactions for the client.[**] *United States v. Epstein*[††] decision supports the concept that a willful blindness instruction is appropriate if the following holds true:

- The defendant claims a lack of knowledge.
- Facts suggest a conscious course of deliberate ignorance.
- The instruction, taken as a whole, cannot be misunderstood as mandating an inference of knowledge.

An appellate court in *United States v. Pizana*[‡‡] held that U.S. Code 1957 prohibited a wider range of activity than generally considered as money laundering. The court interpreted the breadth of Section 1957 to reach almost any bank transaction conducted by a defendant.

Federal Jurisdiction

Federal jurisdiction for Sections 1956 and 1957 is based on the "Commerce Clause" of the U.S. Constitution. Accordingly, for the federal government

[*] 217 F.3d 15, 23 (1st Cir. 2000).
[†] 167 F.3d 1055, 1066 (6th Cir. 1999).
[‡] 421 F.3d 707, 723 (8th Cir. 2005).
[§] *United States v. Henry*, 325 F.3d 93, 104 (2nd Cir. 2003).
[¶] 186 F.3d 928,943 n.8 (9th Cir. 1999).
[**] 454 F.3d 149, 155–56 (3rd Cir. 2006).
[††] 426 F.3d 431,440 (1st Cir. 2005).
[‡‡] 421 F.3d 707, 725 (8th Cir. 2005).

to have jurisdiction, the transaction in question must affect interstate commerce or involve a financial institution that is engaged in, or the activities of which affect, interstate or foreign commerce in any way or degree. The courts have required only "minimal effects" on interstate commerce to satisfy the jurisdiction requirement. For example, transactions considered sufficient to confer federal jurisdiction include payment of a co-conspirator's cash bond to correctional officers, intrastate money transfer violating a loan agreement with an out-of-state company, or purchase of a car or stolen jewelry.

In *United States v. Koller*,* a court held that using a financial institution for purchasing a money order was sufficient nexus for interstate commerce, even if only tangentially related to money laundering. However, in *United States v. Grey*,† the court held that a defendant's transfer of $200 to a club manager to "feed" a video poker pot was insufficient to establish the "effect on commerce" element of the money laundering statute without showing that the particular money used had traveled in interstate commerce.

Multiple Offenses

The more sophisticated money laundering schemes generally utilize several institutions in different jurisdictions and countries. Accordingly, the illegal proceeds pass through several institutions before they reach their final intended destination. Each transaction constitutes a separate offense. As the Senate Report explains,

> Each transaction involving "dirty money" is intended to be a separate offense. For example, a drug dealer who takes $1 million in cash from a drug sale and divides the money into smaller lots and deposits it in 10 different banks (or in 10 different branches of the same bank) on the same day has committed 10 distinct violations of the new statute. If he then withdraws some of the money and uses it to purchase a boat or condominium, he will have committed two more violations, one for the withdrawal and one for the purchase.‡

Summary

- The purpose of the Bank Fraud Statute is to protect the interests of the federal government as an insurer of financial institutions.
- Title 18, Section 1344 of the U.S. Code is commonly referred to as the Bank Fraud Statute (BFS).

---

* 956 F.2d 1408, 1411 (7th Cir. 1992).
† 56 F.3d 1219, 1224–25 (10th Cir. 1995).
‡ U.S. Senate Committee. (1986). *On the Judiciary, the Money Laundering Crimes Act of 1986*. Senate Report No. 99-433. Pages 12–14.

- The BFS established a variety of offenses that could be committed against financial institutions.
- 18 U.S. Code 1344 was enhanced by the Financial Institutions Reform, Recovery, and Enforcement Act of 1989 (FIRREA) and the Crime Control Act of 1990.
- The crimes under BFS are specific intent crimes in that the knowledge element of the BFS requires the government to establish that the defendant had the intent to defraud a financial institution.
- If the government establishes the required intent, the government does not need to prove that the defendant received benefits or meant to do harm to the bank.
- Section 1344 requires a scheme or artifice to defraud a financial institution.
- In 1970, the U.S. enacted the Currency and Foreign Transaction Reporting Act, which is commonly referred to as the Bank Secrecy Act (BSA).
- The BSA was designed to address tax evasion and organized crime use of financial institutions to launder money.
- Presently, a bank must maintain records covering a wide range of business transactions, including checks, money orders drawn, or deposits in amounts in excess of $100 and foreign financial transactions in excess of $10,000.
- Money laundering is the process by which one conceals the existence, illegal source, or illegal application of income, and disguises that income to make it appear legitimate.
- The current efforts of the government in its antimoney laundering efforts are designed to target a wide range of profitable criminal activities, including narcotics trafficking, terrorism activities, illegal sales of weapons, human trafficking, fraud, political corruption, and child pornography.

QUESTIONS IN REVIEW

1. What constitutes money laundering?
2. What are the purposes of money laundering statutes?
3. Explain the rationale behind requiring banks to keep certain records and make certain reports to the government.
4. What constitutes a financial transaction for purposes of Section 1956?
5. Discuss the intent requirement in the money laundering statutory crimes.

Racketeer and Organized Crime

6

Chapter Objectives

After studying this chapter, the reader should be able to do the following:

- Understand the concept behind the RICO statutes.
- Explain the process by which the statutes were developed.
- Explain the problems that the lawmakers had in defining racketeering activity.
- List the three substantive offenses that were prohibited by the Corrupt Organization Act.
- Explain the congressional intent in enacting RICO.
- Define the key terms of racketeering activity, patterns of racketeering activity, and enterprise.
- List the three structural features that are necessary to constitute an enterprise.
- Describe the four different criminal violations that are proscribed by RICO.

Introduction

Where did the name RICO originate?

> In the 1931 Hollywood film *Little Caesar*, Edward G. Robinson, playing the role of Caesar Enrico Bandello (aka Rico), dies at the hands of the police while uttering the famous last words: "Is this the end of Rico?"*

The federal government's primary statutory weapon in the fight against organized crime is the Racketeer Influenced Corrupt Organizations Act of 1970 (RICO). The legislative journey that culminated in the enactment of RICO in 1970 started in 1967, when Senator Roman Hruska of Nebraska introduced two bills designed to facilitate the application of antitrust laws

---

* Little Caesar (film). (2010). Available at http://www.filmsite.org/littc.html [Retrieved on February 17, 2010].

to the problem of organized crime.* One bill, Senate Bill 2048 (1967), was proposed as an amendment to the Sherman Antitrust Act to prohibit the use of intentionally and deliberately unreported income from one line of business into another line of business. The second bill, S. 2049 (1967), was designed to prohibit the investment in legitimate business enterprises of income derived from specified criminal activities, such as gambling, bribery, narcotics, and other violations typically associated with organized crime.[†]

In introducing the bills, Senator Ramon Hruska remarked that the cancerous growth of organized crime threatened American society. He described organized crime as a tightly knit cartel that generated large amounts of cash through illegal activities. According to Senator Hruska, organized crime families coupled the illicit cash with threats of violence and extortion to gain monopoly control of legitimate businesses in all areas of the economy. In his analysis of the problem, Senator Hruska identified four methods by which organized crime gained control of legitimate businesses:

(1) Investing concealed profits acquired from gambling and other illegal enterprises
(2) Accepting business interests in payment of the owners' gambling debts
(3) Foreclosing on usurious loans
(4) Using various forms of extortion

Senator Hruska said the existing antitrust laws had features useful in fighting the infiltration of legitimate business by organized criminal elements. He specifically noted Sections 1 and 2 of the Sherman Act with their prohibitions of combinations in restraint of trade and monopolies, the provisions in the antitrust laws for private civil lawsuits and their provision for use in immunity for grand jury witnesses, and their civil investigative demand procedures.

Hruska said that his proposed Sherman Act amendment, S. 2048, would enable antitrust law enforcement agencies to discover promptly the source of funds in a business through certain discovery techniques and it would also add the sanction of private treble damage suits. Senator Hruska claimed that his proposal, limiting it to intentionally unreported income, stressed the fact that the evil to be curbed was the unfair competitive advantage inherent in the large amount of illicit funds available to organized crime.

---

* The research on the background of RICO was adapted from Cliff Roberson. (2011). *Racketeer Influenced Corrupt Organizations and Other Civil and Criminal Forfeitures.* 16th edition. Fort Worth: Knowles Publishing Company. [A three-volume reference for attorneys handling RICO cases.]
[†] Senator Roman Hruska [NE]. (June 3–6, 1969). "Hearings on Criminal Activities Profit Act." *Congressional Record (91st Congress, 1st session).* Vol. 115. Pages 9780–9788.

Hruska stated that the companion bill, S. 2049, would prohibit investment in legitimate business enterprises of income derived from such criminal activities as gambling, bribery, and narcotics. A full range of criminal and civil sanctions would be made available to law enforcement officials and private citizens adversely affected by the illegal investments.

In introducing the Corrupt Organizations Act of 1969, Senator John McClellan spoke of the need to end the infiltration of legitimate business by organized crime. He said that the laws as they existed were inadequate to remove criminal elements from legitimate endeavor organizations.*

McClellan said that the bill drew from antitrust remedies but that he did not intend the act to import the great complexity of antitrust law enforcement into the federal criminal code. The purpose of the bill was to end infiltration of legitimate business enterprises directly, as persons involved in acquiring or running an organization by a method proscribed in the act could be removed from the organization. The main provisions of the Corrupt Organizations Act of 1969 are generally parallel to those that were enacted as RICO in 1970, with some significant differences.

In Section 1961(1), "racketeering activity" was defined to include, on both the state and federal levels, any act involving the danger of violence to life, limb, or property punishable by imprisonment for more than one year; any act indictable under the federal criminal code involving bribery, sports bribery, counterfeiting, interstate shipment of stolen property, theft from employee benefit plans, or extortionate credit transactions; transmission of wagering information, jury tampering, obstructing criminal investigations, Hobbs Act violations, Travel Act violations, or bribery in employee benefit plans; transportation of stolen goods or securities, selling or receiving stolen goods, and Mann Act violations; and certain labor law violations. Conspiracy to commit any of the enumerated acts was also a predicate offense in the Corrupt Organization Act. The critical term "pattern of racketeering activity," a subject, as will be seen, of intense litigation under RICO as finally enacted, was defined as at least one act occurring after the effective date of the Act.

The Corrupt Organizations Act contained three substantive offenses: (1) unlawful investment in an enterprise; (2) unlawful acquisition of an enterprise; and (3) unlawful participation in an enterprise through a pattern of racketeering activity. These provisions as originally proposed survived as § 1962(a), (b), and (c) of RICO. There was no provision proscribing conspiracy to violate the Act as there is in § 1962(d) of RICO.

McClellan's proposal did not provide for a private civil action but did provide for civil suits by the United States. In addition to a possible 20-year

* Senator John McClellan [TN]. (April 18, 1969). "Hearing on civil RICO: The temptation and impropriety of judicial restriction." *Congressional Record (91st Congress, 1st session)*. Vol. 115. Pages 9567–9571.

prison sentence, fine, and forfeiture, the proposed Act contained civil remedies such as divestiture of interest, dissolution, and prohibition of culpable parties from engaging in the same line of business.

In March and June of 1969, hearings were held by the subcommittee on Criminal Laws and Procedures of the Senate Judiciary Committee concerning S. 30, the proposed Organized Crime Control Act of 1969, and such related proposals as S. 1623 and S. 1861. In the six days devoted to the judiciary committee hearings on the various antiorganized crime measures, relatively little attention was given to the McClellan–Hruska proposals to incorporate antitrust enforcement concepts in the fight against organized crime.

On June 3, 1969, Will Wilson, Assistant Attorney General of the Crime Division of the United States Justice Department, testified that the Justice Department preferred the incorporation of the proposed Corrupt Organizations Act, S. 1861, into the Organized Crime Control Act instead of Senator Hruska's Criminal Activities Profit Act, S. 1623.*

Also on June 3, 1969, the Committee heard testimony on S. 1861 and S. 1623 from Donald F. Taylor, a corporate executive appearing on behalf of the Chamber of Commerce of the United States. Taylor indicated that while the Chamber was not taking an official position on the various bills before the committee, it "particularly" approved of the objectives of S. 1623 and S. 1861. Taylor said that, in looking at the two bills, it appeared that S. 1861, the Corrupt Organizations Act, incorporated most of the basic features of S. 1623 and suggested a single comprehensive bill combining the two bills would be the best approach to follow. He suggested that the definition of "racketeering activity" in S. 1861 be expanded to include narcotics traffic, sales, and use.†

On June 4, 1969, the committee heard testimony from Lawrence Speiser, director of the Washington, D.C., office of the American Civil Liberties Union (ACLU). He was critical of the proposed Corrupt Organizations Act, stating that the ACLU was concerned by the enormous and virtually unlimited breadth of the criminal provisions of the proposed statute, noting that the bill failed to confine its reach to the limited aim of foreclosing opportunities by organized crime for investment in, or takeover of, legitimate organizations. The ACLU said that S. 1861 was potentially dangerous as it would be applicable in areas far removed from organized crime. The ACLU criticized the definition of racketeering activity in the Corrupt Organizations Act as broad enough to encompass every state or federal felony. Turning the focus to § 1962(a) of the Act, which, like § 1962(a) of the current Act, proscribed the direct or indirect investment of racketeering proceeds into an enterprise,

---

* Will Wilson. (June 3, 1969). "Hearing on Senate Bills 1861 and 1863." *Congressional Record (91st Congress, 1st session)*. Vol. 115. Pages 9782–9783.
† Donald F. Taylor. (June 3, 1969). "Hearing on Senate Bills 1861 and 1863." *Congressional Record (91st Congress, 1st session)*. Vol. 115. Pages 9780–9782.

the ACLU claimed that authors of anti–Vietnam War books, such as Norman Mailer, could conceivably be subjected to prosecution under the proposed law, as their works could be profiting indirectly from the broadly defined racketeering activity. The ACLU also stated lawyers defending accused racketeers could find their fees in danger as being directly or indirectly derived from racketeering.*

The ACLU, after expressing concern about the vagueness of some of the statutes' terminology, also expressed reservations concerning the proposed civil remedies in the act, the concept of public depositions, and the broad scope of the civil investigative demand provisions.

Following the close of the hearings, Deputy Attorney General Richard Kleindienst wrote Senator McClellan to express the views of the Justice Department on S. 1861. While stating that the bill had great merit, the Justice Department, according to Kleindienst, had several suggestions for the bill.

One significant suggested change was to redefine the term "racketeering activity" in #§ 1961(1)(a) of the bill from "any act involving the danger of violence to life, limb, or property indictable under state a federal law" to a narrower definition, including a range of generic state offenses. The Justice Department also proposed redefining the pattern of racketeering activity to require at least two acts instead of one.

With respect to the language of the proposed § 1962(a) of the bill dealing with illegal investment of racketeering income, the Department suggested adding language referring to 18 U.S.C. § 2, which defines principals in criminal offenses. It also suggested exempting limited purchases of stock on the open market from the reach of § 1962(a).

The Department was generally supportive of the criminal penalties, the forfeiture provisions, and the civil investigative demand. In fact, Kleindienst indicated that the Department felt that the potential of the various civil equitable remedies in the Act for damaging organized crime was possibly greater than the penal. It did not, however, recommend inclusion of a private civil action.

Two other agencies, the Department of the Treasury and the Small Business Administration, also commented on the bill. The Treasury Department suggested various technical amendments while the Small Business Administration stated that it would defer to the Justice Department.

On December 18, 1969, the Organized Crime Control Act of 1969 was reported to the full Senate with S. 1861, the Corrupt Organizations Act, incorporated as Title IX of the Act. In reporting the bill, Senator McClellan described the purpose of Title IX as being the prohibition of the infiltration of legitimate organizations by racketeers or the proceeds of racketeering

---

* Lawrence Speiser. (June 4, 1969). "Hearing on Senate Bills 1861 and 1863." *Congressional Record (91st Congress, 1st session)*. Vol. 115. Pages 9786–9787.

activities. He said civil remedies that paralleled those available in the anti-trust field were to be made available to prevent racketeering activity.

Two members of the Senate Judiciary Committee, Senators Philip Hart of Michigan and Edward Kennedy of Massachusetts, filed individual views to criticize the scope of the bill, saying it went beyond organized crime.

On January 21, 1970, the Organized Crime Control Act with Title IX, Racketeer Influenced and Corrupt Organizations, was called up for Senate debate. The proposed RICO Act differed from Senator McClellan's original Corrupt Organizations Act in several respects. The definition of "racketeering activity" in #§ 1961(1)(a) was limited to generic state predicate offenses involving murder, kidnapping, gambling, arson, robbery, bribery, extortion, or dealings in narcotics. The federal predicate offenses in #§ 1961(1)(b) were expanded to include mail, wire, and securities fraud as well as other new predicates. The collection of unlawful debt was also added as a statutory violation, and a new section, 1962(d), making conspiracy to violate the act an offense, was also added. The term "pattern of racketeering" was redefined to require proof of two acts of racketeering instead of one. There was no provision, however, for a private civil treble damages remedy.

As the Senate debate began, Senator McClellan addressed himself to Title IX of the Act, RICO. He said Title IX was aimed at removing organized crime from legitimate organizations by providing a means of wholesale removal of organized crime from the organizations, preventing its return and forfeiting its ill-gotten gains. He said that Title IX used three main devices: criminal forfeiture, civil remedies derived from antitrust, and civil investigative procedures.

McClellan noted that Title IX would revise the old concept of forfeiture. He also said that Title IX would use the antitrust remedies of divestiture, dissolution, and prohibition of future activity to attack organized crime. To emphasize his point, he gave the Senate a list of many types of businesses infiltrated by organized crime to which Title IX could apply.

McClellan noted that Title IX would revise the old concept of forfeiture. He also said Title IX would utilize the antitrust remedies of divestiture, dissolution, and prohibition of future activity to attack organized crime. To emphasize his point, he gave the Senate a list of many types of businesses infiltrated by organized crime to which Title IX could apply.

The potential scope of Title IX was also addressed by Senator Hruska, who called the proposed RICO statute novel, promising, and ingenious. He said the purpose of Title IX was to remove the influence of organized crime from legitimate business by attacking its property interests and by removing its members from control of legitimate businesses acquired or operated by unlawful racketeering methods. Like Senator McClellan, he praised Title IX's civil remedies.

The provisions of Title IX were also lauded by Senator Robert Byrd of West Virginia. He said RICO was a carefully structured program that could drastically curtail—or eventually eradicate—the vast expansion of the economic power of organized crime outside the rules of fair competition. He praised the antitrust weapons of injunction, dissolution, divestiture, and reorganization as being time-tested, powerful, and a major deterrent to the expansion of organized crimes' economic power.

On January 22, 1970, Senator Joseph Tydings of Maryland took the Senate floor to describe Title IX, the proposed RICO Act, as one of the more ingenious provisions of the bill and as very important. Senator Warren Magnuson of Washington, a member of the Senate Commerce Committee, raised a question as to the scope and impact of Title IX, asking Senators Hruska and McClellan "... whether Title IX is directed mainly at a situation in which money from criminal activities is transferred into some kind of business that may be legitimate, in interstate commerce, but the proceeds from crime would be used in that business." Senator McClellan responded that "... if it is illegal gambling, engaged in by syndicates, or shylocking, or whatever, and those funds are used for investment in legitimate business in interstate commerce, that would constitute a crime under Title IX." Senator Hruska added, in response to another query from Senator Magnuson, that Title IX might cover the transportation of illegal proceeds from one state to another. Support was also expressed for Title IX by Senator Hugh Scott of Pennsylvania, who called it constructive and said that it would help the poor by ending infiltration of ghetto businesses.

When the Senate debate resumed on January 23, 1970, Senator Strom Thurmond also spoke favorably of Title IX. He said the provision would make it possible to expose the activities of racketeers in gaining inroads into legitimate business through the use of antitrust devices. He called it an important provision to eliminate an avenue for the disposition of ill-gotten gains through legitimate business.

The Organized Crime Control Act, with Title IX, RICO, included, passed the Senate by a vote of 73 to 1, the lone dissenter being Senator Lee Metcalf of Montana. Senators Hart and Kennedy, who had previously filed written dissents criticizing the legislation, including Title IX, voted for it on final passage. Following passage by the Senate, S. 30, the Organized Crime Control Act was referred on January 26, 1970 to the House Judiciary Committee.

Hearings on S. 30, the Organized Crime Control Act of 1970, and related bills were held before a subcommittee of the Committee on the Judiciary of the House of Representatives for a total of eight days: May 20, 27; June 10, 11, 17; July 23; and August 5, 1970. In a testimony before the subcommittee on May 21, 1970, Attorney General John Mitchell described the RICO provision of S. 30 as enabling the full panoply of antitrust weapons to attack organized crimes' "property." Mitchell stated he wanted to see the enduring principles of the antitrust laws used against organized crime (Hearings on Senate Bill 30 and Related Proposals, Organized Crime Control, Subcommittee No. 5, 91

Cong. 2nd Session, Subcommittee report, p. 157). He further introduced into the hearing record a report by the Department of Justice describing Title IX as having tremendous potential for destroying organized crimes' grip on America's free enterprise system.*

On June 10, 1970, the subcommittee heard from Sheldon H. Elsen, Chairman of the Committee on Federal Legislation of the Association of the Bar of the City of New York. In conjunction with his testimony, Elsen presented the subcommittee with the Association's analysis of S. 30, including its comments on Title IX, RICO. The analysis was sharply critical of the RICO concept, claiming that RICO would probably have only limited effect on organized crime and could create complacency by appearing to offer a solution to organized crime but not really doing so. While the civil provisions were described as promising, the criminal provisions of RICO were said to add little to existing law other than to increase penalties that would be dependent on a difficult burden of proof. The report also criticized RICO for "dangerous inroads against individual liberties."†

The Association's analysis stated that Title IX was both overregulated and underregulated and was not adequately focused on organized crime. The analysis said that the proposed 18 U.S.C. #§ 1962(a), proscribing investment of funds obtained through a pattern of racketeering, created the illusion of legal consequences. The Association claimed that proving the crimes making up a pattern of racketeering would be almost impossible and tracing illegal funds would be an insuperable burden on prosecutors.

Moreover, the report said, the list of crimes defined as racketeering activity went clearly beyond those considered characteristically violated by organized crime. The report specifically criticized inclusion of theft from interstate shipment, #18 U.S.C. § 659, unlawful use of telephone credit, #18 U.S.C. § 1343, and the predicates dealing with narcotics offenses.

In sum, the Association concluded that Title IX was seriously deficient. In elaborating on the Association's analysis in his testimony, Elsen said that RICO was too broad. Although the basic concept of RICO was good, the proposed law needed a great deal of work.

Additional criticism of RICO was presented to the subcommittee by Professor Herman Schwartz, Professor of Law, State University of New York at Buffalo, who said that he was puzzled by the rationale of Title IX. He agreed with the Association of the Bar of the City of New York that proposed

* John Mitchell [Attorney General]. (June 6, 1970). Testimony reported in Hearings on Senate Bill 30 and Related Proposals, Organized Crime Control, Subcommittee No. 5, 91 Cong. 2nd Session, Subcommittee Report. Page 157.
† Sheldon H. Elsen. (June 10, 1970). Testimony reported in Hearings on Senate Bill 30 and Related Proposals, Organized Crime Control, Subcommittee No. 5, 91 Cong. 2nd Session, Subcommittee Report. Page 192.

that Section 1962(a) was virtually unenforceable and said that RICO was a frighteningly broad shotgun approach to organized crime.*

Also on June 10, 1970, the subcommittee received a report from Vincent L. Broderick, Chairman of the Committee on Federal Legislation of the New York County Lawyer Association, relative to the Organized Crime Control Act. Broderick's report criticized the pattern of racketeering concept set forth in Title IX, stating that it was questionable if any two illegal acts made a pattern of anything, and criticized the inclusion of such offenses as securities fraud with the definition of racketeering activity. The terms of Section 1962(a) relating to illegal investment also received criticism for being overly broad, and the proposed forfeiture provision was called an "unwarranted departure for existing law."†

In conclusion, the New York City Lawyers Association recommended narrowing the overly broad definition of racketeering, requiring more than two isolated acts for a pattern of racketeering, eliminating #§ 1962(a), and enacting §#§ 1964 through 1968.

As the House hearings were proceeding, Senator John McClellan responded to attacks on Title IX, particularly those made by the Association of the Bar of the City of New York. He said that Title IX was aimed at the removal of organized crime from legitimate organizations by the use of three primary devices: criminal forfeiture, antitrust-based civil remedies, and civil investigative procedures.

McClellan gave particular attention to the Association's claim that Title IX's list of racketeering offenses included "offenses often committed by persons not engaged in organized crime." McClellan said that the enumerated racketeering offenses lent themselves to commercial exploitation, unlike such offenses as rape, and were commonly committed by participants in organized crime. He said, "It is impossible to draw an effective statute which reaches most of the commercial activities of organized crime, yet does not include offenses commonly committed by persons outside organized crime as well."

McClellan noted that the commission of a single racketeering offense by itself did not create liability under RICO. The violator would have to engage in a pattern of violations and use that pattern to obtain or operate interest in an enterprise. McClellan also took issue with attacks on Title IX by the ACLU. He rejected criticism of the pattern requirement by stating that the Senate Judiciary Committee report on Title IX indicated that its target was

---

* Herman Schwartz. (June 9, 1970). Testimony reported in Hearings on Senate Bill 30 and Related Proposals, Organized Crime Control, Subcommittee No. 5, 91 Cong. 2nd Session, Subcommittee Report. Page 189.
† Vincent L. Broderick. (June 9, 1970). Testimony reported in Hearings on Senate Bill 30 and Related Proposals, Organized Crime Control, Subcommittee No. 5, 91 Cong. 2nd Session, Subcommittee Report. Page 190.

not sporadic activity and that showing a pattern would require continuity of the activity plus relationship of the acts.

McClellan further responded to attacks on #§ 1962(a), the illegal investment provision, stating that tracing of illegal funds was difficult but not insuperable.

On June 11, 1970, the House subcommittee heard from the Chamber of Commerce of the United States, which enthusiastically endorsed RICO. Aaron Kohn, Managing Director of the Metropolitan Crime Commission of New Orleans and also a member of the Chamber, described Title IX as a lawful and constructive authority to challenge organized crime's abuse of free enterprise.*

On June 17, 1970, the ACLU presented its objections to Title IX through the testimony of Lawrence Speiser, Director of the Washington, D.C., office of the ACLU. The ACLU, as it had during the Senator's consideration of S. 30, criticized Title IX for an overly broad definition of pattern of racketeering activity and for giving, in #§ 1968, virtually unlimited investigative powers to the government through the civil investigative demand procedure.

The subcommittee also heard from United States Representative Sam Steiger of Arizona on June 17, 1970. He said that he was especially enthusiastic about RICO and described the civil provisions as likely to be much more effective than any existing authority as a means of protecting legitimate businesses from organized crime.†

Significantly, Steiger suggested amending Title IX to "add a private civil damage remedy to Title IX, similar to the private damage remedy found in the antitrust laws." Steiger said, "[n]ot every businessman, of course, will wish to take advantage of such a remedy, but those who have been wronged by organized crime should at least be given access to a legal remedy." Steiger followed up his testimony with a letter on June 30, 1970, specifically proposing an amendment of RICO to provide for a private civil action for treble damages.

On July 23, 1970, the proposed private civil RICO action received further support from Edward L. Wright, President-elect of the American Bar Association (ABA), who told the subcommittee that the ABA recommended amendment of RICO to include the civil remedy of authorizing private damage suits based upon the concept including sections of the Clayton Antitrust Act, which authorized private treble damage suits.‡

* Aaron Kohn. (June 11, 1970). Testimony reported in Hearings on Senate Bill 30 and Related Proposals, Organized Crime Control, Subcommittee No. 5, 91 Cong. 2nd Session, Subcommittee Report. Page 193.
† Rep. Sam Steiger [AZ]. (June 17, 1970). Testimony reported in Hearings on Senate Bill 30 and Related Proposals, Organized Crime Control, Subcommittee No. 5, 91 Cong. 2nd Session, Subcommittee Report. Page 195.
‡ Edward L. Wright. (June 23, 1970). Testimony reported in Hearings on Senate Bill 30 and Related Proposals, Organized Crime Control, Subcommittee No. 5, 91 Cong. 2nd Session, Subcommittee Report. Page 221.

Wright also presented the subcommittee with a report from the Criminal Law Section of the ABA, which recommended that the pattern requirement be changed to require three acts of racketeering, at least two of which occurred within five years of each other. The Criminal Law Section also supported the private cause of action under RICO.

On August 5, 1970, the subcommittee concluded its hearing on S. 30 with testimony from several Justice Department officials, including Assistant Attorney General Will Wilson and Ronald L. Gainer of the Criminal Division.

The House rejected the amendment proposed by Biaggi. The bill then passed by a vote of 341 to 26. It included, as should be noted, a liberal construction clause. On October 12, 1970, the Senate took up S. 30 as amended by the House. It passed by a voice vote as Senators McClellan and Hruska said that the House changes in the bill were not significant. No conference was held between the Senate and the House to harmonize the Senate and House versions of the bill. President Nixon signed the Organized Crime Control Act of 1970 into law on October 15, 1970, with RICO as Title IX.

In review of the legislative history of RICO, several points stand out regarding congressional intent.

1. The drafters of RICO, by removing the statute from the antitrust context in which it was originally proposed, did so to avoid bogging potential plaintiffs down in legalistic battles over such issues as standing, proximate cause, and direct or indirect injury. As will be seen, however, this is actually what has happened to many RICO plaintiffs.
2. RICO was clearly intended to supply a remedy for both competitors of racketeering enterprises and the immediate, direct victims of racketeering.
3. RICO was never intended to be limited to the Mafia, La Cosa Nostra, or other such groups; the defeat of the Biaggi amendment and the remarks of Congressman Poff referring to organized crime as simply a functional or descriptive term make the point clear.
4. The scope of RICO was deliberately expanded to encompass several different types of fraud and other crimes not totally characteristic of traditional organized crime.
5. Congress consistently rejected efforts to narrow the scope of the important new remedies it was creating, even though certain members, by using language that would be echoed in some subsequent judicial interpretations of RICO, claimed that the law was too broad, was too vague, or gave prospective litigants an unfair weapon to damage or destroy business rivals.

It has been speculated that the name and acronym were selected in a sly reference to the movie *Little Caesar*, which featured a notorious gangster named Rico. The original drafter of the bill, Robert G. Blakey, refused to confirm or deny this.* Robert G. Blakey remains the country's foremost expert on RICO; his former student Michael Goldsmith also gained a reputation as one of the nation's leading RICO experts.[†]

While Rico's career in organized crime had been terminated, the film's implied message is that the mob survived as a never-ending circulation of elites. The methods employed by the police to put an end to organized crime are shown to be quite ineffective. The police simply wait out the gang, hoping that one of the mobsters will grow tired of the rackets and willingly become an informant on his fellow gangsters. The specially appointed crime commissioner is killed early in the film by Rico, never to be replaced. Prosecutors and judges are pictured as themselves corrupt, making the job of convicting mobsters nearly impossible. What our cities need, according to the movie's foreword, is a more effective way of eliminating organized crime.

Overview

The RICO statute (18 U.S.C. §§ 1961–1968) prohibits any "person" from "investing in," "acquiring," or "conducting the affairs of" an "enterprise" engaged in or affecting interstate and foreign commerce by means of a "pattern" of "racketeering activity," including collection of an unlawful debt, and also prohibits conspiring to accomplish these goals.

18 U.S. Code § 1961 defines several key terms pertaining to RICO. "Racketeering activity" is defined as any act or threat involving certain generic state felonies—murder, kidnapping, gambling, arson, robbery, bribery, extortion and narcotics trafficking #§ 1961(1) (A) (J)—and acts indictable or punishable under certain federal statutes, including, inter alia, bribery, counterfeiting, gambling, extortion, obstruction of justice, labor law violations, mail fraud, wire fraud, bankruptcy fraud, fraud in the sale of securities, violation of the Currency Transaction Reporting Act, and narcotics dealing.

"Pattern of racketeering activity" is defined as at least two acts of racketeering activity committed within 10 years of each other, one of which occurred since the enactment of the statute in 1970.

"Enterprise" is defined as "any individual, partnership, corporation, association or other legal entity" as well as "any union or group of individuals associated in fact although not a legal entity."

* Robert G. Blakey. (1980). "Racketeer and Corrupt Organizations (RICO)." *Temple Law Quarterly*. Vol. 53. Pages 1009–1019.
† Michael Goldsmith. (1988). "RICO and enterprise criminality: A response to Gerard E. Lynch." *Columbia Law Review*. Vol. 88. Pages 774–778.

UNITED STATES V. SCOTT

2011 U.S. APP. LEXIS 11463 (9TH CIR. CAL. JUNE 8, 2011)

Steve Loren Scott was convicted in the United States District Court for the Central District of California under 18 U.S.C.S. § 1962(d) of Racketeer Influenced and Corrupt Organizations Act (RICO) conspiracy. Scott appeals his conviction and 220-month sentence after being found guilty by a jury of one count of RICO conspiracy, 18 U.S.C. § 1962(d), for participating in violent acts undertaken by the Aryan Brotherhood (AB) prison gang.

The court noted that the AB was a violent prison gang that started in California prisons but eventually spread to the federal prison system. Its members, most of whom are white prisoners, engaged in a conspiracy to use violence and traffic drugs to maintain a position of power in prisons and to discipline other members. The gang operated under a "blood in/blood out" rule, meaning that one had to spill blood to become a member and only left the AB when dead. The federal AB was run by a three-man commission. A council, which had authority over day-to-day operations of a particular prison, reported to the commission.

Scott was a prospective AB member in 1992 while imprisoned at the Leavenworth federal penitentiary. He allegedly became a member after stabbing Ismael Benitez-Mendez, who had attacked another AB member. Several years later, the AB, including Scott, entered into a violent and deadly war with the D.C. Blacks, another federal prison gang composed of mostly black inmates. The catalyst for the war was the attack on an elderly white inmate at the Marion prison around 1996 by Walter Johnson ("Butch" or "Prince"), a member of the D.C. Blacks. Soon thereafter, the AB commission, through commissioner T.D. Bingham, sent a letter to members at the Lewisburg prison declaring war. As a result, two inmates at Lewisburg, who were members of the D.C. Blacks, were killed by the AB. Around that time, Scott was appointed to head the business department of the AB.

As the war raged between the two prison gangs, Scott discussed with other members how to make and store weapons and passed around a "hit list" of D.C. Black members to attack. He was also promoted and became a member of the AB council. In 2000, during the ongoing war, Scott stabbed Erving Bond, a black inmate, in the shower.

Scott objected to the trial court's instruction, which stated, in part, "But once you have made the determination from the evidence that a conspiracy existed and who the members are, you can then, and only then, use all of the statements made by an alleged co-conspirator against any of those persons you find to also have been conspirators."

Scott's conviction was affirmed by the appellate court.

18 U.S. Code § 1962 list four activities that are controlled by RICO:

(a) Using or in, or establish an enterprise involved in illegal activities.
(b) Acquiring or maintaining an interest in, or control of, an enterprise through a pattern of racketeering activity.
(c) Conducting or participating in the conduct of an enterprise's affairs through a pattern of racketeering activity.
(d) Conspiring to violate 18 U.S. Code § 1962(a), (b), or (c).

RICO may be prosecuted as a civil or criminal violation. Section 1963 defines the criminal penalties, including forfeitures of property, and § 1964 provides for various civil remedies, including the following: allowing federal district courts to prevent violations by ordering divestiture of any interest in an enterprise and restricting future activities of the violator; civil actions by the Attorney General in which injunctive relief is available; and a private right of action for treble damages, costs, and attorney's fees to any person injured in his business or property by reason of a violation of § 1962.

What Is an Enterprise?

The U.S. Supreme Court answered this question in *Boyle v. United States*.* The Boyle case was probably one of the most important cases decided by the Supreme Court on RICO. The U.S. Courts of Appeals had disagreed on the question of whether an associated-in-fact enterprise required a showing of an ascertainable structure that was distinct from that inherent in the pattern of racketeering. Boyle was charged with a series of bank thefts that were allegedly conducted by a loosely organized group and did not appear to have had a leader or hierarchy. The trial court had refused the defense's proposed instruction that the government was required to prove that the RICO enterprise had an ascertainable structural hierarchy distinct from the charged predicate acts. The trial court instead instructed the jury that an association of individuals without structural hierarchy could form an enterprise.

The Supreme Court held that an association-in-fact enterprise had to have a "structure." However, the instructions did not have to include the term "structure," and that the jury was correctly and adequately instructed. The Court noted that the enumerated enterprises under 18 U.S.C. #§ 1961(4) broadly encompassed any group of individuals associated in fact and were

---

* 129 S. Ct. 2237 (2009).

UNITED STATES V. TURKETTE

452 U.S. 576 (U.S. 1981)

Novia Turkette was convicted under RICO, 18 U.S.C.S. §§ 1961–1968, for conspiracy to conduct and participate in the affairs of an enterprise, engaged in interstate commerce, through a pattern of racketeering activities. The enterprise conducted illegal activities. The appellate court reversed the judgment and held that the term "enterprise" as used in RICO applied only to legitimate enterprises, not illegitimate enterprises. The Supreme Court reversed the appellate court's judgment. The language and structure of RICO were not limited in its application to legitimate enterprises. Further, the legislative history indicated that Congress intended the term "enterprise" to include legitimate as well as illegitimate enterprises.

The judgment reversing the defendant's conviction under RICO was reversed because, based upon the legislative history and language, RICO applied to legitimate enterprises as well as illegitimate enterprises.

not limited to "business-like entities." The Court imposed the requirement that three structural features were necessary to constitute an enterprise:

(1) A purpose
(2) Relationships among those associated with the enterprise
(3) Sufficient longevity to permit pursuit of the purpose

The Court stated that additional structural features such as hierarchy or a chain of command were not required.

RICO in Criminal Cases

The RICO statutes have undergone periodic amendment since 1970, but they are largely unchanged in its basic provisions. RICO contains severe criminal penalties for persons engaging in a "pattern of racketeering activity" or "collection of an unlawful debt" that has a specified relationship to an "enterprise" affecting interstate commerce. "Racketeering activity" is defined to include major state felonies involving murder, robbery, extortion, and several other serious offenses, and more than thirty serious federal offenses, including extortion; counterfeiting; interstate theft and gambling offenses; narcotics violations; and mail, wire, and securities fraud. For RICO purposes, a pattern is defined as two or more of the specified state or federal crimes occurring within a statutorily prescribed time period. An "unlawful debt" is a debt arising from illegal gambling or loan sharking activities. "Enterprise" is broadly defined to include any individual, partnership, corporation, association, or other legal entity, and any group of individuals associated in fact although not a legal entity. For example, a narcotics ring can be a RICO enterprise, as can a large or small business or a government agency, such as a police department.

Four different criminal violations (including conspiracy) are proscribed by RICO. Section 1962(a) makes it a crime to invest the proceeds of a pattern of racketeering activity or collection of an unlawful debt in an enterprise affecting interstate commerce. For example, a narcotics trafficker violates this provision if he or she purchases a legitimate business with the proceeds of multiple drug transactions.

Section 1962(b) makes it unlawful to acquire or maintain an interest in an enterprise affecting interstate commerce through a pattern of racketeering activity or collection of an unlawful debt. An organized crime figure violates this provision if he or she takes over a legitimate business through a series of extortionate acts or arsons designed to intimidate the owners into selling out.

Section 1962(c) makes it a crime to conduct the affairs of an enterprise affecting interstate commerce through a pattern of racketeering activity or collection of an unlawful debt. An automobile dealer violates this provision if he or she uses the facilities of the dealership to operate a stolen car ring.

Section 1962(d) expressly makes it a crime to conspire to commit any of the three substantive RICO offenses.

Section 1963 of the act contains strong criminal penalties for violating any provision of § 1962: twenty years in prison and a fine of $25,000 or up to twice the gross profits of the offense, in addition to forfeiture of the defendant's interest in an enterprise connected to the offense and interests acquired through racketeering activity. Section 1963 also permits the government to seek pretrial (and even preindictment) restraining orders to prevent the dissipation of assets subject to forfeiture.

Section 1961(1) (b) includes as racketeering activity "any act which is indictable under" any of a list of federal criminal statutes. This provision is narrower than subdivision (A) because the federal offense must be an "act" that is "indictable" under a listed statute; attempts and conspiracies cannot be used as predicate offenses unless they are expressly included within the terms of the listed statute. Thus, for example, a conspiracy to violate the Hobbs Act, 18 U.S.C. § 1951, is a RICO predicate, because § 1951(a) expressly makes conspiracy a crime; conspiracy to conduct an illegal gambling business, on the other hand, cannot be a RICO predicate, because 18 U.S.C. § 1955 does not expressly make conspiracy a crime.*

---

* *United States v. Ruggiero*, 726 F.2d 913 (2nd Cir. 1984), and *United States v. Brooklier*, 685 F.2d 1208 (9th Cir. 1982).

Section 1961(1) defines "racketeering activity" to mean any crime that is enumerated in subdivision (A), (B), (C), (D), or (E) of this subsection. That list contains all of the offenses that constitute racketeering activity; no crime can be a part of a RICO "pattern of racketeering activity" unless it is expressly included in this subsection. The listed crimes are commonly called "predicate crimes or offenses" because they provide the underlying basis of a RICO violation. The different introductory wording of subdivisions (A), (B), (C), (D), and (E) is significant: subdivision (A) includes "any act or threat involving" the named offenses; subdivisions (B), (C), and (E) include "any act which is indictable under" the listed statutes; and subdivision (D) includes "any offense involving" the named categories of offenses. A major consequence of these differences in wording is that under some circumstances, conspiracies, or attempts to commit the crimes listed in subdivisions (A) and (D) have been held to be proper RICO predicates, whereas a conspiracy or attempt to commit an offense within subdivision (B) or (C) cannot be a RICO predicate unless attempt or conspiracy to commit the offense is specifically included in the statutory offense, and thus is "indictable under" the listed statute. Examples of the different results under the various subdivisions are set forth below, in connection with the discussions of the various predicate offenses.

Pattern of Racketeering

The term "pattern of racketeering activity" is one of the most important in the RICO statute, as it defines a key element of each substantive RICO offense in § 1962. In the statute, the elements of a pattern are set out in § 1961(5), which states that a pattern of racketeering activity requires at least two acts of racketeering activity, one of which occurred after the statute became law in 1970 and the last of which occurred within 10 years after the commission of a prior act of racketeering (excluding any period of imprisonment).

It is clear from the definition that a pattern of racketeering activity must contain at least two acts of racketeering activity, as defined in § 1961(1). The violations may be federal offenses, state offenses, or a combination of the two. Moreover, they need not have been previously charged.*

The U.S. Supreme Court in *H.J. Inc. v. Nw. Bell Tel. Co.*† stated that Congress had intended a "common sense" approach to the determination of the pattern of racketeering element in RICO cases. The Court stated that Congress had envisioned more stringent proof requirements than simply showing the commission of two qualifying crimes (predicate offenses) to

---

* *United States v. Parness*, 503 F.2d 430 (2nd Cir. 1974).
† 492 U.S. 229 (1989).

constitute a pattern, and it was the intent of Congress that to prove a pattern of racketeering activity, the prosecutor was required to prove that the predicate acts of racketeering are related and, in addition, that those predicates amount to or pose a threat of continuing criminal activity.

In one U.S. Court of Appeals case, defendants had engaged in at least a two-year scheme involving repeated international travel to convince the laborers to borrow thousands of dollars to travel to the United States only to find upon their arrival that things were not as promised. The Court in finding a pattern of racketeering held that there was no reason to suppose that this allegedly systematic victimization would not have continued indefinitely.*

In *New Burnham Prairie Homes, Inc. v. Village of Burnham*,† the court considered a RICO action based on an alleged wrongful withholding of building permits by a village official. The U.S. Court of Appeals affirmed the district court's action in granting summary judgment on the RICO claim by holding that the single scheme allegedly inflicted only a single injury and that this did not constitute a pattern of racketeering. The plaintiffs had argued that they had suffered numerous injuries through difficulties that arose when their building projects were delayed.

RICO in Civil Cases

While there are substantial similarities in the elements of criminal and civil RICO actions, there are also major differences between them. Both actions require proof of interaction between a formal or informal entity, the RICO enterprise and a pattern of racketeering activity, proof of which is made by showing a series of violations of certain federal state crimes within a 10-year period. The civil RICO action also is subject to a variety of issues common to all civil litigation. Civil RICO actions, like criminal RICO actions, require proof of criminal acts, but the context of that proof is circumscribed by the application of civil procedural and substantive law concepts rather than the proof beyond reasonable doubt that is required for criminal actions.

Jennings v. Auto Meter Products ‡ contains a general discussion on federal civil RICO. As noted in Jennings, Congress passed RICO in an effort to combat organized, long-term criminal activity. The appellate court noted that although § 1964(c) provides a private civil action to recover treble damages for violations of RICO's substantive provisions, the statute was not intended to allow plaintiffs to turn garden-variety state law fraud claims into federal RICO actions. The court noted that to establish a violation of § 1962(c),

---

* *Abraham v. Singh*, 480 F.3d 351 (5th Cir. La. 2007).
† 910 F.2d 1474 (7th Cir. 1990).
‡ 495 F.3d 466 (7th Cir. 2007).

UNITED STATES V. JOSEPH

781 F.2D 549 (6TH CIR. MICH. 1986)

Frank Joseph sought review of the judgment of the United States District Court for the Eastern District of Michigan, convicting him of attempting to collect an extension of credit by extortion in violation of 18 U.S.C.S. § 894, and of racketeering activity and conspiracy under RICO, 18 U.S.C.S. § 1961 et seq.

Joseph was convicted of racketeering activities. The court found that, in convicting him under 18 U.S.C.S. § 894, the district court relied on evidence that it had previously declared inadmissible. Because there was no independent proof that a collection or attempted collection was made, that extortionate means were used, and that Joseph knowingly participated as required by § 894, the evidence was clearly insufficient to support the conviction. The count under § 894 had been one of the predicate acts relied upon for the conviction under 18 U.S.C.S. § 1962(c), and its exclusion meant that there was insufficient evidence for conviction under § 1962(c). The court found, however, that with respect to the conspiracy count under 18 U.S.C.S. § 1962(d), it was not necessary to prove that the defendant agreed to personally commit the requisite acts, but only that he agreed that another violation of 18 U.S.C.S. § 1962(c) occured by committing two acts of racketeering activity. Even though one of the predicate acts relied upon by the district court was insufficient, a finding of guilt was not foreclosed because the defendant may have agreed that others would commit predicate acts.

The court reversed the defendant's convictions with respect to the counts under 18 U.S.C.S. § 894 and 18 U.S.C.S. § 1962(c), and remanded with respect to the count under 18 U.S.C.S. § 1962(d) for further proceedings.

on which Jennings relies in part, a plaintiff must show the following four elements by a preponderance of the evidence:

- Conduct
- Of an enterprise
- Through a pattern
- Of racketeering activity

The Jennings court noted that a pattern of racketeering activity consists, at the very least, of two predicate acts of racketeering committed within a 10-year period.* In order to prevent attempts to turn routine commercial

* 18 U.S.C. § 1961(5).

disputes into civil RICO actions, courts have carefully scrutinized the pattern requirement to forestall RICO's use against isolated or sporadic criminal activity and to prevent RICO from becoming a surrogate for garden-variety fraud actions properly brought under state law. The Jennings's court noted that to fulfill the pattern requirement, plaintiffs must satisfy the "continuity plus relationship" test: the predicate acts must be related to one another (the relationship prong) and pose a threat of continued criminal activity (the continuity prong).

In 18 U.S.C. § 1964(c), a civil remedy is provided to "any person" who is injured in his or her business or property by virtue of a violation of 18 U.S.C. § 1962. "Person" is defined to include any individual or entity capable of holding a legal or beneficial interest in property.*

Potential defendants in federal civil RICO actions include those persons who are found to have invested in, maintained or acquired an interest in, or participated in, an enterprise through a pattern of racketeering activity or conspired to do any of those things. The term "person," for RICO purposes, is broad, including any individual or entities capable of having a beneficial interest in property. Governmental units such as counties and cities are considered as "persons" for civil RICO actions and thus may be sued. A few courts, however, have held that counties and cities are inappropriate RICO defendants because they lack the capacity to form the criminal intent required to violate the statute.

State RICO Statutes

RICO statutes have been enacted in most states, Puerto Rico, and the Virgin Islands. Many of these statutes have both criminal and civil applications, although some of them do not authorize private suits. While many of these statutes bear a structural resemblance to the federal RICO statute, there are significant differences between the state laws and the federal law. A number of the state laws, for example, incorporate many state law violations as predicate offenses that are not encompassed by the federal RICO law. Some of the state RICO laws have longer limitation periods than the federal law and also authorize various types of relief to private litigants not available under federal law, such as recovery for personal injury and the right to equitable remedies. State RICO statutes also may have elements that are easier for litigants to establish. Criminal prosecutions under state RICO laws are often not subject to review by one agency such as the U.S. Department of Justice, but can be commenced by any district attorney. Some states have broadened

---

* 18 U.S.C. § 1961(e).

UNITED STATES V. ROBERTS

749 F.2D 404 (7TH CIR. ILL. 1984)

Fred Roberts, property owner, sought review of an order from the U.S. District Court for the Northern District of Illinois, Eastern Division, which required him to forfeit an automobile pursuant to 18 U.S.C.S. § 1963. The forfeiture was agreed to in a plea bargain, in which the appellant pleaded guilty to mail fraud, 18 U.S.C.S. § 1341, and activity in violation of RICO, 18 U.S.C.S. § 1961 et seq.

Roberts pleaded guilty to a violation of RICO, 18 U.S.C.S. § 1961 et seq. As part of the plea agreement, he agreed to forfeit an automobile. The court affirmed the order requiring Roberts to forfeit the automobile because, on the basis of concessions made in the plea agreement, a jury would have been justified in finding that the automobile was the property of an enterprise conducted in violation of RICO. The appellate court noted that the trial court was under a special burden in dealing with forfeitures resulting from pleas of guilty to violations of RICO, 18 U.S.C.S. § 1961 et seq. As in the case of any guilty plea, the court must make such inquiry as shall satisfy it that there is a factual basis for the plea. The mere fact that the defendant has agreed that an item is forfeitable, in a plea agreement, does not make it so; the trial court must ascertain whether it falls into one of the two forfeiture categories in 18 U.S.C.S. § 1963(a). The possibility of error in determining whether an item falls under one of these two headings is considerably greater than the possibility of error in determining the maximum jail sentence prescribed by law. A defendant's waiver of his right to trial cannot be said to have a factual basis, where a forfeiture of property is involved, unless the property is in fact subject to forfeiture.

The RICO defendant who has not distinguished his funds from those of the illegal enterprise does not, in virtue of that alone, expose all his personal assets to forfeiture. At the same time, he cannot be allowed to protect assets by claiming that although they were purchased with corporation funds, the assets were really purchased for personal use.

The appellate court affirmed the order requiring Roberts to forfeit an automobile because, on the basis of concessions made in the plea agreement, the automobile was an asset of an enterprise conducted in violation of RICO.

their RICO laws by incorporating federal predicates in the statute. There are also state statutes that authorize the reward of punitive damages in addition to treble damages.

Conversely, state RICO laws may force challenges based on state laws and state constitutional principles that are not present in federal civil RICO litigation. In a number of states, courts have also indicated a willingness to apply federal RICO case law to the interpretation of state statutes.

Summary

- RICO is the federal government's primary statutory weapon in its fight against organized crime.
- During the congressional hearing on the statutes, there were four distinct methods by which organized crime obtained control of legitimate businesses: (1) investing concealed profits acquired from gambling and other illegal enterprises, (2) accepting business interests in payment of the owners' gambling debts, (3) foreclosing on usurious loans, and (4) using various forms of extortion.
- The Corrupt Organizations Act contained three substantive offenses: (1) unlawful investment in an enterprise, (2) unlawful acquisition of an enterprise, and (3) unlawful participation in an enterprise through a pattern of racketeering activity. These provisions as originally proposed survived as § 1962(a), (b), and (c) of RICO.
- One criticism of RICO was that the scope of the bill, saying it went beyond organized crime.
- The RICO statute (18 U.S.C. §§ 1961–1968) prohibits any "person" from "investing in," "acquiring," or "conducting the affairs of" an "enterprise" engaged in or affecting interstate and foreign commerce by means of a "pattern" of "racketeering activity," including collection of an unlawful debt, and also prohibits conspiring to accomplish these goals.
- "Pattern of racketeering activity" is defined as at least two acts of racketeering activity committed within 10 years of each other, one of which occurred since the enactment of the statute in 1970.
- "Enterprise" is defined as "any individual, partnership, corporation, association or other legal entity" as well as "any union or group of individuals associated in fact although not a legal entity."
- 18 U.S. Code § 1962 lists four activities that are controlled by RICO: (a) using or in, or establish an enterprise involved in illegal activities, (b) acquiring or maintaining an interest in or control of, an enterprise through a pattern of racketeering activity, (c) conducting or participating in the conduct of an enterprise's affairs through a

pattern of racketeering activity, and (d) conspiring to violate 18 U.S. Code § 1962(a), (b), or (c).

- RICO may be prosecuted as a civil or criminal violation.

QUESTIONS IN REVIEW

1. What were the methods identified by Congress by which organized crime obtained control of legitimate businesses?
2. What were the three substantive offenses targeted in the Corrupt Organizations Act?
3. How does a RICO prosecution under the civil procedure differ from one under the criminal procedures?
4. Define "patterns of racketeering activity."
5. Define "enterprise" as referred to in the RICO statutes.
6. What are the four activities that are prohibited by the federal RICO statutes?

Crimes Involving
Public Officials

7

Chapter Objectives

After studying this chapter, you should be able to do the following:

- List the elements of the federal crimes of bribery and illegal gratuity.
- Describe the differences between bribery and illegal gratuity.
- Explain the types of intent involved in bribery and illegal gratuity offenses.
- Discuss the problems with establishing honest-services fraud.
- Discuss what constitutes criminal conflict of interest.

Introduction

There are a number of federal statutory crimes that were enacted to deter and punish public officials who are involved in acts of corruption. Those crimes include bribery and illegal gratuity, illegal outside income by government employees, kickbacks, and the honest-services crimes.

Bribery and Illegal Gratuity

The present federal bribery and illegal gratuity crimes are based on the Federal Conflict-of-Interest Law enacted in 1962. The distinction between the crimes of bribery and illegal gratuity is that bribery requires the government to have a specific intent in giving or demanding something of value whereas the crime of illegal gratuity does not require a specific intent to receive or give something of value.

The crime of illegal gratuity requires only that an illegal gratuity be given for or because of an official act. Both bribery and illegal gratuity apply to present and future public officials. The crime of illegal gratuity, unlike bribery, applies to former officials. For example, to commit the crime of bribery, the offender must be either a present public official or a future offender at the time of the criminal act. Note that the status of the defendant refers to the status at the time of the act, not the time of prosecution. Accordingly, a former executive may be prosecuted for bribery if he or she committed the act either during his or her service as a public officer or prior to accepting the position.

Another major difference between the two offenses is that bribery requires that the subject of misconduct be for or because of an officer act, whereas an illegal gratuity requires only that a gratuity be given.

The conflict of interest crimes created or modified by the 1962 legislation include the following:

- 18 U.S. Code 201(b): Making the offering or receipt of a bribe to or by a public official or witness a crime.
- 18 U.S. Code 201(c): Making the offering or receipt of illegal gratuity to or by public official or witness a crime.
- 18 U.S. Code 203 prohibited the unauthorized compensation of government officials for representing persons before the government.
- 18 U.S. Code 205 prohibited government officials from representing persons prosecuting claims against the federal government or before the federal government.
- 18 U.S. Code 207 restricted the postemployment activities of former federal government executive branch officials. [Note: This statute only applies to former officials of the executive branch and not to former congressional personnel.] The 1962 statute restricted the employment of former executives for one year. This restriction was extended to two years by the Honest Leadership and Open Government Act of 2007.*
- 18 U.S. Code 208 prohibited executive branch officials from participating in matters that affect their financial interest.

Elements of Bribery and Illegal Gratuities

To convict a person of bribery, generally, the government must establish the following:

- A thing of value was either offered, given, or promised to a recipient or
- A recipient demanded, sought, received, or accepted something of value, done by a present or future public official
- For an official act
- With corrupt intent or intent to influence

* Public Law No. 110-81, Sections 101 and 121 (2007).

To prove the offense of illegal gratuity, the government must establish the following:

- A thing of value was given, offered, or promised to (or, in the case of a recipient, demanded, sought, received, or accepted by)
- A present, past, or future public official
- For or because of any official act performed or to be performed by such public official

Public Official or Witness

The requirement that the bribery or illegal gratuity be directed at a public official or a witness has provided some interesting cases. The Supreme Court and the federal appellate courts have interpreted the term "public official" broadly. In general, it is a person who occupies a position involving public trust with official federal responsibilities. In some cases, because state and local officials are involved in implementing federal programs, they may be considered as a "public official" for purposes of federal bribery and illegal gratuity crimes. In the Dixson case, it was stated that Congress intended for such local officials to be covered by the statute, with the conclusion that employment by the United States or some other similarly formal contractual or agency bond is not a prerequisite to prosecution under the federal bribery statute.[*]

Title 18, U.S. Code has defined public official as a

- Member of Congress,
- Delegate, or
- Resident Commissioner,
- Either before or after such an official has qualified, or an officer, or
- Employee or person acting for or on behalf of the United States, or
- Any department, agency or branch of Government thereof, including the District of Columbia, in any official function, under or by authority of any such department, agency, or branch of Government, or a juror[†]

A person who has been selected to be a public official is defined as any person who has been nominated or appointed to be a public official or has been officially informed that such person will be so nominated or appointed.[‡] A "witness" is defined as any person who testifies at a trial, hearing, or other

[*] 465 U.S. at 497–98.
[†] 18 U.S. Code 201(a)(1).
[‡] 18 U.S.C. 201(a)(1) and 201(a)(2).

proceeding. This includes any proceedings before any court; any committee of the Senate, House, or both; or any agency, commission, or officer authorized by the laws of the United States to hear evidence or take testimony.

The court in *United States v. Kenney* concluded that a defense contractor employee who did not have the final say but whose recommendations were given sufficient weight to influence the outcome of the decisions at issue was a public official for the purposes of Section 201(c).*

The court in *Dixon v. United States* stated that Congress never intended the open-ended definition of public official in Section 201(a) to be given a cramped reading.† The court noted that the interpretation of the meaning of "public official" was not intended to bring all employees of local organizations that administer federal funds within the definition of "public official" and that the term "public official" applied only to those individuals who possess some degree of official responsibility for carrying out a federal program or policy.‡ The court in that decision indicated that a person merely receiving federal assistance is not sufficient to be considered as a "public official."

The actual ability of a public official to complete the objective of the scheme is not important. Mere misrepresentation as to the scope of the official's authority has been sufficient. Even undercover agents acting as public officials qualify under the statutes as a public official.§ An immigration inspector's promise to commit immigration fraud was sufficient to sustain a conviction for bribery even if the inspector did not have the authority to perform on his promise.¶

Thing of Value

The term "thing of value" is broadly defined by the courts. It includes checks and negotiable instruments. The courts have found that it also includes the promise of future employment, overseas travel, sexual acts, shares of stock, and any item that the recipient subjectively believes to have value even if it has little or no commercial value.** The Court in *United States v. Williams* upheld a lower court's decision that worthless shares of stock were things of value to the defendant senator because he had a subjective belief that they were valuable.††

---

* 185 F.3d 1217, 1221–22 (11th Cir. 1999).
† 465 U.S. 482, 496 (1984).
‡ *United States v. Dixon*, 536 F.2d 1388 (2nd Cir. 1976).
§ *United States v. Romano*, 879 F.2d 1056, 1060 (2nd Cir. 1989).
¶ *United States v. Vega*, 184 F. App'x 236, 242 (3rd Cir. 2006).
** *United States v. Ostrander*, 999 F.2d 27, 31 (2nd Cir. 1993) and *United States v. Crozier*, 987 F.2d 893, 901 (2nd Cir. 1993).
†† *United States v. Williams*, 705 F.2d 603 (2nd Cir. 1983).

The item of value need not be conveyed to the official; it can be conveyed to a third party for the benefit of the official, e.g., the awarding of a public contract to the senator's son is a thing of value to the senator. The fact that the receipt of the thing of value may be delayed until after the individual is no longer a public official is immaterial. The promise of a thing of value has been held to include the promise to testify in court proceedings.

Official Act Requirement

Under both the bribery and illegal gratuity offenses, an "official act" is required. An official act is defined by 18 U.S. Code 201(a)(3) as any decision or action on any question, matter, cause, suit, proceeding or controversy, which may be pending or may be brought before any public official in the official's official capacity, or in such official's place of trust or profit.

The U.S. Supreme Court has taken a narrow definition of the phrase "official capacity." The Court stated in *United States v. Sun-Diamond Growers of California* that 18 U.S. Code 201 requires a showing that a gift was motivated by the recipient's capacity to exercise governmental power or influence in the donor's favor without necessarily showing that it was connected to a particular official act.* The Court, in that case, noted that a broad interpretation of Section 201 would criminalize the giving of token gifts during public ceremonies—a sports jersey for the President during a White House visit by the sports team, school cap for the Secretary of Education during a high school visit, and complementary lunch from the farmers during a visit by the Secretary of Agriculture—all assuredly official acts in some sense.† Note: In a prosecution under Section 201, the government must allege and establish some particular act.

The required act may be a failure to act. For example, the court held that the failure to report a licensing violation by a massage parlor constituted an official act.‡

Prosecution and Informant Agreements

A thing of value has been held to include a promise of leniency by a federal prosecutor, although there is a serious question as to whether leniency-induced testimony is included in the concept.§ Note in the Singleton case, that the court held that when a federal prosecutor enters into a plea agreement with a defendant, the plea agreement is between the United States

---

* 526 U.S. 398, 406–07 (1999).
† Id. at 407.
‡ *United States v. Alan*, 231 F.3d 26, 32 (D.D.C. 2000).
§ *United States v. Singleton*, 144 F.3d 1343, 1348 (10th Cir. 1998).

government and the defendant; therefore, the prosecutor does not receive a thing of value.*

In *United States v. Dawson*, a U.S. Court of Appeals held that a government payment of 20% of the proceeds from the government sale of illegal narcotics was not a violation of the bribery or illegal gratuity statutes.[†] In *United States v. Barnett*,[‡] a federal appellate court concluded that a government payment of $7,500 to a witness for assistance and testimony in a murder-for-hire prosecution was not in violation of 18 U.S. Code 201(c). The court noted that government payments for assistance and testimony in criminal cases were not prohibited by the U.S. Code.

The *United States v. Feng*[§] case concluded that the government's offer of letters recommending asylum on behalf of testifying witnesses was not a violation of the federal antigratuity statute because immigration benefits or leniency should not be differentiated from criminal leniency.

Intent

As noted earlier in this chapter, the major distinction between the crimes of bribery and illegal gratuity is that bribery requires the government to have a specific intent in giving or demanding something of value whereas the crime of illegal gratuity does not require a specific intent to receive or give something of value. In *United States v. Jennings*,[¶] an appellate court stated that a goodwill gift to an official to foster a favorable business climate, given simply with the generalized hope or expectation of ultimate benefit on the part of the donor, did not constitute a bribe.

Intent Required to Establish Bribery

To establish a bribery offense under Section 201(b), the government must prove a corrupt intent to influence, or be influenced in, the performance of an official act. The Supreme Court has stated that this element requires proof of a *quid pro quo*, i.e., a specific intent to give or receive something of value in exchange for an official act. While the Court has indicated a requirement of a *quid pro quo*, the Court has stated that it need not be fully executed and that bribery requires only the specific intent of performing an official act in return for something of value. Vague expectations of some future benefit do not satisfy the statutory intent requirement.

---

* *United States v. Singleton*, 165 F.3d 1297, 1299–1301 (10th Cir. 1999).
† *United States v. Dawson*, 425 F.3d 389, 394–95 (7th Cir. 2005).
‡ *United States v. Barnett*, 197 F.3d 138, 145 (5th Cir. 1999).
§ 277 F.3d 1151, 1153–54 (9th Cir. 2002).
¶ 160 F.3d 1006, 1013 (4th Cir. 1998).

The specific intent requirement to establish bribery may be established by circumstantial evidence.* The promises need not be specifically correlated to a particular official act, as long as the offeror of the bribe intended for the payment to induce the official to adopt a specific course of action. In addition, a payment or promise need not alter a public official's actual course of conduct, as long as the parties to the transaction possessed corrupt intent.[†]

Question: Candidate Jamison is running for the U.S. Senate. She has promised that if elected, she will reduce the taxes on foreign stock profits. Based on this promise, Fred makes a large contribution to her campaign fund. Does this constitute bribery?

An appellate court in *United States v. Tomblin*[‡] stated that intending to make a campaign contribution does not constitute bribery, even though many contributors hope that the official will act favorably because of their contributions. In *United States v. Allen*, the court noted that accepting a campaign contribution does not equal taking a bribe unless the payment is made in exchange for an explicit promise to perform or not perform an official act.[§]

A goodwill gift to an official to foster a favorable business climate, given simply with the generalized hope or expectation of ultimate benefit on the part of the donor, does not constitute a bribe.[¶]

Intent in Illegal Gratuity Offenses

To establish an illegal gratuity offense under Section 201(c)(1), the government needs only to prove that the gratuity was given or accepted for or because of any official act. Corrupt intent or a *quid pro quo* agreement need not be established. The court, in *United States v. Bustamante*, held that it was sufficient for the government to show that the defendant was given the gratuity simply because he held public office.[**]

In *United States v. Schaffer*, the court stated that a gratuity can be given with the intent to induce a public official to propose, take, or shy away from some future official act.[††] Under the rule in this case, it would be an offense to give a gift if it was given in the hope that when the particular official actions move to the forefront, the public official will listen hard to, and hopefully be swayed by, the giver's proposals, suggestions, and/or concerns. It would appear that maybe the authors committed the offense when they made

---

* *United States v. Jennings*, 160 F.3d 1006 (4th Cir. 1998).
† *United States v. Quinn*, 359 F.3d 666 (4th Cir. 2004).
‡ 46 F.3d 1369, 1379 (5th Cir. 1995).
§ 10 F.3d 405, 411 (7th Cir. 1993).
¶ *United States v. Jennings*, 160 F.3d 1006, 1013 (4th Cir. 1998).
** 45 F.3d 933 (5th Cir. 1995).
†† 183 F.3d 833, 842 (D.C. Cir. 1999).

donations to their favorite presidential candidate with the goal of getting him elected in order to have a president more favorable to their business or political beliefs.

Lesser Included Offense

Since the illegal gratuity offense does not require a showing of specific intent, it is often used by prosecutors as a lesser included offense to bribery. If the prosecutor cannot establish the specific intent, then he or she may consider prosecuting the defendant under the lesser included offense of taking or offering an illegal gratuity.*

Criminal Conflict of Interest

The use of a public office for private gain is prohibited by 18 U.S. Code 203. The offense applies to the public official receiving the unauthorized compensation and also to the individual attempting to influence a public official.

The elements of the criminal conflict of interest offense are as follows:

- The person was covered by the statute (generally a public official),
- In connection with a particular matter in which influence was sought, demanded, accepted, or agreed to receive compensation
- With corrupt intent
- To provide services before a particular governmental forum

Section 203 applies to all individuals employed by the federal government. This includes members of Congress, federal judges, and employees of the executive, legislative, and judicial branches. It also covers those who knowingly give, promise, or offer compensation to public officials for representational services rendered or to be rendered in the future. The statute exempts retired military officers who are not otherwise government employees, individuals working under grants for the benefit of the national interest, those giving testimony under oath or statements under penalty of perjury, and those representing family members or other personal fiduciaries.

Section 203 prohibits public officials from accepting compensation for representational services in relation to a particular matter in which the United States is a party or has a direct and substantial interest. Section 203 is violated only when compensation is demanded, sought, received, accepted, or agreed upon by a public official or knowingly given, promised, or offered

---

* *United States v. Patel*, 32 F.3d 340 (8th Cir. 1994).

to a public official. The offense does not require specific intent nor an intent to be corrupted or influenced. The acceptance of an unauthorized compensation is all that the government needs to establish in a trial under Section 203.

There are some exceptions under Section 203. Section 205 allows government employees to provide unpaid representation to a person who is the subject of disciplinary, loyalty, or other personnel administrative proceedings if it is not inconsistent with the employees' duties. The *pro bono* exception ensures that government employees with grievances against their employer-agency will have representation in those proceedings without having to hire a private attorney. This exception, however, has been interpreted as applying only to administrative proceedings, and not to representation before a court. Two Georgetown University Law students who also worked for the government, however, were prohibited from participating in an appellate litigation clinic representing indigent clients because of the potential for a conflict of interest between their duties to their employers and their duties to their clients.*

Another exception is that special government employees may represent parties who are grant recipients or who are under contract with the federal government, if the head of the federal agency involved certifies that such representation is necessary. Federal employees may also testify in court proceedings even if the case is against the United States.

Postemployment Activities

The Revolving Door Statute, Title 18 U.S. Code 207, limits lobbying by individuals after they leave government service. For example, covered employees or appointees are forbidden to lobby any employee or officer of their former agency for a period of two or five years after the termination of their employment. Time period depends on the nature of the prior federal employment. The employees covered by Section 207 are classified according to their positions, pay grades, and tenure of employment.

Section 207 applies to instances where a former official, acting as agent or attorney or otherwise representing anyone else, has contact with the federal government knowingly and with the intent of influencing the government. The key issue is whether the defendant actually represented another party after leaving federal employment. For example, in *United States v. Schaltenbrand*, a former Air Force reserve officer who worked for a private contractor attended a meeting between the Air Force and his new employer. The Eleventh Circuit, applying principles of agency law, held that the defendant could not be considered a representative or agent for purposes of

---

* *United States v. Bailey*, 498 F.2d 677 (D.C. Cir. 1974).

Section 207 because he did not have actual or apparent authority to bind the principal.*

To prove a violation under Section 207, the government must establish that the defendant had participated personally and substantially by having official responsibility for the particular matter. For example, in *United States v. Medico Industries, Inc.*, a former Army procurement officer attempted to alter a series of contracts initially negotiated while he was still on active duty.† The court concluded that the defendant had been involved personally and substantially in the particular matter. The court stated also that if the matter was just within his job description, but he did not work on it himself, the officer would be free to represent a private party after leaving the government.

In *Kelley v. Brown*, the Secretary of Veterans Affairs attempted to disqualify an attorney from representing a client by arguing that the attorney had a conflict of interest because he initially appeared in the case on behalf of the Secretary of Veterans Affairs. The Veterans Appeals Court disagreed and held that the attorney's prior involvement had not been substantial, as his duties were limited to reviewing, signing, and filing two minor pleadings.‡ The court concluded that the pleadings failed to meet Section 207's requirement that the proposal be the same particular matter in which the former federal employee participated personally and substantially.

The majority of cases arising under this restriction are not criminal cases, but claims that government contracts awarded to former government employees should be void. It is noted that such claims have generally been unsuccessful.

Acts Affecting Financial Interest

Title 18 U.S. Code 208 generally prohibits an officer or employee of the executive branch from personally and substantially participating in any particular matter in which, to his or her knowledge, the officer, his or her spouse, general partner, or organization with which they are involved has a financial interest. This section was enacted to ensure honesty in the Government's business dealings by preventing federal agents who have interests adverse to those of the Government from advancing their own interests at the expense of the public's welfare, and to preserve the integrity of the decision-making process. Courts have interpreted Section 208 broadly in order to achieve the objectives.

---

* 930 F.2d 1554 (11th Cir. 1991).
† *United States v. Medico Indus., Inc.*, 784 F.2d 840 (7th Cir. 1986).
‡ *Kelly v. Brown*, 9 Vet. App. 37, 39 (1996).

Illegal Outside Salaries for Federal Employees

Title 18 U.S. Code 209 prohibits the receipt or payment of a salary as compensation, except from the Government, for services rendered as an officer or employee of the Executive Branch, an executive agency, or the District of Columbia government. The statute has no intent or *mens rea* requirement. The elements of a Section 209(a) offense are as follows:

- A nongovernment party
- Makes a contribution or supplementation to
- The salary of an executive branch official
- As compensation for his services as an officer or employee of the executive branch

When determining whether the payment was for government services, subjective intent is not a relevant inquiry. The purpose of the statute is to avoid improper *quid pro quos*. It was drafted with the intent to proscribe any gift giving or salary supplementation, regardless of the payment's purpose.

In *Crandon v. United States*, the Supreme Court held that severance payments made to future federal employees before they begin government service do not violate the statute.* The Court determined that Congress intended to help the government attract personnel with special knowledge and skills, and that Section 209 accordingly applies only to those persons who are employed by the government at the time the outside payments are received.

Honest-Services Fraud

Honest-services fraud refers to a 28-word sentence of 18 U.S.C. § 1346: "For the purposes of this chapter, the term, scheme or artifice to defraud includes a scheme or artifice to deprive another of the intangible right of honest services."

The first federal mail-fraud statute was enacted in 1872. Later in 1909, Congress added the language to 18 U.S. Code 1346 that prohibited any scheme or artifice to defraud, or for obtaining money or property by means of false or fraudulent pretenses, representations, or promises. The statute, more commonly known as the Honest-Services Doctrine, criminalized both schemes to defraud and schemes for obtaining money and property via fraudulent methods. The section protects the public from traditional fraudulent schemes that enrich the purveyor of the fraud at the expense of the

---

* 359. 494 U.S. 152 (1990).

EXCERPTS FROM *SKILLING V. UNITED STATES* DECISION

Founded in 1985, Enron Corporation grew from its headquarters in Houston, Texas, into the seventh highest-revenue-grossing company in America. Petitioner Jeffrey Skilling, a longtime Enron officer, was Enron's chief executive officer from February until August 2001, when he resigned. Less than four months later, Enron crashed into bankruptcy, and its stock plummeted in value. After an investigation uncovered an elaborate conspiracy to prop up Enron's stock prices by overstating the company's financial wellbeing, the Government prosecuted dozens of Enron employees who participated in the scheme. In time, the Government worked its way up the chain of command, indicting Skilling and two other top Enron executives. These three defendants, the indictment charged, engaged in a scheme to deceive investors about Enron's true financial performance by manipulating its publicly reported financial results and making false and misleading statements. Count 1 of the indictment charged Skilling with, inter alia, conspiracy to commit "honest-services" wire fraud, 18 U. S. C. §§ 371, 1343, 1346, by depriving Enron and its shareholders of the intangible right of his honest services. Skilling was also charged with over 25 substantive counts of securities fraud, wire fraud, making false representations to Enron's auditors, and insider trading.

...Section 1346, which proscribes fraudulent deprivations of "the intangible right of honest services," is properly confined to cover only bribery and kickback schemes. Because Skilling's alleged misconduct entailed no bribe or kickback, it does not fall within the Court's confinement of § 1346's proscription....

To satisfy due process, "a penal statute must define the criminal offense with sufficient definiteness that ordinary people can understand what conduct is prohibited and in a manner that does not encourage arbitrary and discriminatory enforcement.... The void-for-vagueness doctrine embraces these requirements. Skilling contends that § 1346 meets neither of the two due-process essentials. But this Court must, if possible, construe, not condemn, Congress' enactments. Alert to § 1346's potential breadth, the Courts of Appeals have divided on how best to interpret the statute. Uniformly, however, they have declined to throw out the statute as irremediably vague. This Court agrees that § 1346 should be construed rather than invalidated....

Interpreted to encompass only bribery and kickback schemes, § 1346 is not unconstitutionally vague. A prohibition on fraudulently depriving another of one's honest services by accepting bribes or kickbacks presents neither a fair-notice nor an arbitrary-prosecution problem. As to fair notice, it has always been clear that bribes and kickbacks constitute honest-services fraud, *Williams v. United States*, 341 U. S. 97, 101, and the statute's *mens rea* requirement further blunts any notice concern, see, e.g., *Screws v. United States*, 325 U.S. 91, 101–104. As to arbitrary prosecutions, the Court perceives no significant risk that the honest-services statute, as here interpreted, will be stretched out of shape....

victim as well as fraudulent schemes that enrich the purveyor of the fraud as well as a complicit third party and deprive the victim of only honest services.

In *Skilling v. United States*,* the U.S. Supreme Court addressed the conviction of an officer of a corporation who was alleged to have denied the corporation's shareholders honest services by committing fraud regarding the corporation's finances. Skilling's attorneys argued that Section 1346 was a facially invalid violation of due process because (1) the statute was not definite enough to be understood by an ordinary person and (2) the statute was so vague it encouraged arbitrary enforcement. The Court acknowledged that a broad interpretation of the statute could run afoul of the void-for-vagueness doctrine. The Court interpreted the right to honest services to be violated only when the perpetrator of the fraud received a bribe or kickback from a third party. The Court also found that a corporate officer convicted of fraudulently paying himself noncompetition fees and failing to disclose such fees had not violated Section 1346, because there was no bribe or kickback from a third party.

After the Skilling case, to be convicted under section 1346,

- An individual must
- Defraud the victim of honest services
- By accepting a bribe or kickback

Summary

- A number of federal statutory crimes were enacted to deter and punish public officials who are involved in acts of corruption.
- The present federal bribery and illegal gratuity crimes are based on the Federal Conflict-of-Interest Law enacted in 1962.

* 130 S. Ct. 2963 (2010).

- The distinction between the crimes of bribery and illegal gratuity is that bribery requires the government to have a specific intent in giving or demanding something of value whereas the crime of illegal gratuity does not require a specific intent to receive or give something of value.
- The crime of illegal gratuity requires only that an illegal gratuity be given for or because of an official act.
- Another major difference between the two offenses is that bribery requires that the subject of misconduct be for or because of an officer act, whereas an illegal gratuity requires only that a gratuity be given.
- The Supreme Court and the federal appellate courts have interpreted the term "public official" broadly. In general, it is a person who occupies a position involving public trust with official federal responsibilities.
- The term "thing of value" is broadly defined by the courts. It includes checks and negotiable instruments.
- The courts have found that a "thing of value" also includes promise of future employment, overseas travel, sexual acts, shares of stock, and any item that the recipient subjectively believes to have value even if it has little or no commercial value.
- Under both the bribery and illegal gratuity offenses, an "official act" is required.
- To establish a bribery offense under section 201(b), the government must prove a corrupt intent to influence, or be influenced in, the performance of an official act.
- To establish an illegal gratuity offense under section 201(c)(1), the government needs only to prove that the gratuity was given or accepted for or because of any official act.
- The use of a public office for private gain is prohibited by 18 U.S. Code 203.
- Section 203 applies to all individuals employed by the federal government.
- The Revolving Door Statute, Title 18 U.S. Code 207, limits lobbying by individuals after they leave government service.
- Title 18 U.S. Code 208 generally prohibits an officer or employee of the executive branch from personally and substantially participating in any particular matter in which, to his or her knowledge, the officer, his or her spouse, general partner, or organization with which they are involved has a financial interest.
- Honest-services fraud refers to a 28-word sentence of 18 U.S.C. § 1346: "For the purposes of this chapter, the term, scheme or artifice to defraud includes a scheme or artifice to deprive another of the intangible right of honest services."

QUESTIONS IN REVIEW

1. How did the Supreme Court limit the scope of honest-services fraud in the Skilling decision?
2. What are differences in required intent between bribery and illegal gratuities?
3. Explain the types of misconduct involved in the criminal conflict of interest crimes.
4. Why are there restrictions on the postemployment activities of former federal officials?
5. What are the elements of honest-services fraud?

Practicum

Gerald Green is a candidate for the U.S. House of Representatives. Green knows that the president, who is of the same political party as Green, will ask for Green's recommendation (if Green is elected) for a federal judgeship that is open in Green's district. Green approaches Fred Loyate, an attorney friend. He tells Fred that if Fred will act as his campaign manager and Green gets elected, Green will ensure that Fred is appointed to the federal judgeship.

Question: What crimes if any has Green committed?

Obstruction of Justice

8

Chapter Objectives

After studying this chapter, you should be able to do the following:

- Explain what constitutes obstruction of justice.
- Discuss the crime of perjury.
- List the elements of obstruction of justice and perjury.
- Explain which proceedings are protected by the obstruction of justice crimes.
- Explain why prosecutors often prosecute the defendant for perjury rather than the underlying charges.
- Explain what constitutes a material statement for perjury purposes.

Introduction

Obstruction of justice is defined in the U.S. Code as any "interference with the orderly administration of law and justice." The crime is governed principally by 18 U.S. Code 1501–1520. Those U.S. Code sections are designed to protect the integrity of judicial proceedings before the federal judiciary and other governmental bodies. While the code sections address many particular categories of behavior, only the provisions that have been given the most expansive treatment by courts and involve white-collar crimes are discussed in this chapter.

In white-collar crime investigations, the prosecutor frequently charges crimes involving misconduct that is related to the investigation such as perjury and obstruction of justice rather that prosecuting the defendant for the underlying offenses. Generally, this decision is based on the evidence available to the prosecutor, and frequently, he or she lacks evidence on the underlying crime such as insider trading. Note: Martha Stewart was not convicted of insider trading, but of giving false statements to the investigator. In this chapter, generally, only the federal crimes will be discussed, but in most cases, there are similar state statutes protecting state proceedings.

Omnibus Obstruction Provision

> Section 1503 is designed to "achieve the twin goals of protecting the partici-
> pants in a specific federal proceeding and preventing a miscarriage of justice
> in a case pending in a federal court."[*]

18 U.S. Code 1503(a) provides that an individual is guilty of influencing or injuring an officer who corruptly, or by threats or force, or by any threatening letter or communication, endeavors to influence, intimidate, or impede any grand or petit juror, or officer in or of any court of the United States, or officer who may be serving at any examination or other proceeding before any United States magistrate judge or other committing magistrate, in the discharge of his duty, or injures any such grand or petit juror in his person or property on account of any verdict or indictment assented to by him, or on account of his being or having been such juror, or injures any such officer, magistrate judge, or other committing magistrate in his person or property on account of the performance of his official duties, or corruptly or by threats or force, or by any threatening letter or communication, influences, obstructs, or impedes, or endeavors to influence, obstruct, or impede, the due administration of justice.[†] Section 1503 is commonly considered as the Omnibus Obstruction Provision.

The maximum punishment for conviction of this offense may be enhanced if the crime occurs in connection with a trial of a criminal case, and the act in violation of this section involves the threat of physical force or physical force.

Section 1503 protects the judicial process in two ways.

- The specific language of the statute forbids corruptly influencing any grand or petit juror or officer of the court by threats or force, or by letter or communication.
- The last section of 1503 is considered as the "Omnibus Clause." It is a catch-all provision that generally prohibits any conduct that interferes with the due administration of justice.

The U.S. Supreme Court noted that the Omnibus Clause serves as a catch-all and is far more general in scope than the earlier clauses in the statute. The Court held that acts prosecuted under the "catch-all" clause must have the "natural and probable" effect of interfering with the due administration of justice. Section 1503 applies to both civil and criminal proceedings.[‡]

---

[*] David Cylkowski and Ryan Thornton. (Spring 2011). "Obstruction of justice." *American Criminal Law Review.* Vol. 48. Issue 2. Pages 955–976.
[†] *United States v. Aguilar,* 515 U.S. 593 (1995).
[‡] *United States v. Aguilar* (1995), p. 598.

Section 1503 applies to both actual and attempted obstructions of justice. To obtain a conviction, the government is required to prove the following:

- A nexus between the misconduct in question and a federal judicial proceeding.
- That the defendant knew of or had notice about the proceeding.
- That the defendant acted corruptly with the intent to obstruct or interfere with the proceeding or due administration of justice.

A federal court in *United States v. Erickson** affirmed a conviction where the evidence established that the defendant had altered documents subpoenaed after they were subpoenaed by a grand jury. In *United States v. Quattrone,*† a federal appellate court noted that a conviction can be upheld where a defendant merely knows of a "category of documents" requested by a grand jury subpoena and seeks to hide them. In another case, the defendant was convicted under Section 1503 when the evidence established that the subpoenaed corporate minutes had been altered after the date of the subpoena and that some of the original minutes were missing.‡ The *United States v. Gravely* case held that documents do not have to be under subpoena to constitute obstruction of justice; what is required is that the defendant is aware that the grand jury will likely seek documents in its investigation and the defendant interfered with the production of those documents.§

Most federal courts have interpreted Section 1503 to require the existence of a pending judicial proceeding as a prerequisite for conviction under 1503. Section 1503 does not give authority to prosecute obstruction of an independent government investigation or official proceeding not connected with a pending judicial proceeding.¶ Note: The defendant may, however, be guilty of a violation of U.S. Code 1505, which is discussed later in this chapter.

The U.S. Court of Appeals for the Ninth Circuit has held that aiding and abetting illegal aliens by assisting them escape from custody is not obstruction of justice since "custody" is not a pending judicial proceeding.** In *United States v. Macari*, a court held that an investigation by the Federal Bureau of Investigation (FBI) does not constitute a pending proceeding under 1503 unless it is an extension of a grand jury investigation.†† In *United States v. Davis*, the court held that a wiretap investigation of a defendant is not a pending judicial

---

* 561 F.3d 1150, 1159 (10th Cir. 2009).
† 441 F.3d 153, 171 (2nd Cir. 2006).
‡ *United States v. Brooks*, 111 F.3d 365, 373 (4th Cir. 1997).
§ 840 F.2d 1156, 1160 (4th Cir. 1988).
¶ *United States v. Macari*, 453 F.3d 926, 936 (7th Cir. 2006).
** *Salazar-Luviano v. Mukasey*, 551 F.3d 857, 862 (9th Cir. 2008).
†† *United States v. Macari*, 453 F.3d at 936 (2005).

proceeding and is thus insufficient to invoke 1503.* A grand jury investigation is a "pending judicial proceeding" for the purpose of 1503, where the grand jury has been impaneled and the witness had signed a written agreement to testify.[†]

In *United States v. Aguilar*,[‡] the Supreme Court noted that a defendant must know that his or her actions will affect the judicial proceedings to have the requisite intent to obstruct. The *United States v. Erickson*[§] held that if there is no knowledge of the pending proceeding, there is no specific intent to obstruct the proceeding.

Q: The defendant lied to the FBI. At the time, the defendant did not have knowledge of a grand jury proceeding. Has he violated Section 1503? [¶]

Agency Provision

18 U.S. Code 1505 is similar to the earlier discussed Section 1503, except 1505 applies to a proceeding before departments, agencies, and committees. For example, 1505 would apply to the misconduct of preventing a person from testifying before the U.S. Congress or other nonjudicial proceeding involving the U.S. Government.

To establish a violation of Section 1505, the prosecutor must prove that the following:

- The defendant was aware of the proceedings.
- There is a pending proceeding before a department or agency of the United States.
- The defendant intentionally and corruptly endeavored to influence, obstruct, or impede the proceeding.

There is no requirement that the defendant is successful in his or her attempt to obstruct the proceeding, only that an attempt to do so was made. Under 1505, the term "proceeding" includes both the investigative and adjudicative functions of a department or agency. Whether a meeting constitutes a proceeding is a question of law to be decided by the trial judge. Section 1505 has been applied to the "investigative aspect" of agency proceedings, which reaches most agency activity conducted before an investigation is formally

---

* 183 F.3d 231, 240 (3rd Cir. 1999).
† *United States v. Vesich*, 724 F.2d 451, 455 (5th Cir. 1984).
‡ 515 U.S. 593, 599 (1995).
§ 561 F.3d 1150, 1159 (10th Cir. 2009).
¶ While the defendant may be guilty of providing a false statement, he is not guilty of obstruction of justice under Section 1503. See *United States v. Forman*, 180 F.3d 766, 768 (6th Cir. 1999).

commenced. The section applies even if the matter investigated will later be tried before a criminal court. The defendant is considered as culpable if his or her conduct has the natural and probable effect of obstructing justice.

The "corrupt" requirement has been interpreted expansively to include both subtle threats and acts of force and includes all acts conducted with an improper purpose. It is not defense that a defendant believed that the pending proceeding was illegitimate or unjust. The "corrupt" requirement has been interpreted to include both subtle threats and acts of force. It generally includes all acts conducted with an "improper purpose."

What constitutes a proceeding is a question of law and therefore is decided by the trial judge. The term "proceeding" encompasses both the investigative and adjudicative functions of a department or agency. A few U.S. district courts have determined that an agency must have "rule-making or adjudicative authority" for an act to come under Section 1505.*

Obstructing an Investigation

18 U.S. Code 1510 is used to deter the coercion of potential witnesses by subjects of federal criminal investigations prior to the initiation of judicial proceedings. It is an extension of Sections 1503 and 1505 and is designed to provide potential witnesses and informants with the same protection afforded to witnesses, jurors, and others involved in judicial, administrative, or congressional proceedings.

Witness Tampering and Retaliation

The U.S. Congress passed the Victim and Witness Protection Act of 1982 (VWPA) because of its concern that testifying victims and other witnesses had little hope of protection from the government if they were harassed or threatened. The VWPA provides for both criminal sanctions and civil remedies. The elements of the federal crime of witness tampering are set forth in 18 U.S. Code 1512. That section provides that a person is guilty of witness tampering under the following circumstances:

- Whoever kills or attempts to kill another person, with the intent to
- Prevent the attendance or testimony of any person in an official proceeding

---

* *United States v. Adams*, 472 F. Supp. 2d 811, 817 n.8 (W.D. Va. 2007).

- Prevent the production of a record, document, or other object, in an official proceeding; or
- Prevent the communication by any person to a law enforcement officer or judge of the United States of information relating to the commission or possible commission of a Federal offense or a violation of conditions of probation, parole, or release pending judicial proceedings

The second subsection of 1512 applies to any official proceedings of a federal government agency. That subsection provides, in part, that

- Whoever uses physical force or the threat of physical force against any person, or attempts to do so, with the intent to
- Influence, delay, or prevent the testimony of any person in an official proceeding; or
- Cause or induce any person to
- Withhold testimony, or withhold a record, document, or other object, from an official proceeding
- Alter, destroy, mutilate, or conceal an object with the intent to impair the integrity or availability of the object for use in an official proceeding; or
- Evade legal process summoning that person to appear as a witness, or to produce a record, document, or other object, in an official proceeding; or
- Be absent from an official proceeding to which that person has been summoned by legal process; or
- Hinder, delay, or prevent the communication to a law enforcement officer or judge of the United States of information relating to the commission or possible commission of a Federal offense or a violation of conditions of probation, supervised release, parole, or release pending judicial proceedings;
- Is guilty of a violation of Section 1512

Other misconducts that are prohibited by Section 1512 include the following:

- Evading a legal process which summons a person to appear as a witness, or to produce a record, document, or other object, in an official proceeding; or
- The absence from an official proceeding to which such person has been summoned by legal process; or
- Hindering, delaying, or preventing the communication to a law enforcement officer or judge of the United States of information relating to the commission or possible commission of a Federal offense or a violation of conditions of probation, supervised release, parole, or release pending judicial proceedings

18 U.S. Code 1513 is designed to protect a witness, victim, or an informant from retaliation. That section provides that

- Whoever kills or attempts to kill another person with the intent to retaliate against any person for
- The attendance of a witness or party at an official proceeding, or any testimony given or any record, document, or other object produced by a witness in an official proceeding; or
- Providing to a law enforcement officer any information relating to the commission or possible commission of a Federal offense or a violation of conditions of probation, supervised release, parole, or release pending judicial proceedings;
- Is guilty of a federal crime

Section 1513 may also be violated by the following:

- Knowingly engaging in any conduct and thereby causes bodily injury to another person or damages the tangible property of another person, or threatens to do so, with the intent to retaliate against any person for
- The attendance of a witness or party at an official proceeding, or any testimony given or any record, document, or other object produced by a witness in an official proceeding; or
- For giving any information relating to the commission or possible commission of a Federal offense or a violation of conditions of probation, supervised release, parole, or release pending judicial proceedings given by a person to a law enforcement officer

It is an affirmative defense, as to which the defendant has the burden of proof by a preponderance of the evidence, that the conduct consisted solely of lawful conduct and that the defendant's sole intention was to encourage, induce, or cause the other person to testify truthfully.

Section 1512(b) requires that the defendant "knowingly" commit a prohibited act. However, it does not require that the defendant act with a corrupt purpose. It is sufficient that the defendant performed one of the other enumerated acts with the intent to "influence" testimony. The prosecution need not prove that the defendant knew of the federal nature of the proceeding with which he or she tampered.

Section 1512 focuses on a defendant's attempt to impede justice, rather than on his success. Accordingly, the prosecution does not have to prove actual intimidation of the witness, only that the threats had a tendency to intimidate. The threats or intimidating acts that form the basis for the prosecution can be either explicit or implicit in the defendant's conduct.

The "misleading conduct" requirement focuses on the defendant's actions rather than his intent. Misleading conduct occurs only when the defendant uses coercive or deceptive conduct, including situations where the defendant deliberately lies or makes culpable omissions to witnesses.

Corrupt persuasion is the act or acts of deterring or attempting to influence testimony through sheer persuasion with a corrupt purpose. In addition to the purpose of corrupt persuasion, courts have considered the "persuader's" knowledge of whether his conduct was unlawful. The statute requires joining the meanings of "knowingly" and "corruptly," thus limiting criminal liability to those who are conscious of their wrongdoing. Apparently absent dishonesty merely impeding an investigation does not constitute corrupt persuasion.

As to the requirement to establish that a defendant intended to influence the testimony, the government need only show that the defendant was aware that the natural and probable consequences of his actions would be to influence the testimony of a witness. Under 1512, whether or not the defendant actually influenced any testimony is immaterial. Likewise, under the crime of retaliation, the prosecution must establish an intent to threaten retaliation, but need not establish an intent to carry out the threat.

The prosecution does not need to establish by direct evidence that the defendant knew that a witness was an informant; the jury may infer the intent to retaliate. The intent to retaliate is a question of fact to be decided by a jury. The intent to retaliate does not require an intent to carry out the threat; rather, the defendant must simply intend to communicate the threat of retaliation.

Civil Action to Restrain Harassment of a Victim or Witness

Pursuant to U.S. Code 1514, the government, victim, or witness may file a civil action in a U.S. District Court to obtain a temporary restraining order (TRO) prohibiting harassment of a victim or witness in a Federal criminal case. In order to issue a TRO, the court needs to find from specific facts shown by an affidavit or by verified complaint that there are reasonable grounds to believe that harassment of an identified victim or witness in a Federal criminal case exists, or that such order is necessary to prevent and restrain an offense.

The district court may issue a temporary restraining order without written or oral notice to the adverse party or such party's attorney in a civil action under this section if the court finds, upon written certification of facts by the attorney for the government, that such notice should not be required and that there is a reasonable probability that the government will prevail on the merits. Any TRO issued without notice shall be endorsed with the date and hour of issuance and be filed forthwith in the office of the clerk of the court issuing the order. The temporary TRO will expire at a specific time, not to exceed 14 days from issuance; however, the court, for good cause shown before expiration of such order, may extend the expiration date of the order for up to 14 days or for such longer period agreed to by the adverse party.

When a TRO is issued without notice, the motion for a protective order shall be set down for hearing at the earliest possible time and takes precedence over all matters except older matters of the same character, and when such motion comes on for hearing, if the attorney for the government does not proceed with the application for a protective order, the court shall dissolve the TRO.

The term "harassment" means

- A course of conduct directed at a specific person
- That causes substantial emotional distress in such person; and
- Serves no legitimate purpose

The term "course of conduct" means a series of acts over a period of time, however short, indicating a continuity of purpose.

Perjury

The integrity of governmental processes depends in large part on the truthfulness of statements made under oath.[*]

If a person testifies falsely after taking the oath or writes a false statement on a document supported by an affidavit, he or she has committed the crime of perjury. The person must be aware that the testimony or statement is false. The states have their own laws on perjury when the offense takes place in a state court or in relation to a state agency. Untrue testimony or falsely sworn documents relating to a federal court or administrative agency can result in federal perjury charges. The penalty for a federal offense is generally more severe than the sentence for a similar state law offense.

The essence of the crime of perjury is willful making while under oath an untruth statement in a material statement. Section 1621 applies only to testimony the defendant willfully stated or to which the defendant subscribed with knowledge of its falsity. The prosecution is required to establish beyond a reasonable doubt that the speaker had a willful intent and that the speaker knew the testimony was false. The intent element is not satisfied by false testimony provided as a result of confusion, mistake, faulty memory, or inconsequential inconsistencies or conflicts in a witness's testimony.

[*] Daniel J. McGinn-Shapiro. (Spring 2011). "Perjury." *American Criminal Law Review.* Vol. 48. No. 2. Page 997.

The federal perjury statute is 18 USC 1621. The elements of perjury are the following:

- A false statement
- On a material issue
- Made willfully and with knowledge that it was false
- Under oath (by someone authorized to administer the oath, and
- Before an authorized tribunal, officer, or person

A material issue is an issue that, in one way or another, determines the outcome of a legal proceeding. If the false statement would not or could not change the final disposition of a legal proceeding, then it is arguably immaterial and not a basis for perjury charges. The sentence for this charge is a maximum of five years in prison.

In perjury cases, the courts have construed the phrase "before a competent tribunal, officer, or person" broadly and have applied Section 1621 to a wide range of circumstances, including testimony before a grand jury and testimony before a congressional committee.

The Whole Truth

Q: If a witness was asked on cross-examination at a civil trial, "Has the corporation ever had a foreign bank account?" and the witness stated, "We do not have a foreign bank account," did the witness commit perjury when the government establishes that the company had recently (before the trial) closed its only foreign bank account?

In *Bronston v. United States*,* the Supreme Court held that a misleading but literally true answer could not provide the basis for a prosecution for perjury. If no false statement has been made, even the alleged intent of the witness to mislead by evasion or nonresponse is irrelevant. The court noted that fancy footwork in crafting a response might preclude actionable perjury if there is literal truth in the answer.

Materiality

A false statement must be material to be actionable under federal perjury crimes. The burden of proving materiality rests on the prosecution. Consider the following scenario: A high school math teacher was being prosecuted for having sex with one of her students who was under the age of 17. The prosecutor, trying to

---

* 145 F.3d 1289 (11th Cir. 1998).

establish that the teacher was an adult, asked her, "How old are you?" The defendant answered, "34." The defendant's actual age was 38. Did she commit perjury? Probably not, because whether she was 34 or 38, she was still an adult.

A statement is not immaterial simply because it does not resolve an issue in the tribunal before whom it is uttered. The courts have held that a statement is material if it tends to enhance or impugn the credibility of a material witness, even in instances where the statement is unrelated to charges in a criminal trial. False statements may be considered to be material if truthful answers would likely have led to the discovery of admissible evidence in the underlying case.

In *United States v. Regan*,[*] a federal appellate court held that a false statement is material if it has the effect or tendency to impede or dissuade a grand jury investigation. In *United States v. Kross*,[†] the defendant argued that his answer to an attorney's question was not material because the attorney knew the correct answer before asking the question. The appellate court held that the statement was material and that the defendant had committed perjury.

A statement is material if the statement could have potentially aided a grand jury investigation. It is the statement's potential—but not its actual—effect on a grand jury that determines the statement's materiality.[‡] The individual making the false statement may be prosecuted even if the original case is dismissed.[§]

Fifth Amendment

A defendant may be prosecuted for false statements made while under a grant of immunity. The grant of immunity may protect a defendant from prosecution for past crimes, but it does not protect false testimony that may frustrate the administration of justice. While the Fifth Amendment grants suspects the privilege to remain silent without risking contempt, it does not give any individual the right to lie. Once a defendant chooses to speak and deceive the court, the Fifth Amendment will no longer shield him or her.[¶]

Perjury Trap

In *United States v. Crisconi*,[**] a federal appellate court stated that a perjury trap was in violation of the Due Process Clause when the government abuses the grand jury process by using investigatory powers to secure indictment for perjury on matters that are not material or germane to the legitimate investigation of a grand jury.

---

[*] 103 F.3d 1072, 1081 (2nd Cir. 1997).
[†] 14 F.3d 751, 755 (2nd Cir. 1994).
[‡] *United States v. Goguen*, 723 F.2d 1012, 1019 (1st Cir. 1983).
[§] *United States v. Akram*, 152 F.3d 698, 701 (7th Cir. 1998).
[¶] *Kansas v. Ventris*, 129 S.Ct. 1841, 1845 (2009).
[**] 520 F. Supp. 915, 920 (D. Del. 1981).

Often it is easier for the government to prove perjury than the underlying crime. Is it legal for the government to have the grand jury call a defendant in order to create an opportunity for the witness to commit perjury? While the courts have held that the government may not use a grand jury to lay a trap, it is difficult to establish that the only reason the witness was called was to set the trap. If the grand jury testimony relates to the crimes under investigation, generally, the courts will not accept a "perjury trap" claim.

Crime of False Declaration

In addition to perjury, federal criminal statutes provide the crime of false declaration where the act occurred before a court or grand jury. Under 18 USC 1623, prosecutors can charge a person with making a false declaration if the prosecutor can prove the following:

- A false statement
- On a material issue
- Made with knowledge that it was false
- Under oath
- Made before or in relation to a court or grand jury

The sentencing for a false declaration is the same as the punishment for perjury. The false declarations crime was added by the Organized Crime Control Act of 1970 and is intended to be used for perjury committed before a court or grand jury. The perjury statute is applicable to a broader range of conduct, including statements before a tribunal, officer, or person, whereas the false declarations statute only applies to statements before a court or grand jury. Federal prosecutors have discretion on which statute to use to prosecute a person for perjury.

The crimes apply to witness testimony and written statements made on legal documents. Any document that contains an affidavit, verification, certification, sworn declaration, or oath can be the basis of a perjury charge. In most cases, the document does not need to be supported by an oath. Rather, it can be supported by a declaration that it is true (also referred to as a certificate or verification). However, the declaration needs to be substantially in a form described by 26 USC 1746. It should read as follows:

I declare (or certify, verify, or state) under penalty of perjury under the laws of the United States of America that the foregoing is true and correct. Executed on (date). (Signature).

A false declaration in the form established by 26 USC 1746 can result in federal perjury charges.

The filing of false federal income tax forms may be prosecuted as perjury under the federal tax statues.* In addition, making a false statement to the Immigration and Naturalization Service (INS) can also result in federal perjury charges.† False statement charges for denying involvement in a crime is considered as a federal crime.

Subornation of Perjury

Section 1622 of Title 18 U.S. Code makes subornation of perjury a crime. To commit this offense, the defendant must have persuaded a witness to perjure him or herself. The witness must actually have committed perjury. It is not necessary that the witness be threatened with physical harm; having been persuaded may be sufficient.

Summary

- Obstruction of justice is defined in the U.S. Code as any interference with the orderly administration of law and justice.
- Those U.S. Code sections are designed to protect the integrity of judicial proceedings before the federal judiciary and other governmental bodies.
- In white-collar crime investigations, the prosecutor frequently charges crimes involving misconduct that is related to the investigation, such as perjury and obstruction of justice.
- The U.S. Supreme Court noted that the Omnibus Clause serves as a catch-all and is far more general in scope than the earlier clauses in the statute. The Court held that acts prosecuted under the "catch-all" clause must have the "natural and probable" effect of interfering with the due administration of justice. Section 1503 applies to both civil and criminal proceedings.
- Most federal courts have interpreted Section 1503 to require the existence of a pending judicial proceeding as a prerequisite for conviction under 1503.
- The defendant must know that his or her actions will affect the judicial proceedings to have the requisite intent to obstruct. The *United States v. Erickson* held that if there is no knowledge of the pending proceeding, there is no specific intent to obstruct the proceeding.

---

* 26 U.S. Code 7206.
† 8 U.S. Code 1357.

- 18 U.S. Code 1505 is similar to the earlier discussed Section 1503, except that 1505 applies to proceedings before departments, agencies, and committees.
- There is no requirement that the defendant has successfully obstructed the proceeding, only that an endeavor was made.
- 18 U.S. Code 1510 is used to deter the coercion of potential witnesses by subjects of federal criminal investigations prior to the initiation of judicial proceedings.
- The U.S. Congress passed the Victim and Witness Protection Act of 1982 because of its concern that testifying victims and other witnesses had little hope of protection from the government if they were harassed or threatened.
- If a person testifies falsely after taking the oath, or writes a false statement on a document supported by an affidavit, he or she has committed the crime of perjury.
- The person must be aware that the testimony or statement is false.
- The states have their own laws on perjury when the offense takes place in a state court or in relation to a state agency.
- Untrue testimony or falsely sworn documents relating to a federal court or administrative agency can result in federal perjury charges.

Practicum

Consider this scenario: John works for a brokerage firm. He has received a subpoena to testify before a congressional committee about issues involving the stock exchange. What if John's employer remarks to John the day before the hearing that testifying before the congressional committee could mean new regulations and the new regulations would result in fewer employees for the company. The employer suggests to John that he should tailor his testimony so that the committee does not see the need to add new regulations and that if the hearing results in the company having to lay off employees, the fact that John testified would be considered in determining which employees to dismiss. Has the employer violated Section 1505?

QUESTIONS IN REVIEW
1. What does the government need to establish to prove an obstruction of justice charge?
2. What are the primarily differences between Sections 1503 and 1505?
3. What constitutes perjury?
4. How does making a false declaration differ from perjury?
5. What constitutes witness tampering?

Sanctions for White-Collar Criminals

9

Chapter Objectives

After studying this chapter, you should be able to do the following:

- Explain the sanctions available to the judge in cases involving white-collar criminals.
- Discuss when white-collar criminals should be imprisoned.
- Explain the concept of civil asset forfeitures.
- Describe and explain the functions of sentencing guidelines.
- Explain why taking a person's assets under civil asset forfeiture and then prosecuting the person in a criminal court is not double jeopardy.

Introduction

By sanctions, we are actually referring to punishments. Punishment has been defined as a government authorized imposition of a deprivation of freedom, privacy, or goods to which the person would otherwise have a right or the imposition of special burdens because the individual receiving the punishment has been found guilty of some crime.* As we cover the aspects of punishments in this chapter, ask yourself if those aspects apply equally to the white-collar criminal.

As noted by Masters and Roberson, unlike common criminals, the white-collar criminal tends to be mature, middle-class or higher, white, and male.† Sutherland, in his famous work on white-collar crime, observed the following:

> Those who become white-collar criminals generally start their careers in good neighborhoods and good homes, graduate from college with idealism, and, with little selection on their part, get into a particular business situation in

---

* Dennis Rodder. (2009). *White-Collar Crime: What Sanctions or Punishment Should Be Imposed*. Norderstedt, Germany: GmbH.
† Ruth Masters and Cliff Roberson. (1989). *Inside Criminology*. Englewood Cliffs, NJ: Prentice-Hall.

SHAMING AS A SANCTION FOR WHITE-COLLAR CRIMINALS

Would it be a cruel and unusual punishment to require Martha Stewart to open her television programs with a picture of her in a prison uniform?

which criminality is practically a folkway, becoming inducted into that system of behavior just as into any other folkway.*

Professor Dan Kahan wonders whether it might be more effective in deterring white-collar crime by imposing extensive shaming sanctions on the white-collar criminal rather than extensive prison terms.† In discussing the Rajaratnam insider trading case, would it be more effective if, rather than a couple of years in prison, Rajaratnam would be required every business day to ring the opening bell at the stock exchange while wearing his prison jumpsuit, or if Martha Stewart's magazines and television shows had to include an image of her eating in the federal prison's mess hall along with other convicted felons when she was imprisoned? What if anyone convicted of a white-collar offense were required for decades to post a large sign on their lawns that highlighted to all their neighbors that the homeowner was a criminal? Would shaming work for white-collar offenders because they, unlike petty robbers and muggers, live in a nice, safe, white-collar world?

The authors have discussed the sentencing process with numerous judges. The overwhelming majority of the judges indicated that the sentencing process was the most difficult task in trying a criminal case. Near the end of this chapter is a sentencing memorandum by U.S. District Court Judge Marvin E. Frankel. In his memorandum, Judge Frankel discusses the issues involved in determining an appropriate sentence for a white-collar criminal.

The U.S. Federal courts are involved primarily in three types of criminal cases: illegal substance, bank robberies, and white-collar crime. In addition, many states have followed the federal scheme for determining sanctions in cases involving white-collar crimes. The following Crime Reporter Box provides excerpts from the federal rules of criminal procedure involving the sentencing of a person convicted in a federal court.

---

* Edwin H. Sutherland. (1940). "White-Collar Criminality." *American Sociological Review*. Vol. 5. Page 32.
† Douglas A. Berman. (October 18, 2011). "Seeking better deterrence, should we try extensive shaming of white-collar criminals?" Posted at http://sentencing.typepad.com/sentencing_law_and_policy/2011/10/seeking-better-deterrence-should-we-try-extensive-shaming-of-white-collar-criminals.html [Accessed on August 14, 2012].

FEDERAL RULES OF CRIMINAL PROCEDURE
(EXCERPTS FROM RULE 32.
SENTENCING AND JUDGMENT)

(b) Sentencing

    (1) In General. The court must impose sentence without unnecessary delay.

    (2) Changing Time Limits. The court may, for good cause, change any time limits prescribed in this rule.

(c) Presentence Investigation.

    (1) Required Investigation.

        (A) In General. The probation officer must conduct a presentence investigation and submit a report to the court before it imposes sentence unless:

            (i) 18 U.S.C. § 3593 (c) or another statute requires otherwise; or

            (ii) The court finds that the information in the record enables it to meaningfully exercise its sentencing authority under 18 U.S.C. § 3553, and the court explains its finding on the record.

        (B) Restitution. If the law permits restitution, the probation officer must conduct an investigation and submit a report that contains sufficient information for the court to order restitution.

    (2) Interviewing the Defendant. The probation officer who interviews a defendant as part of a presentence investigation must, on request, give the defendant's attorney notice and a reasonable opportunity to attend the interview.

(d) Presentence Report.

    (1) Applying the Advisory Sentencing Guidelines. The presentence report must:

        (A) Identify all applicable guidelines and policy statements of the Sentencing Commission;

        (B) Calculate the defendant's offense level and criminal history category;

        (C) State the resulting sentencing range and kinds of sentences available;

        (D) Identify any factor relevant to:

            (i) The appropriate kind of sentence, or

            (ii) The appropriate sentence within the applicable sentencing range; and

    (E)   Identify any basis for departing from the applicable sentencing range.

  (2) Additional Information. The presentence report must also contain the following:

    (A) The defendant's history and characteristics, including:

       (i)   Any prior criminal record;

      (ii) The defendant's financial condition; and

     (iii) Any circumstances affecting the defendant's behavior that may be helpful in imposing sentence or in correctional treatment;

    (B) Information that assesses any financial, social, psychological, and medical impact on any victim;

    (C) When appropriate, the nature and extent of nonprison programs and resources available to the defendant;

    (D) When the law provides for restitution, information sufficient for a restitution order;

    (E) If the court orders a study under 18 U.S.C. § 3552(b), any resulting report and recommendation;

    (F) A statement of whether the government seeks forfeiture under Rule 32.2 and any other law; and

    (G) Any other information that the court requires, including information relevant to the factors under 18 U.S.C. § 3553(a).

  (3) Exclusions. The presentence report must exclude the following:

    (A) Any diagnoses that, if disclosed, might seriously disrupt a rehabilitation program;

    (B) Any sources of information obtained upon a promise of confidentiality; and

    (C) Any other information that, if disclosed, might result in physical or other harm to the defendant or others.

(e) Disclosing the Report and Recommendation.

  (1) Time to Disclose. Unless the defendant has consented in writing, the probation officer must not submit a presentence report to the court or disclose its contents to anyone until the defendant has pleaded guilty or nolo contendere, or has been found guilty.

  (2) Minimum Required Notice. The probation officer must give the presentence report to the defendant, the defendant's attorney, and an attorney for the government at least 35 days before sentencing unless the defendant waives this minimum period.

(3) Sentence Recommendation. By local rule or by order in a case, the court may direct the probation officer not to disclose to anyone other than the court the officer's recommendation on the sentence.

(f) Objecting to the Report.

(1) Time to Object. Within 14 days after receiving the presentence report, the parties must state in writing any objections, including objections to material information, sentencing guideline ranges, and policy statements contained in or omitted from the report.

(2) Serving Objections. An objecting party must provide a copy of its objections to the opposing party and to the probation officer.

(3) Action on Objections. After receiving objections, the probation officer may meet with the parties to discuss the objections. The probation officer may then investigate further and revise the presentence report as appropriate.

(g) Submitting the Report. At least 7 days before sentencing, the probation officer must submit to the court and to the parties the presentence report and an addendum containing any unresolved objections, the grounds for those objections, and the probation officer's comments on them.

(h) Notice of Possible Departure from Sentencing Guidelines. Before the court may depart from the applicable sentencing range on a ground not identified for departure either in the presentence report or in a party's prehearing submission, the court must give the parties reasonable notice that it is contemplating such a departure. The notice must specify any ground on which the court is contemplating a departure.

(i) Sentencing.

(1) In General. At sentencing, the court:

(A) Must verify that the defendant and the defendant's attorney have read and discussed the presentence report and any addendum to the report;

(B) Must give to the defendant and an attorney for the government a written summary of—or summarize in camera—any information excluded from the presentence report under Rule 32(d)(3) on which the court will rely in sentencing, and give them a reasonable opportunity to comment on that information;

(C)   Must allow the parties' attorneys to comment on the probation officer's determinations and other matters relating to an appropriate sentence; and

(D)   May, for good cause, allow a party to make a new objection at any time before sentence is imposed.

Purposes of Criminal Sanctions

In discussing the purposes of criminal sanctions, various ideologies are presented. For purposes of studying this chapter, ideology refers to the belief system adopted by a group and consists of assumptions and values. The assumptions are beliefs about the way the world is constituted, is organized, and operates. Values, however, are beliefs about what is moral and desirable.* There are numerous methods to classify ideologies. Three popular classifications based on political theories that influence our corrections system are conservative, liberal, and radical.

The conservative ideology tends to accept the concept that human beings are rational, possess free will, and voluntarily commit criminal misconduct. Accordingly, criminals should be held accountable for their actions. Punishment should be imposed to inflict suffering on the criminal because the suffering is deserved and because it will deter future crime. The punishment imposed should fit the crime. This ideology, because of its view on the causes of human behavior generally, does not accept the concept of rehabilitation as an attractive objective of punishment.

The liberal ideology tends to view human behavior as greatly influenced by social circumstances including one's upbringing, material affluence, education, peer relationships, etc. Accordingly, human behavior is more than a simple product of free choice. All of the social influences are important factors in shaping our conduct. Viewing criminal behavior as a product of both social circumstances and individual actions, liberals are more likely to support rehabilitation as the proper purpose of criminal punishment. Most liberals tend to be receptive to a wider range of aims for criminal punishment, including deterrence.

The radical ideology rejects both the conservative and liberal ideologies. To them, crime is a reflection of the status of our present social system. Crime is only a natural consequence of our social system. According to the radicals,

---

* Alexis M. Durham III. (1994). *Crisis and Reform: Current Issues in American Punishment*. Boston: Little, Brown, and Company. Pages 16–18.

fundamental changes in the socioeconomic basis of society are required in order to control crime.

The ultimate purpose of criminal sanctions is generally considered to be the maintenance of our social order. Herbert Packer contends that the two major goals of criminal sanctions are to inflict suffering upon the wrong-doers and the prevention of crime.*

Robert Dawson sees the major purpose of the criminal justice system as the identification in a legally acceptable manner of those persons who should be subjected to control and treatment in the correctional process.† According to Dawson, if the corrections process does not properly perform its task, the entire criminal justice system suffers. An inefficient or unfair correctional process can nullify the courts, prosecutors, and police alike. Conversely, the manner in which the other agencies involved perform their tasks has an important impact upon the success of the process: a person who has been unfairly dealt with prior to conviction is a poor subject for rehabilitation.

The four popular goals of criminal sanctions are retribution, deterrence, incapacitation, and rehabilitation. From the 1940s to the 1980s, rehabilita-tion was considered by most as the primary goal of our system. Since the 1980s, retribution has received popular support.

Retribution

Retribution generally means "getting even." Retribution is based on the ideology that the criminal is an enemy of society and deserves severe pun-ishment for willfully breaking its rules. Retribution is often mistaken as revenge. There are, however, important differences between the two. Both retribution and revenge are primarily concerned with punishing the offender and neither is overly concerned with the impact of the punishment on the offender's future behavior or behavior of others. Unlike revenge, however, retribution attempts to match the severity of the punishment to the seri-ousness of the crime. Revenge acts on passion, whereas retribution follows specific rules regarding the types and amounts of punishment that may be inflicted. The Biblical response of an "eye for an eye" is a retributive response to punishment. While the "eye for eye" concept is often cited as an excuse to use harsh punishment, it is less harsh than revenge-based punishment, which does not rule out "two eyes for an eye" punishment. Sir James Stephen, an English judge, expressed the retributive view by stating that "the punish-ment of criminals was simply a desirable expression of the hatred and fear

---

* Herbert L. Packer. (1968). *The Limits of Criminal Sanction.* Stanford, CA: Stanford University Press. Page 33.
† Robert O. Dawson. (1969). *Sentencing: The Decision as to Type, Length, and Conditions of Sentence.* Boston: Little, Brown, and Company.

aroused in the community by criminal acts."* This line of reasoning conveys the message that punishment is justifiable because it provides an orderly outlet for emotions that, if denied, may express themselves in socially less acceptable ways. Another justification under the retribution ideology is that only through suffering punishment can the criminal expiate his sin. In one manner, retribution treats all crimes as if they were financial transactions. You got something or did something; therefore, you must give something of equivalent value (suffering).

Retribution is also referred to as "just deserts." The just deserts movement reflects the retribution viewpoint and provides a justifiable rationale for support of the death penalty. This viewpoint has its roots in a societal need for retribution. It can be traced back to the individual need for retaliation and vengeance. The transfer of the vengeance motive from the individual to the state has been justified based on theories involving theological, aesthetic, and expiatory views. According to the theological view, retaliation fulfills the religious need to punish the sinner. Under the aesthetic view, punishment helps reestablish a sense of harmony through requital and thus solves the social discord created by the crime. The expiatory view is that guilt must be washed away (cleansed) through suffering. There is even a utilitarian view that punishment is the means of achieving beneficial and social consequences through the application of a specific form and degree of punishment deemed most appropriate for the particular offender after a careful individualized study of the offender.[†]

Deterrence

Deterrence is a punishment viewpoint that focuses on future outcomes rather than past misconduct. It is also based on the theory that creating a fear of future punishments will deter crime. It is based on the belief that punishments have a deterrent effect. There is substantial debate as to the validity of this concept. Specific deterrence specifically deters the offender, whereas general deterrence works generally on others who might consider similar acts. According to this viewpoint, the fear of future suffering motivates individuals to avoid involvement in criminal misconduct. This concept assumes that the criminal is a rational being who will weigh the consequences of his or her criminal actions before deciding to commit them.

One of the problems with deterrence is determining the appropriate magnitude and nature of punishment to be imposed in order to deter future

---

[*] Herbert L. Packer. (1968). *The Limits of Criminal Sanction*. Stanford: Univ. of Stanford Press. Page 37.

[†] Elmer H. Johnson. (1974). *Crime, Correction, and Society*. Homewood, IL: Dorsey Press. Page 173.

criminal misconduct. For example, an individual who commits a serious crime and then feels bad about the act may need only slight punishment to achieve deterrent effects, whereas a professional shoplifter may need severe fear-producing punishments to prevent future shoplifting.

Often, increases in crime rates and high rates of recidivism are used to cast doubt that the deterrence approach is effective. Recidivism may cause some doubt on the efficacy of special deterrence, but it says nothing about the effect of general deterrence. In addition, unless we know what the crime rate or rates of recidivism would be if we did not attempt to deter criminal misconduct, the assertions are unfounded. Are we certain that the rates would not be higher had we not attempted to deter criminals?

Incapacitation

At least while the prisoner is in confinement, he is unlikely to commit crimes on innocent persons outside of prison. To this extent, confinement clearly helps reduce criminal behavior. Under this viewpoint, there is no hope for the individual as far as rehabilitation is concerned; therefore, the only solution is to incapacitate the offender. Marvin Wolfgang's famous study of crime in Philadelphia indicated that while chronic offenders constituted only 23% of the offenders in the study, they committed over 61% of all the violent crimes.[*] Accordingly, the supporters of the incapacitation viewpoint contend that incapacitating the 23% would have prevented 61% of the future violent crimes. This approach has often been labeled the "nothing else works" approach to corrections. According to this viewpoint, we should make maximum effective use of the scarce prison cells to protect society from the depredations of such dangerous and repetitive offenders. This approach is present in California's "Three Strikes and You're Out" statute.

There are two variations in the incapacitation viewpoint. Collective incapacitation refers to sanctions imposed on offenders without regard to their personal characteristics, such as all violent offenders. Selective incapacitation refers to incapacitation of certain groups of individuals who have been identified as high-risk offenders, such as robbers with a history of drug use. Under selective incapacitation, offenders with certain characteristics or history would receive longer prison terms than others convicted of the same crime. The purpose of incapacitation is to prevent future crimes, and the moral concerns associated with retribution are not as important as the reduction of future victimization.[†] As Herbert Packer stated, "Incapacitation is a mode of punishment that uses the fact that a

---

[*] Marianne W. Zawitz (Ed.). (1983). *Report to the Nation on Crime and Justice*. Washington, D.C.: Bureau of Justice Statistics, U.S. Government Printing Office. Page 35.

[†] Durham (1994), p. 26.

person has committed a crime as a basis for predicting that he will commit future crimes."* Packer also states that the logic of the incapacitative position is that until the offender stops being a danger, we will continue to restrain him. Accordingly, he contends that pushed to its logical conclusion, offenses that are regarded as relatively trivial may be punished by imprisonment for life.

Rehabilitation

The rehabilitation approach is that punishment should be directed toward correcting the offender. This approach is also considered the "treatment" approach. This approach considers the criminal misconduct as a manifestation of a pathology that can be handled by some form of therapeutic activity. While this viewpoint may consider the offender as "sick," it is not the same as the medical approach. Under the rehabilitation viewpoint, we need to teach the offender to recognize the undesirability of his or her criminal behavior and make significant efforts to rid themselves of that behavior. The main difference between the rehabilitation approach and the retribution approach is that under the rehabilitation approach, the offenders are assigned to programs designed to prepare them for readjustment or reintegration into the community, whereas the latter approach is more concerned with the punishment aspects of the sentence. Packer sees two major objections to making rehabilitation the primary justification for punishment. First, we do not know how to rehabilitate offenders. Second, we know little about who is likely to commit crimes and less about what makes them apt to do so. As long as we are ignorant in these matters, Packard contends that punishment in the name of rehabilitation is gratuitous cruelty.[†]

Imprisonment

In 2012, Raj Rajaratnam, the Sri Lanka-born hedge fund billionaire at the center of the biggest insider-trading case in U.S. history, was sentenced to 11 years behind bars—the stiffest punishment ever handed out for the crime of insider trading. The trial judge in announcing the sentence called it "an assault on the free markets that are a fundamental element of our democratic society. There may not be readily identifiable victims, but when the playing field is not level, the integrity of the marketplace is called into question and the public suffers." Federal prosecutor Reed Brodsky said that insider

* Packer (1963), p. 49.
† Packer (1963), pp. 55–57.

trading "makes a mockery of the principle that no one participant has an unfair advantage through thievery." He said Rajaratnam corrupted at least 20 fellow traders and insiders, and at least 19 public companies were victims of his crimes. The federal prosecutor stated to the trial judge at the sentencing that "today you sentence a man who is the modern face of illegal insider trading. He is arguably the most egregious insider trader to face sentencing in a courthouse in the United States."*

Question: The discussion on the purposes of sanctions is traditionally considered when dealing with common street level crimes. Do the earlier discussed purposes apply to white-collar criminals?

Criminal Fines

Generally, statutes creating white-collar crimes provide for punishment to include criminal fines. Unlike the common street criminal who generally has few assets, most white-collar criminals are affluent. Accordingly, the use of criminal fines and civil asset forfeitures are common when a white-collar criminal is convicted. Civil asset forfeiture is discussed in a later section of this chapter.

In August 2012, a New York bank was forced to pay a fine of $340 million to the state of New York for allegedly laundering money to Iran over a time period of seven years. The bank is also being investigated by the federal government. It appears that the action by the state of New York set a bare minimum for the fine that the federal government will seek. It is unlikely that the federal authorities will seek a lesser fine than that set by the state authorities. According to one estimate, the federal penalty will be at least $360 million, making the combined penalty one of the largest ever assessed for money-laundering charges. It is speculated that federal officials did not act earlier because they were tracking money-laundering allegations against the bank with other countries subject to sanctions.[†]

In addition to criminal fines, civil asset forfeitures, and other sanctions, the defendant may be barred from his or her profession. For example, it is not unusual to bar an individual convicted of a securities-related crime from holding a necessary license or working in that trade. An attorney convicted of a fraud is generally barred from practicing law.

---

* As reported in an AP Alert—Legal Author: LARRY NEUMEISTER; Associated Press; Loaded Date: 10/13/2011 APALERTLEGAL 22:15:13 (Available in Westlaw) [Accessed on August 15, 2012].
† See blog at: http://www.criminallawlawyerny.com/2012/08/bank-to-pay-hefty-fine-for-allegedly-laundering-money-to-iran.shtml [Accessed on August 28, 2012].

Sentencing Guidelines

The Sentencing Reform Act of 1984 changed the concept of federal sentencing. The act created the United States Sentencing Commission as an independent agency in the judicial branch. The act also directed the Commission to develop guidelines and policy statements for sentencing courts to use when sentencing offenders convicted of federal crimes. The Commission was empowered with ongoing responsibilities to monitor the guidelines and recommend to the U.S. Congress changes in criminal statutes.

The Reform Act of 1984 called for consistent sentencing ranges, taking into account the seriousness of the criminal conduct, the defendant's criminal record, just punishment, rehabilitation, and deterrence. It also abolished parole, while allowing 54 days of credit a year for good behavior. Judges were then advised to choose a sentence from within the guideline range, unless the court identified a factor the Commission failed to consider that should result in a different sentence.

In 1989, the U.S. Supreme Court upheld the constitutionality of the commission as a judicial branch agency.* In 2005, the Supreme Court held that the Sixth Amendment of the U.S. Constitution applies to the sentencing guidelines.† The Court in that case determined that the Federal Sentencing Guidelines were *only advisory* and *not mandatory* on the sentencing judges.

The Commission consists of seven voting members appointed by the President, and confirmed by the Senate, and two nonvoting members. Included among their responsibilities are the following:

- Establishing effective and efficient sentencing and policies, practices, and guidelines for the Federal courts regarding the appropriate form and severity of punishment for offenders convicted of Federal crimes.
- Collecting, analyzing, and distributing information as the resource hub on crime and sentencing issues for the Executive Branch, Congress, the courts, criminal justice practitioners, academicians, and the public.
- Providing training to judges, prosecutors, probation officers, the defense bar, and other members of the criminal justice community on how best to apply the guidelines they create.
- Monitoring and evaluating the use of the guidelines and recommending improvements in federal sentencing practices and other related policies.

* *Mistretta v. United States*, 488 U.S. 361 (1989).
† *United States v. Booker*, 543 U.S. 220 (2005).

MISTRETTA V. U.S.
488 U.S. 361, 109 S.CT. 647(1989)

[In the Mistretta case, the defense counsel contended that the U.S. Sentencing Commission exceeded its authority by increasing the base sentences for white-collar criminals. Prisoners challenged the constitutionality of the Sentencing Commission. The U.S. District Court for the Western District of Missouri, Sachs, J., 682 F.Supp. 1033, determined that the sentencing guidelines were constitutional, and a notice of appeal was filed. Granting certiorari before judgment in the Court of Appeals, the Supreme Court, Justice Blackmun, held that the sentencing guidelines were constitutional, amounting to neither excessive delegation of legislative power, nor violation of separation of powers principle.]

The court noted in its opinion:

> There is no doubt that the Sentencing Commission has established significant, legally binding prescriptions governing application of governmental power against private individuals—indeed, application of the ultimate governmental power, short of capital punishment... Average prior sentences were to be a starting point for the Commission's inquiry, but it could and regularly did deviate from those averages as it thought appropriate. It chose, for example, to prescribe substantial increases over average prior sentences for white-collar crimes such as public corruption, antitrust violations, and tax evasion. For antitrust violations, before the Guidelines only 39% of those convicted served any imprisonment, and the average imprisonment was only 45 days, whereas the Guidelines prescribe base sentences (for defendants with no prior criminal conviction) ranging from 2 to 8 months to 10 to 16 months, depending upon the volume of commerce involved.
>
> The Commission also determined when probation was permissible, imposing a strict system of controls because of its judgment that probation had been used for an "inappropriately high percentage of offenders guilty of certain economic crimes."

Financial Sanctions

Consider the Ford Pinto case as an indication of the problems involving the use of financial sanctions. On August 10, 1978, a Ford Pinto was rear-ended. The Pinto burst into flames killing three teenage girls. In September 1978, Ford Motor Company was indicted in Elkhart, IN, on three charges of reckless homicide. The company was charged with recklessly designing and manufacturing the automobile in such a manner as would be likely to cause the automobile to burn up on rear-end impact. If convicted, the maximum punishment would have been a fine of $30,000. Since the defendant was a corporation, it could not be incarcerated. At the time, the Ford Motor Company was the fourth largest corporation in the world.

The Pinto, a small car, was developed to sell for about $2000 (late 1960 prices). The design was completed on a rushed schedule. For design reasons, the gas tank was placed behind, rather than over, the rear axle of the automobile. When the automobile was hit from behind, the gas tank could be crushed against the rear axle and the car had a tendency to burst into flames. Evidence was presented that the company was aware of the problem and that the car could have been modified for a cost of $15.30 per car, but apparently, the executives and the board decided to go ahead with the present design to save money.

The company contended that it was not sociopathic and did not randomly victimize its customers, but was rather a responsible citizen that obeyed federal regulations and carefully weighed all factors in manufacturing a product that the public wanted: a small affordable American car. The Ford Motor Company was found not guilty by the jury on March 13, 1980. The maximum penalty had the company been convicted was only $30,000, but why did the Ford Motor Company spend millions of dollars in legal fees and expenses in defending this case? Fining the Ford Motor Company $30,000 would have been the equivalent of fining an individual making $150,000 a year a quarter.*

Plea Waivers

In August 2012, a female defendant pleaded guilty in a Missouri court to a parking meter fraud scandal in St. Louis. In the plea agreement, the woman agreed to cooperate with the police in an ongoing investigation into allegedly inflated contracts and apparent ghost employees of her firm.

Her business had been under contract with the St. Louis City Treasurer's office. The defendant admitted that she paid one ghost employee at the specific direction of the St. Louis Treasurer's office. The ghost employees, as well as a fourth person who is believed to have blackmailed the woman, are still being investigated and have not been charged with any crime or identified to the public.

By choosing a guilty plea, she assumes that she will have a reduced penalty for the admitted crimes. She also agreed to work with investigators to identify other misconduct. Her case involves many different members of

---

* Francis T. Cullen, William J. Maakestad, and Gary Cavendar. (1987). *Corporate Crime under Attack*. Cincinnati: Anderson. Page 251.

both public and private companies as well as complex contracts and subcontracts. The legal issues were quite complex, as were the issues surrounding possible misconduct in the Treasurer's office.

Why Would a Prosecutor Agree to a Lesser Sentence in This Case?

Plea Statement Waivers

During plea agreement negotiations, the defendant made several statements that were later used against him in his trial when plea negotiations failed. Normally, statements made during plea negotiations are not admissible in court should the negotiations fail, but in this case, prior to starting the negotiations, the prosecutor demanded that the defendant waive this right and allow the government to use any statement made during negotiations if the defendant presented evidence at trial that conflicted with any statements made during negotiations. The question before the appellate court was whether or not this waiver was effective.

In *United States v. Sylvester*,[*] defendant Donald Sylvester sought to overturn his felony conviction, arguing that the district court erred in allowing the prosecution to use—in its case-in-chief—statements that Sylvester made during failed plea negotiations, when he, as a condition to negotiations, knowingly and voluntarily waived his right to object to such use. The U.S. Court of Appeals for the Fifth Circuit stated that it found no convincing reason for not allowing the use of such statements. The appellate court noted that in analyzing plea-statement waivers. He first discerned a "background presumption that legal rights generally, and evidentiary provisions specifically, are generally subject to waiver by voluntary agreement of the parties." Thus, without affirmative indication that Congress intended to proscribe waiver of statutory protections, including evidentiary rules, voluntary agreements to waive these protections are presumptively enforceable. The appellate court found no indication of any congressional disfavor toward waiver, either in the rules' text or in their attendant Advisory Committee's Notes.

In determining whether a plea statement waiver was effective, the judge considered the need to ensure the integrity of the judicial system. The appellate court contended that accepting the waiver did not question the integrity of the system because the "admission of plea statements for impeachment purposes enhances the truth-seeking function of trials and will result in more accurate verdicts." The court opined that when the prosecution seeks to enforce a waiver allowing it to use plea statements for impeachment,

[*] No. 08-30586. 5th Cir., September 18, 2009.

the defendant under any view of the evidence has made a false statement, either to the prosecutor during the plea discussion or to the jury at trial. And making the jury aware of the inconsistency will tend to increase the reliability of the verdict without risking institutional harm to the federal courts.

In addition, the appellate court contended that the waiver was not at odds with Federal Rule of Evidence 410's goal of encouraging voluntary settlement. Even if a waiver discourages some defendants from negotiating, it is also true that prosecutors may be unwilling to proceed without it. Instead of precluding negotiation over an issue, a sounder way to encourage settlement is to permit the interested parties to enter into knowing and voluntary negotiations without any arbitrary limits to their bargaining chips.

Deferred Prosecution Agreements

Deferred prosecution agreements (DPAs) are agreements between the government and a defendant that the prosecution will be deferred if the defendant assists the government in an ongoing investigation, testifies against other defendants, or completes a period of rehabilitation. If the defendant fails to complete the terms of the agreement, then he or she will be prosecuted for the original crimes.

Mark Beeley and John G. Zadkovich contend that DPAs have been a feature of the U.S. legal system for many years. The researchers claim that these agreements have generally been viewed as a success and an invaluable tool in the arsenal of prosecutors in a modern commercial environment, particularly in the field of corruption. The researchers claim that the prohibition of using DPAs in the United Kingdom legal system is being increasingly questioned. The U.K. solicitor general and the director of the Serious Fraud Office have sought to address this apparent deficiency and have been strongly advocating for the introduction of DPAs into the U.K. This has culminated in the U.K. Ministry of Justice's recently released consultation paper on the subject. The U.K. DPA aims to increase self-reporting by corporations by providing a degree of certainty and efficiency. Its broad intention is to take the best of the U.S. system and complement it with the U.K. legal system.*

Civil Forfeitures

Civil asset forfeiture is the process by which the United States government, or a state government, takes property from an individual when the

---

* Mark Beeley and John G. Zadkovich. (July 2012). "Deferred prosecution agreements: The U.K. proposal." *West Law Journal—White-Collar Crime.* Pages 1–3.

government claims that the property was either used in a crime or purchased with the proceeds of a crime. Property or belongings that were allegedly part of a criminal act, or the proceeds of a crime, can be seized by the government.

The civil asset forfeiture concept is an outgrowth of the drug war and rests on the legal theory that property can be guilty of a crime. Once authorities establish a nexus between a piece of property and criminal activity—most commonly drug cases, but also prostitution, driving while intoxicated (DWI), and white-collar crime—the owner must prove his innocence or lose his or her property, even if he or she is never charged with an underlying crime. In most jurisdictions, seized cash and the proceeds from the auctioned property go back to the police departments and prosecutors' offices responsible for the seizure. The scheme, which creates unsavory incentives for public officials, became popular because of a 1984 federal bill designed to encourage aggressive enforcement. After a number of forfeiture cases had made national headlines, Congress reformed the federal civil forfeiture law in 2000.

Frequently, the Government seeks to forfeit all or nearly all of a defendant's assets. As noted by one defense attorney, the government often threatens to take everything owned by a defendant except the shirt off his (or her) back. In addition, there is the threat of a criminal prosecution in addition to the asset forfeitures. The individual may be prosecuted later for either (1) misconduct relating to the source of the funds used to obtain the property, (2) the use of the property, or (3) false statements made in the course of the civil forfeiture proceeding itself.

The first step for the Government in a civil asset forfeiture case is generally to obtain possession of the property at issue under 21 U.S. Code § 881(b) (authorizing seizure of property without issuance of judicial process). If the Government has already obtained possession of the property in connection with a prior administrative forfeiture proceeding, then no new steps need be taken by the Government to physically obtain possession of the property. In these circumstances, the Government starts civil forfeiture by filing a complaint, obtaining a summons and warrant for the arrest of the property, and providing effective notice to interested parties.

If the Government does not possess the property at the time, the civil forfeiture proceeding begins. The property may be real estate, which the Government does not seize and forfeit administratively, or it may be worth more than $500,000.00 in value, or there may be some other reason why the Government does not want to proceed administratively initially. In these instances, the Government can obtain physical possession of the property and seize it pending later forfeiture by using a search warrant under 21 U.S. Code § 881(d), 18 U.S. Code 981(b), and Federal Rule of Criminal Procedure 41.

Double Jeopardy and White-Collar Crime

Under the federal constitution, the Fifth Amendment states, in part, "...nor shall any person be subject for the same offense to be twice put in jeopardy." This protection is commonly known as the protection against double jeopardy. The courts have recognized certain exceptions to this protection. One of the exceptions is the civil asset forfeiture procedures. Technically, in the civil asset forfeiture procedures, the defendant is the property, not the owner of the property.*

In *United States v. Hudson*, by a 9–0 ruling, the U.S. Supreme Court said that federal prosecutors could bring criminal bank fraud charges against three former Oklahoma bank directors, even though they earlier had paid large fines to the U.S. Treasury Department for having secretly loaned themselves money.

Rehnquist in the court's opinion stated that this "does not prohibit the imposition of any additional sanction that could, in common parlance, be described as punishment. The clause protects only against the imposition of multiple criminal punishments for the same offense, and then only when such occurs in successive proceedings."

In a case of insider trading, the Securities and Exchange Commission (SEC) may quickly impose a fine and bar the violator from further trading. After an additional investigation, the SEC may then bring a criminal charge against the same person.

A second double jeopardy issue that is frequently involved in white-collar crime cases involves prosecuting the defendant in both the federal court and the state court for the same misconduct. For example, if a person was convicted in a state court for theft because of misconduct, which involves embezzlement from a bank (a state crime), the person could also be convicted in a federal court for embezzlement involving a federally insured bank, a federal crime.

As noted in the earlier mentioned case involving alleged money laundering by a New York bank, the State of New York fined the bank, and the federal government is also considering the assessment of fines against the bank for the same misconduct. In addition, both the federal government and the state government may bring criminal action against the bank and its executives. Technically, the state and federal government are two different sovereigns. The bank could be tried in state criminal court for violations of state criminal laws and in federal court for violations of federal criminal law.

---

* *Hudson v. United States*, 522 U.S. 93 (1997).

UNITED STATES V. BERGMAN
416 F.SUPP. 496 (S.D.N.Y., 1976)
SENTENCING MEMORANDUM

FRANKEL, District Judge.

Defendant is being sentenced upon his plea of guilty to two counts of an 11-count indictment. The sentencing proceeding is unusual in some respects. It has been the subject of more extensive submissions, written and oral, than this court has ever received upon such an occasion. The court has studied some hundreds of pages of memoranda and exhibits, plus scores of volunteered letters. A broad array of issues has been addressed. Imaginative suggestions of law and penology have been tendered. A preliminary conversation with counsel, on the record, preceded the usual sentencing hearing. Having heard counsel again and the defendant speaking for himself, the court postponed the pronouncement of sentence for further reconsideration of thoughts generated during the days of studying the briefs and oral pleas. It seems fitting now to report in writing the reasons upon which the court concludes that defendant must be sentenced to a term of four months in prison.

I. DEFENDANT AND HIS CRIMES

Defendant appeared, until the last couple of years, to be a man of unimpeachably high character, attainments, and distinction. A doctor of divinity and an ordained rabbi, he has been acclaimed by people around the world for his works of public philanthropy, private charity, and leadership in educational enterprises. Scores of letters have come to the court from across this and other countries reporting debts of personal gratitude to him for numerous acts of extraordinary generosity. (The court has also received a kind of petition, with fifty-odd signatures, in which the signers, based upon learning acquired as newspaper readers, denounce the defendant and urge a severe sentence. Unlike the pleas for mercy, which appear to reflect unquestioned facts inviting compassion, this document should and will be disregarded.) In addition to his good works, defendant has managed to amass considerable wealth in the ownership and operation of nursing homes, in real estate ventures, and in a course of substantial investments.

Beginning about two years ago, investigations of nursing homes in this area, including questions of fraudulent claims for Medicaid funds, drew to a focus upon this defendant among several others. The results that concern us were the present indictment and two state indictments. After extensive pretrial proceedings, defendant embarked upon elaborate plea negotiations with both state and federal prosecutors. A state guilty plea and the instant plea were entered in March of this year. (Another state indictment is expected to be dismissed after defendant is sentenced on those to which he has pled guilty.) As part of the detailed plea arrangements, it is expected that the prison sentence imposed by this court will comprise the total covering the state as well as the federal convictions.

For purposes of the sentence now imposed, the precise details of the charges, and of defendant's carefully phrased admissions of guilt, are not matters of prime importance. Suffice it to say that the plea on Count One (carrying a maximum of five years in prison and a $10,000 fine) confesses defendant's knowing and willful participation in a scheme to defraud the United States in various ways, including the presentation of wrongfully padded claims for payments under the Medicaid program to defendant's nursing homes. Count Three, for which the guilty plea carries a theoretical maximum of three more years in Prison and another $5,000 fine, is a somewhat more "technical" charge. Here, defendant admits to having participated in the filing of a Partnership return which was false and fraudulent in failing to list people who had bought Partnership interests from him in one of his nursing homes, had paid for such interests, and had made certain capital withdrawals.

The conspiracy to defraud, as defendant has admitted it, is by no means the worst of its kind; it is by no means as flagrant or extensive as has been portrayed in the press; it is evidently less grave than other nursing home wrongs for which others have been convicted or publicized. At the same time, the sentence, as defendant has acknowledged, is imposed for two federal felonies including, as the more important, a knowing and purposeful conspiracy to mislead and defraud the Federal Government.

II. THE GUIDING PRINCIPLES OF SENTENCING

Proceeding through the short list of the supposed justifications for criminal sanctions, defense counsel urges that no licit purpose could be served by defendant's incarceration. Some of these arguments are plainly sound; others are not.

The court agrees that this defendant should not be sent to prison for "rehabilitation." Apart from the patent inappositeness of the concept to this individual, this court shares the growing understanding that no one should ever be sent to prison for rehabilitation. That is to say, nobody who would not otherwise be locked up should suffer that fate on the incongruous premise that it will be good for him or her. Imprisonment is punishment. Facing the simple reality should help us to be civilized. It is less agreeable to confine someone when we deem it an affliction rather than a benefaction. If someone must be imprisoned—for other, valid reasons—we should seek to make rehabilitative resources available to him or her. But the goal of rehabilitation cannot fairly serve in itself as grounds for the sentence to confinement.

Equally clearly, this defendant should not be confined to incapacitate him. He is not dangerous. It is most improbable that he will commit similar, or any, offenses in the future. There is no need for "specific deterrence."

Contrary to counsel's submissions, however, two sentencing considerations demand a prison sentence in this case:

First, the aim of general deterrence, the effort to discourage similar wrongdoing by others through a reminder that the law's warnings are real and that the grim consequence of imprisonment is likely to follow from crimes of deception for gain like those defendant has admitted.

Second, the related, but not identical, concern that any lesser penalty would, in the words of the Model Penal Code, 7.01(1)(c), "depreciate the seriousness of the defendant's crime."

Resisting the first of these propositions, defense counsel invoked Immanuel Kant's axiom that "one man ought never to be dealt with merely as a means subservient to the purposes of another." In a more novel, but equally futile effort, counsel urges that a sentence for general deterrence "would violate the Eighth Amendment proscription against cruel and unusual punishment." Treating the latter point first, because it is a short subject, it may be observed simply that if general deterrence as a sentencing purpose were now to be outlawed, as against a near unanimity of views among state and federal jurists, the bolt would have to come from a place higher than this.

As for Dr. Kant, it may well be that defense counsel mistake his meaning in the present context. Whether or not that is so, and without pretending to be an authority on that score, we take the widely accepted stance that a criminal punished in the interest of general deterrence is not being employed "merely as a means...." Reading Kant to mean that every man must be deemed more than the instrument of others, and must "always be treated as an end in himself," the humane principle is not offended here. Each of us is served by the enforcement of the law—not least a person like the defendant in this case, whose wealth and privileges, so long enjoyed, are so much founded upon law. More broadly, we are driven regularly in our ultimate interests as members of the community to use ourselves and each other, in war and in peace, for social ends. One who has transgressed against the criminal laws is certainly among the more fitting candidates for a role of this nature. This is no arbitrary selection. Warned in advance of the prospect, the transgressor has chosen, in the law's premises, "between keeping the law required for society's protection or paying the penalty."

But the whole business, defendant argues further, is guesswork; we are by no means certain that deterrence "works." The position is somewhat over-stated; there is, in fact, some reasonably "scientific" evidence for the efficacy of criminal sanctions as deterrents, at least as against some kinds of crimes. Moreover, the time is not yet here when all we can "know" must be quantifiable and digestible by computers. The shared wisdom of generations teaches meaningfully, if somewhat amorphously, that the utilitarians have a point; we do, indeed, lapse often into rationality and act to seek pleasure and avoid pain. It would be better, to be sure, if we had more certainty and precision. Lacking these comforts, we continue to include among our working hypotheses a belief (with some concrete evidence in its support) that crimes like those in this case—deliberate, purposeful, continuing, nonimpulsive, and committed for profit—are among those most likely to be generally deferrable by sanctions most shunned by those exposed to temptation.

The idea of avoiding depreciation of the seriousness of the offense implicates two or three thoughts, not always perfectly clear or universally agreed upon, beyond the idea of deterrence. It should be proclaimed by the court's judgment that the offenses are grave, not minor or purely technical. Some attention must be paid to the demand for equal justice; it will not do to leave the penalty of imprisonment a dead letter as against "privileged" violators while it is employed regularly, and with vigor, against others. There probably is in these conceptions an element of retributiveness, as counsel urge. And retribution, so denominated, is in some disfavor as a reason for punishment. It remains a factor, however, as Holmes perceived, and as is known to anyone who talks to judges, lawyers, defendants, or people generally. It may become more palatable, and probably more humanely understood, under the rubric of "deserts" or "just deserts." However the concept is formulated, we have not yet reached a state, supposing we ever should, in which the infliction of punishments for crime may be divorced generally from ideas of blame worthiness, recompense, and proportionality.

III. AN ALTERNATIVE, "BEHAVIORAL SANCTION"

Resisting prison above all eke, defense counsel included in their thorough memorandum on sentencing two proposals for what they call a "constructive," and therefore a "preferable" form of "behavioral sanction." One is a plan for Dr. Bergman to create and run a program of Jewish vocational and religious high school training. The other is for him to take charge of a "Committee on Holocaust Studies," again concerned with education at the secondary school level.

A third suggestion was made orally at yesterday's sentencing hearing. It was proposed that Dr. Bergman might be ordered to work as a volunteer in some established agency as a visitor and aide to the sick and the otherwise incapacitated. The proposal was that he could read, provide various forms of physical assistance, and otherwise give comfort to afflicted people.

No one can doubt either the worthiness of these proposals or Dr. Bergman's ability to make successes of them. But both of the carefully formulated "sanctions" in the memorandum involve work of an honorific nature, not unlike that done in other projects to which the defendant has devoted himself in the past. It is difficult to conceive of them as "punishments" at all. The more recent proposal is somewhat more suitable in character, but it is still an insufficient penalty. The seriousness of the crimes to which Dr. Bergman has pled guilty demands something more than "requiring" him to lend his talents and efforts to further philanthropic enterprises. It remains open to him, of course, to pursue the interesting suggestions later on as a matter of unforced personal choice.

IV. "MEASURING" THE SENTENCE

In cases like this one, the decision of greatest moment is whether to imprison or not. As reflected in the eloquent submissions for defendant, the prospect of the closing prison doors is the most appalling concern; the feeling is that the length of the sojourn is a lesser question once that threshold is passed. Nevertheless, the setting of a term remains to be accomplished. And in some respects it is a subject even more perplexing, unregulated, and unprincipled.

Days and months and years are countable with a sound of exactitude. But there can be no exactitude in the deliberations from which a number emerges. Without pretending to a nonexistent precision, the court notes at least the major factors.

The criminal behavior, as has been noted, is blatant in character and unmitigated by any suggestion of necessitous circumstance or other pressures difficult to resist. However metaphysicians may conjure with issues about free will, it is a fundamental premise of our efforts to do criminal justice that competent people, possessed of their faculties, make choices and are accountable for them. In this sometimes harsh light, the case of the present defendant is among the clearest and least relieved. Viewed against the maxima Congress ordained, and against the run of sentences in other federal criminal cases, it calls for more than a token sentence.

On the other side are factors that take longer to enumerate. Defendant's illustrious public life and works are in his favor, though diminished, of course, by what this case discloses. This is a first, probably a last, conviction. Defendant is 64 years old and in imperfect health, though by no means so ill, from what the court is told, that he could be expected to suffer inordinately more than many others of advanced years who go to prison.

Defendant invokes an understandable, but somewhat unworkable, notion of "disparity." He says others involved in recent nursing home fraud cases have received relatively light sentences for behavior more culpable than his. He lays special emphasis upon one defendant whose frauds appear indeed to have involved larger amounts and who was sentenced to a maximum of six months' incarceration, to be confined for that time only on week nights, not on weekdays or weekends. This court has examined the minutes of that sentencing proceeding and finds the case distinguishable in material respects. But even if there were a threat of such disparity as defendant warns against, it could not be a major weight on the scales.

Our sentencing system, deeply flawed, is characterized by disparity. We are to seek to "individualize" sentences, but no clear or clearly agreed standards govern the individualization. The lack of meaningful criteria does indeed leave sentencing judges far too much at large. But the result, with its nagging burdens on conscience, cannot be meaningfully alleviated by allowing any handful of sentences in a short series to fetter later judgments. The point is easy, of course, where Sentence No. 1 or Sentences 1–5 are notably harsh. It cannot be that a later judge, disposed to more leniency, should feel in any degree "bound." The converse is not identical, but it is not totally different. The net of this is that this court has considered and has given some weight to the trend of the other cited sentences (though strict logic might call for none), but without treating them as forceful "precedents" in any familiar sense.

How, then, is the particular sentence adjudged in this case? As has been mentioned, the case calls for a sentence that is more than nominal. Given the other circumstances, however—including that this is a first offense, by a man no longer young and not perfectly well, where danger of recidivism is not a concern—it verges on cruelty to think of confinement for a term of years. We sit, to be sure, in a nation where prison sentences of extravagant length are more common than they are almost anywhere else. By that light, the term imposed today is not notably long. For this sentencing court, however, for a nonviolent first offense involving no direct assaults or invasions of others' security (as in bank robbery, narcotics, etc.), it is a stern sentence. For people like Dr. Bergman, who might be disposed to engage in similar wrongdoing, it should be sufficiently frightening to serve the major end of general deterrence. For all but the profoundly vengeful, it should not depreciate the seriousness of his offenses.

V. PUNISHMENT IN OR FOR THE MEDIA

Much of defendant's sentencing memorandum is devoted to the extensive barrage of hostile publicity to which he has been subjected during the years before and since his indictment. He argues, and it appears to be undisputed, that the media (and people desiring to be featured in the media) have vilified him for many kinds of evildoing of which he has in fact been innocent. Two main points are made on this score with respect to the problem of sentencing.

First, as has been mentioned, counsel express the concern that the court may be pressured toward severity by the force of the seeming public outcry. That the court should not allow itself to be affected in this way is clear beyond discussion. Nevertheless, it is not merely permissible, but entirely wholesome and responsible, for counsel to bring the expressed concern out in the open. Whatever our ideals and mixed images about judges, it would be naive to doubt that judges have sometimes been swept by a sense of popular demand toward draconian sentencing decisions. It cannot hurt for the sentencing judge to be reminded of this and cautioned about it. There can be no guarantees. The sentencer must confront and regulate himself. But it bears reaffirmance that the court must seek to discount utterly the fact of notoriety in passing its judgment upon the defendant. Defense counsel cite reported opinions of this court reflecting what happens in a large number of unreported cases, by the present sentencer and many others, in which "unknown" defendants have received prison sentences, longer or shorter than today's, for white-collar or comparably nonviolent crimes. The overall run of cases, with all their individual variations, will reflect, it is hoped, earnest efforts to hew to the principle of equal treatment, with or without publicity.

Defendant's second point about his public humiliation is the frequently heard contention that he should not be incarcerated because he "has been punished enough." The thought is not without some initial appeal. If punishment were wholly or mainly retributive, it might be a weighty factor. In the end, however, it must be a matter of little or no force. Defendant's notoriety should not in the last analysis serve to lighten, any more than it may be permitted to aggravate, his sentence. The fact that he has been pilloried by journalists is essentially a consequence of the prestige and privileges he enjoyed before he was exposed as a wrongdoer. The long fall from grace was possible only because of the height he had reached. The suffering from loss of public esteem reflects a body of opinion that the esteem had been, in at least some wrongly bestowed and enjoyed. It is not possible to justify the notion that this mode of nonjudicial punishment should be an occasion for leniency not given to a defendant who never basked in such an admiring light at all. The quest for both the appearance and the substance of equal justice prompts the court to discount the thought that the public humiliation serves the function of imprisonment.

Writing, as judges rarely do, about a particular sentence concentrates the mind with possibly special force upon the experience of the sentencer as well as the person sentenced. Consigning someone to prison, this defendant or any other, "is a sad necessity." There are impulses of avoidance from time to time—toward a personally gratifying leniency or toward an opposite extreme. But there is, obviously, no place for private impulse in the judgment of the court. The course of justice must be sought with such objective rationality as we can muster, tempered with mercy, but obedient to the law, which, we do well to remember, is all that empowers a judge to make other people suffer.

Practicum on Sentencing

Assume that you are the district court judge and responsible for determining the sentence in a case involving a popular 64-year-old Jewish rabbi who pleaded guilty to two counts involving knowing and willful participation in a scheme to defraud the United States. The scheme involved federal Medicaid funds being paid to nursing homes. This case was widely reported in the New York newspapers.

What Factors Would You Consider in Determining the Correct Sentence?

Would You Send the Rabbi to Prison?

The following sentencing memorandum was issued by the trial court judge to justify his sentence. [Note: Judge Frankel's citations have been omitted. To check them, go to the case report in volume 416 of the Federal Reporter.]

Summary

- Punishment has been defined as a government authorized imposition of a deprivation of freedom, privacy, or goods to which the person would otherwise have a right, or the imposition of special burdens because the individual receiving the punishment has been found guilty of some crime.
- It might be more effective in deterring white-collar crime by imposing extensive shaming sanctions on the white-collar criminal rather than extensive prison terms.
- The sentencing process may be the most difficult task in trying a criminal case.
- Three popular classifications based on political theories that influence our corrections system are conservative, liberal, and radical.
- The ultimate purpose of criminal sanctions is generally considered to be the maintenance of our social order.
- The four popular goals of criminal sanctions are retribution, deterrence, incapacitation, and rehabilitation.
- Retribution generally means "getting even."
- Retribution is also referred to as "just deserts."
- Deterrence is a punishment viewpoint that focuses on future outcomes rather than past misconduct.
- Incapacitation is based on the concept that at least while the prisoner is in confinement, he is unlikely to commit crimes on innocent persons outside of prison.
- The rehabilitation approach is that punishment should be directed toward correcting the offender.
- Generally, statutes creating white-collar crimes provide for punishment to include criminal fines.
- The Sentencing Reform Act of 1984 changed the concept of federal sentencing.
- The act created the United States Sentencing Commission as an independent agency in the judicial branch.

- The act also directed the commission to develop guidelines and policy statements for sentencing courts to use when sentencing offenders convicted of federal crimes.
- Deferred prosecution agreements are agreements between the government and a defendant that prosecution will be deferred if the defendant assists the government in an ongoing investigation, testifies again other defendants, or completes a period of rehabilitation.
- Civil asset forfeiture is the process by which the United States government, or a state government, takes property from an individual when the government claims that the property was either used in a crime or purchased with the proceeds of a crime.
- Property or belongings that were allegedly part of a criminal act, or the proceeds of a crime, can be seized by the government.
- The civil asset forfeiture concept is an outgrowth of the drug war and rests on the legal theory that property can be guilty of a crime.
- The double jeopardy protection protects only against the imposition of multiple criminal punishments for the same offense, and then only when such occurs in successive proceedings.

QUESTIONS IN REVIEW

1. What purpose is served by sentencing a white-collar criminal to confinement?
2. Explain the functions of the sentencing guidelines.
3. Should the government be allowed to obtain a defendant's assets by civil forfeiture and then prosecute the defendant in a criminal court? Why isn't this double jeopardy?

Control and Prevention of White-Collar Crimes $\underset{\text{10}}{\Large 10}$

Chapter Objectives

After studying this chapter, you should be able to do the following:

- Explain the key issues in controlling white-collar crime.
- Understand the policies contained in the Thompson memo.
- List some of the recent steps taken to reduce white-collar crime.
- Explain why it is important to prosecute white-collar criminals.
- Explain how the FBI's asset forfeiture/money laundering unit functions.
- Explain how the NW3C functions.

Introduction

Many of the concepts discussed in this chapter reflect the personal opinions and biases of the authors. While we realize that it is easy to speculate and guess as to what measures will prevent or reduce crime, it is rare that we get to test those presumptions. In this chapter, some of the various theories on preventing or reducing white-collar crime will be examined.

Both authors agree that to reduce "white-collar" crime, the American public needs to recognize the need to prevent it and its seriousness. It was in his much publicized text, *Thinking about Crime*, in which James Q. Wilson[*]

He argued that the "real" crime was what we have labeled as street crime. Wilson dismisses the importance of white-collar crime by arguing that crimes committed by those with economic and social power are really ambivalent acts for which condemnation is apparently a matter of personal taste. For an excellent discussion on why Wilson is off-track, see Gary Potter's book, *Controversies in White-Collar Crimes.*[†]

As noted on the FBI White-Collar Crime Web site, it is not a victimless crime. A single scam can destroy a company, devastate families by wiping out their life savings, or cost investors billions of dollars (or even all three, as in the Enron case). Today's fraud schemes are more sophisticated than ever,

---

[*] James Q. Wilson. (1975). *Thinking about Crime.* New York: Basic Books.
[†] Gary W. Potter. (2002). *Controversies in White-Collar Crimes.* Cincinnati: Anderson.

and we are dedicated to using our skills to track down the culprits and stop scams before they start.*

The concept that white-collar crime is not real crime needs to be discarded. The public needs to be aware of the damages that occur from this phenomenon.

How a Convicted Felon Would Reduce White-Collar Crime

Convicted felon, former CPA, and former corporate executive Sam Antar on his Web site contends that

> The main pillar of our capitalistic free market economic system, which is a cornerstone of democracy, is the integrity of financial information. Without reliable financial information, capitalism cannot and will not survive. However, the integrity of financial information can only be achieved through building blocks such as sound internal controls and independently verifiable financial information. The well-educated, skilled, and experienced accountant is the first line of defense for the capitalist system.†

Antar proposes that to combat white-collar crime, the nation needs to require a comprehensive approach by law enforcement, the accounting profession, the education establishment, government, and private industry. He proposes a four-prong approach:

- Prevention—Strong internal controls are needed and should be reviewed by competent and independent external auditors. Antar considers strong internal controls as barriers to crime for criminals. Internal controls help businesses operate more efficiently and effectively too.
- Power—Antar advocates legislation like Sarbanes–Oxley and standards issued by the Public Company Accounting Oversight Board (PCAOB) and the American Institute of Certified Public Accountants (AICPA).
- Professionalism—Antar sees the need for a better educated, skilled, trained, experienced, and independent accounting profession. He contends that all efforts at prevention, any legislation, and any standards issued will not be fully effective unless the accounting profession addresses its educational issues.
- Prosecution—According to Antar, aggressive prosecution of white-collar criminals is needed. White-collar criminals must know that they will be prosecuted for their crimes.

---

* As posted at http://www.fbi.gov/about-us/investigate/white_collar/whitecollarcrime [Accessed on June 22, 2011].
† As posted at http://www.whitecollarfraud.com/946562.html [Accessed on June 22, 2011].

- Prison—Strong punishment and accountability for those convicted of white-collar crimes are essential according to Antar. He states that such criminals must be held fully accountable for their actions.

Thompson Memorandum

The Thompson Memorandum refers to a memorandum issued on January 20, 2003, by then U.S. Deputy Attorney General Larry D. Thompson. The subject of the memorandum was "Principles of Federal Prosecution of Business Organizations." The memo contained a set of principles to guide prosecutors as they make the decision whether to seek charges against a business organization. Thompson stated that the principles were derived from the combined efforts of the Corporate Fraud Task Force and the U.S. Attorney General's Advisory Committee in a three-year study.*

The main focus of the revisions was increased emphasis on and scrutiny of the authenticity of a corporation's cooperation. The memo notes that too often, business organizations, while purporting to cooperate with a department investigation, in fact take steps to impede the quick and effective exposure of the complete scope of wrongdoing under investigation. The revisions make clear that such conduct should weigh in favor of a corporate prosecution. The revisions also address the efficacy of the corporate governance mechanisms in place within a corporation, to ensure that these measures are truly effective rather than mere paper programs. While these guidelines refer to corporations, they apply to the consideration of the prosecution of all types of business organizations, including partnerships, sole proprietorships, government entities, and unincorporated associations.

Key Principles to Be Considered in Charging a Corporation

Key principles set forth in the memo to be considered in charging a corporation include the following:

- Corporations should not be treated leniently because of their artificial nature, nor should they be subject to harsher treatment. Vigorous enforcement of the criminal laws against corporate wrongdoers, where appropriate, results in great benefits for law enforcement and the public, particularly in the area of white-collar crime.
- Indicting corporations for wrongdoing enables the government to address and be a force for positive change of corporate culture, alter

* The Thompson Memorandum is posted on the U.S. Department of Justice Web site at http://www.justice.gov/dag/cftf/business_organizations.pdf [Accessed on June 22, 2011].

corporate behavior, and prevent, discover, and punish white-collar crime.

- In all cases involving corporate wrongdoing, prosecutors should consider the factors discussed herein. First and foremost, prosecutors should be aware of the important public benefits that may flow from indicting a corporation in appropriate cases. For instance, corporations are likely to take immediate remedial steps when one is indicted for criminal conduct that is pervasive throughout a particular industry, and thus an indictment often provides a unique opportunity for deterrence on a massive scale. In addition, a corporate indictment may result in specific deterrence by changing the culture of the indicted corporation and the behavior of its employees.
- Certain crimes that carry with them a substantial risk of great public harm, e.g., environmental crimes or financial frauds, are by their nature most likely to be committed by businesses, and there may, therefore, be a substantial federal interest in indicting the corporation.
- Charging a corporation, however, does not mean that individual directors, officers, employees, or shareholders should not also be charged.
- Prosecution of a corporation is not a substitute for the prosecution of criminally culpable individuals within or without the corporation. Because a corporation can act only through individuals, imposition of individual criminal liability may provide the strongest deterrent against future corporate wrongdoing. Only rarely should provable individual culpability not be pursued, even in the face of offers of corporate guilty pleas.
- Corporations are "legal persons," capable of suing and being sued, and capable of committing crimes.
- Under the doctrine of *respondeat superior*, a corporation may be held criminally liable for the illegal acts of its directors, officers, employees, and agents. To hold a corporation liable for these actions, the government must establish that the corporate agent's actions (i) were within the scope of his duties and (ii) were intended, at least in part, to benefit the corporation. In all cases involving wrongdoing by corporate agents, prosecutors should consider the corporation, as well as the responsible individuals, as potential criminal targets.
- Agents, however, may act for mixed reasons—both for self-aggrandizement (both direct and indirect) and for the benefit of the corporation, and a corporation may be held liable as long as one motivation of its agent is to benefit the corporation. Moreover, the corporation need not even necessarily profit from its agent's actions for it to be held liable.

The Thompson Memo noted that in Automated Medical Laboratories, the Fourth Circuit stated that "Benefit is not a 'touchstone' of criminal corporate liability; benefit at best is an evidential, not an operative, fact." Thus, whether the agent's actions ultimately redounded to the benefit of the corporation is less significant than whether the agent acted with the intent to benefit the corporation. The basic purpose of requiring that an agent has acted with the intent to benefit the corporation, however, is to insulate the corporation from criminal liability for actions of its agents, which may be inimical to the interests of the corporation or which may have been undertaken solely to advance the interests of that agent or of a party other than the corporation.

The memo also noted that in *United States v. Automated Medical Laboratories*, 770 F.2d 399 (4th Cir. 1985), the court affirmed the corporation's conviction for the actions of a subsidiary's employee despite its claim that the employee was acting for his own benefit, namely, his "ambitious nature and his desire to ascend the corporate ladder." The court stated, "Partucci was clearly acting in part to benefit AML since his advancement within the corporation depended on AML's wellbeing and its lack of difficulties with the FDA." Similarly, in *United States v. Cincotta*, 689 F.2d 238, 241-42 (1st Cir. 1982), the court held, "criminal liability may be imposed on the corporation only where the agent is acting within the scope of his employment. That, in turn, requires that the agent be performing acts of the kind which he is authorized to perform, and those acts must be motivated—at least in part—by intent to benefit the corporation." Applying this test, the court upheld the corporation's conviction, notwithstanding the substantial personal benefit reaped by its miscreant agents, because the fraudulent scheme required money to pass through the corporation's treasury and the fraudulently obtained goods were resold to the corporation's customers in the corporation's name. As the court concluded, "Mystic—not the individual defendants—was making money by selling oil that it had not paid for."

Charging a Corporation: Factors to Be Considered

The Thompson Memo provides that, generally, prosecutors should apply the same factors in determining whether to charge a corporation as they do with respect to individuals. Thus, the prosecutor should weigh all of the factors normally considered in the sound exercise of prosecutorial judgment: the sufficiency of the evidence; the likelihood of success at trial; the probable deterrent, rehabilitative, and other consequences of conviction; and the adequacy of noncriminal approaches. However, due to the nature of the corporate "person," some additional factors are present.

In conducting an investigation, determining whether to bring charges, and negotiating plea agreements, prosecutors should consider the following factors in reaching a decision as to the proper treatment of a corporate target:

1. The nature and seriousness of the offense, including the risk of harm to the public, and applicable policies and priorities, if any, governing the prosecution of corporations for particular categories of crime.
2. The pervasiveness of wrongdoing within the corporation, including the complicity in, or condemnation of, the wrongdoing by corporate management.
3. The corporation's history of similar conduct, including prior criminal, civil, and regulatory enforcement actions against it.
4. The corporation's timely and voluntary disclosure of wrongdoing and its willingness to cooperate in the investigation of its agents, including, if necessary, the waiver of corporate attorney-client and work product protection.
5. The existence and adequacy of the corporation's compliance program.
6. The corporation's remedial actions, including any efforts to implement an effective corporate compliance program or to improve an existing one, to replace responsible management, to discipline or terminate wrongdoers, to pay restitution, and to cooperate with the relevant government agencies.
7. Collateral consequences, including disproportionate harm to shareholders, pension holders, and employees not proven personally culpable and impact on the public arising from the prosecution.
8. The adequacy of the prosecution of individuals responsible for the corporation's malfeasance.
9. The adequacy of remedies such as civil or regulatory enforcement actions.

The memo notes that as with the factors relevant to charging natural persons, the factors are intended to provide guidance rather than to mandate a particular result. The factors listed are intended to be illustrative of those that should be considered, and they do not constitute a complete or exhaustive list. Some or all of these factors may or may not apply to specific cases, and in some cases, one factor may override all others. The nature and seriousness of the offense may be such as to warrant prosecution regardless of the other factors. Further, national law enforcement policies in various enforcement areas may require that more or less weight be given to certain of these factors than to others.

In making a decision to charge a corporation, the prosecutor generally has wide latitude in determining when, whom, how, and even whether to prosecute for violations of Federal criminal law. In exercising that discretion, prosecutors should consider the general statements of principles that summarize appropriate considerations to be weighed and desirable practices to be followed in discharging their prosecutorial responsibilities. In doing so, prosecutors should ensure that the general purposes of the criminal law—assurance of warranted punishment, deterrence of further criminal conduct, protection of the public from dangerous and fraudulent conduct, rehabilitation of offenders, and restitution for victims and affected communities—are adequately met, taking into account the special nature of the corporate "person."

Cooperation and Voluntary Disclosure

The memorandum places emphasis on cooperation and voluntary disclosures by the individuals or companies who are the focus of a white-collar crime investigation. Note: In the next section, the American Bar Association is critical of this approach.

According to the memorandum, in determining whether to charge a corporation, that corporation's timely and voluntary disclosure of wrongdoing and its willingness to cooperate with the government's investigation may be relevant factors. In gauging the extent of the corporation's cooperation, the prosecutor may consider the corporation's willingness to identify the culprits within the corporation, including senior executives; to make witnesses available; to disclose the complete results of its internal investigation; and to waive attorney–client and work product protection.

The memorandum notes that in investigating wrongdoing by or within a corporation, a prosecutor is likely to encounter several obstacles resulting from the nature of the corporation itself. It will often be difficult to determine which individual took which action on behalf of the corporation. Lines of authority and responsibility may be shared among operating divisions or departments, and records and personnel may be spread throughout the United States or even among several countries. Where the criminal conduct continued over an extended period of time, the culpable or knowledgeable personnel may have been promoted, transferred, or fired, or they may have quit or retired. Accordingly, a corporation's cooperation may be critical in identifying the culprits and locating relevant evidence.

One factor the prosecutor may weigh in assessing the adequacy of a corporation's cooperation is the completeness of its disclosure, including, if necessary, a waiver of the attorney–client and work product protections, both with respect to its internal investigation and with respect to communications between specific officers, directors, and employees and counsel. Such waivers permit the government to obtain statements of possible witnesses, subjects, and targets, without having to negotiate individual cooperation or immunity agreements. In addition, they are often critical in enabling the government to evaluate the completeness of a corporation's voluntary disclosure and cooperation. Prosecutors may, therefore, request a waiver in appropriate circumstances. The Department does not, however, consider waiver of a corporation's attorney–client and work product protection an absolute requirement, and prosecutors should consider the willingness of a corporation to waive such protection when necessary to provide timely and complete information as one factor in evaluating the corporation's cooperation.

In plea agreements in which the corporation agrees to cooperate, the prosecutor should ensure that the cooperation is complete and truthful. To do so, the prosecutor may request that the corporation waive attorney–client and work product protection, make employees and agents available for debriefing, disclose the results of its internal investigation, file appropriate

Chicago law professor Richard Epstein blasted the Thompson Memorandum, the 2003 Justice Department policy statement that laid out guidelines for prosecuting corporations. Epstein contends that the Thompson Memorandum insisted that corporations receive a temporary reprieve only if they purge themselves of individual wrongdoers and agree to extensive government oversight to make them walk the straight and narrow path.

Epstein urges a complete revamp of the way the government thinks about corporate criminal prosecution. He contends that the Department of Justice (DOJ) should engage in unilateral disarmament by disavowing the odious Thompson memo, and rethinking why it ever needs to threaten the nuclear option of a corporate indictment. He also states that Congress should repeal by statute the doctrines of vicarious liability for criminal conduct in a corporate context—because these give the government unwarranted and arbitrary power over corporations. Epstein notes that corporations are just individuals tied together by an elaborate network of contracts, and we do not need yet another sorry reminder of how mindless government policies harm the innocent shareholders whom they are supposed to protect. The government has a vital role in criminal enforcement. So let it go after real, i.e., human, criminals the old-fashioned way, by careful investigation and skilled prosecution.*

* Peter Laffman. (November 26, 2006). "Richard Epstein blasts Thompson Memorandum." Wall Street Journal. Available online at http://blogs.wsj.com/law/2006/11/28/richard-epstein-blasts-thompson-memorandum/ [Accessed on June 22, 2011].

certified financial statements, agree to governmental or third-party audits, and take whatever other steps are necessary to ensure that the full scope of the corporate wrongdoing is disclosed and that the responsible culprits are identified and, if appropriate, prosecuted.

Why Prosecution Is Important

Karen J. Mathis, former President of the American Bar Association (ABA), states that prosecuting white-collar crime is important,* but preventing it is even more so. Mathis claims that one approach used by the U.S. DOJ undermines corporate compliance with the law rather than strengthening it.

The approach Mathis was referring to is the so-called Thompson Memorandum of 2003, which encourages federal prosecutors to condition prosecution and sentencing leniency on waiving confidentiality for communications with lawyers, for corporations suspected of crimes. The effect of the trade-off is to inhibit communication, reducing opportunities for lawyers to guide corporations in compliance with the law.

The ABA had urged the Senate Judiciary Committee in a September 2006 hearing to send a strong message in its oversight capacity to the Justice Department expressing the view that the attorney–client privilege and a related concept, the work product doctrine, are "fundamental principles of our legal system" and must be protected.

The ABA noted that lawyers are "indispensable in helping companies and their officials understand and comply with complex laws." Unless their lawyers enjoy the trust of corporate board members, managers, and operating personnel, those company leaders will not share information freely with them, information the lawyers must have if they are to guide compliance with the law. According to the ABA, there is no room for trust once companies waive their attorney–client privilege, releasing their lawyers from the ethical obligation—and legal ability—to protect confidential communication.

FBI'S Asset Forfeiture/Money Laundering Unit

The mission of the Asset Forfeiture/Money Laundering Unit (AF/MLU) is to promote the strategic use of the asset forfeiture and to ensure that field offices employ the money laundering violation in all investigations, where

---

* As reported on the ABA webpage at http://apps.americanbar.org/abanet/media/oped/ oped.cfm?releaseid=24 [Accessed on June 22, 2011].

appropriate, to disrupt and/or dismantle criminal enterprises.* The asset forfeiture and money laundering process identifies targets and disrupts and dismantles criminal and terrorist organizations and individuals engaged in fraud schemes that target our nation's financial infrastructure.

The implementation of the asset forfeiture process to criminal investigation provides law enforcement with the opportunity to remove the tools of crime from criminal organizations, deprives wrongdoers of the proceeds of their crimes, recovers property that may be used to compensate victims, and deters crimes. The asset forfeiture process can destroy the financial infrastructure of criminal enterprises, return funds to victims of large-scale fraud, and share forfeiture property with state and local law enforcement agencies.

The AF Program and the ML Program provide support to all FBI investigative programs, to include international and domestic terrorism.

Money Laundering

The DOJ defines "money laundering" in the following manner: Money laundering is the process by which criminals conceal or disguise the proceeds of their crimes or convert those proceeds into goods and services. It allows criminals to infuse their illegal money into the stream of commerce, thus corrupting financial institutions and the money supply, thereby giving criminals unwarranted economic power.

The FBI maintains a proactive approach when investigating money laundering. After identifying a specified unlawful activity that generates illicit proceeds, a parallel financial investigation is conducted in order to locate the proceeds and prove their connection to the underlying crime.

Asset Forfeiture

The FBI's AF Program is one of the most successful in all of law enforcement. The bulk of the monies seized are returned to victims of the frauds that generated them. This is unique to the FBI and some other agencies. Most people associate the seizure and forfeiture of assets with narcotics trafficking. Although the FBI does seize assets from drug dealers and other criminals, the White-Collar Crime Program (WCCP) is the largest contributor to the FBI's forfeiture program.

---

* This information for this section was taken from the FBI White Collar Crime Web site at http://www.fbi.gov/stats-services/publications/financial-crimes-report-2009/financial-crimes-report-2009#asset [Accessed on June 22, 2011].

Significant Cases

Cashtrica (New York): FBI New York Agents participated in a joint investigation with Rockland County, NY, law enforcement, targeting La Cosa Nostra (LCN) subjects that were running a multimillion-dollar Internet gambling operation out of Costa Rica. Based on experience garnered in that investigation, agents formulated a plan to attack the entire internet gambling industry by targeting all facets to include online gaming companies, banks, money transfer businesses, and the owners of same. Significant targets included Neteller PLC, Partygaming PLC, Sportingbet PLC, Fireone Group PLC, HSBC, Dresdner Bank, and Canaccord Capital, to name a few. As a result of the investigation to date, the targets listed above, as well as several others, are fully cooperating with the FBI. Key cooperators have recently been tasked to identify companies, individuals, and assets and to conduct consensual recordings. Liaison with Legats in Canada, Europe, South America, and the Bahamas has been necessary for the success of this ongoing investigation into what has become a virtually worldwide criminal industry. This investigation thus far has obtained evidence of money laundering, mail fraud, wire fraud, bank fraud, securities fraud, credit card fraud, and illegal gambling. There has also been clear indication of an expertise in moving vast sums of money around the world while effectively masking the associated transactions. Forfeiture to date amounts to $364,265,995.86.

Hassan Nemazee (New York): Hassan Nemazee is a multimillionaire Iranian–American investment banker. Nemazee is one of the top political donors in the United States. Nemazee obtained approximately $230,000,000 in loans from Bank of America (BoA), HSBC, and other banks. It was determined that the collateral securing the loans was based on false and misleading information. Nemazee was arrested as he was attempting to flee to Italy. A meeting was held with Daylight FoAs, retained by BoA to trace the flow of illegal proceeds. Numerous seizure warrants were executed against various accounts owned/controlled by Nemazee. Having learned that they were in possession of illegal proceeds, Citibank wired $75,000,000 to the U.S. Marshals Asset Forfeiture Account for forfeiture. Plea negotiations with Nemazee's partner are continuing, which could lead to the receipt of another $40 million.

Bernard Madoff (New York): On December 10, 2008, Bernard L. Madoff was arrested for perpetrating the largest Ponzi scheme in history, $64 billion, through the Madoff Investment Advisory (MIA). The fraud involved thousands of victims and numerous targets. The Madoff office space contained approximately 3,000 banking boxes of potential evidence; additionally, a warehouse contained approximately 9,000 more banking boxes of evidence. Madoff conspired with two computer programmers who created a proprietary software system that was used to document false trades and issue bogus statements. The system was the foundation for the Ponzi scheme. The fraudulent documents were so effective that the fraud went on for decades and cleared audits by the SEC as well as major financial institutions. Various institutions and individual funds invested their clients' funds into the Madoff Ponzi scheme. These entities are referred to as "feeder funds" because they "fed" the MIA Ponzi fraud. Without this consistent injection of capital, the fraud could not have been maintained for the length of time that it was. As many as 50 funds fed the MIA. Many of the feeder fund managers appear to have been excessively compensated. Finally, Madoff used an elaborate flow of funds from domestic banks to offshore banks to cloak the fraudulent activity in the MIA.

Forensic Accountant Program

In March 2009, the FBI created the Forensic Accountant Program (FAP) and instituted the Forensic Accountant Unit (FAU) within the Criminal Investigative Division (CID), Financial Crimes Section (FCS). The Forensic Accountant (FoA) position was developed in an effort to attract and retain top-tier accounting professionals who possess the ability to conduct complex, thorough forensic financial investigations.

The FAP is the culmination of years of effort to advance and professionalize the FBI's financial investigative capabilities. The FBI's FoAs will be expected to testify as expert witnesses in judicial proceedings and essentially retain ownership of the financial investigative portion of complex investigations with little guidance from the respective case agent(s).

The mission of the FAU is to support all FBI investigative matters requiring a forensic financial investigation and to ensure that the FBI's financial investigative priorities are continually addressed. The FAU seeks to provide the highest caliber of financial investigative work product and support as well as contribute to the FBI's intelligence cycle. The FAU is developing and implementing a rigorous training curriculum and partnering with an array of public and private organizations in an effort to cultivate a workforce that provides superior results both in the field offices and at FBI headquarters.

Forensic Accountant Core Training Session Training Course

In fiscal year (FY) 2009, the FAU initiated the development of a rigorous training curriculum titled the Forensic Accountant Core Training Session (FACTS). FACTS is a comprehensive introductory program of instruction designed to increase an FoA's proficiency in the critical areas necessary to conduct a financial investigation. This extensive course will develop the FoA's aptitude and knowledge in handling a financial investigation according to pertinent rules and regulations across a wide variety of subject matters. The FAU developed the FACTS training curriculum and will be responsible for administering the training. The material covered will focus primarily on providing an overview of FBI programs and systems, financial investigative topics and techniques, resources available to develop an investigation, legal training, and expert witness-testifying techniques.

BankScan Initiative

BankScan is an FBI in-house-created software application that translates physical bank and credit card statements into an electronic medium, thus dramatically decreasing the time-consuming data entry process. In FY 2009, FAU deployed the BankScan training initiative "Train the Trainer" with the goal of full field office deployment by the end of FY 2010. The Train the Trainer initiative was completed, and each field office "Trainer" received the requisite training and was supplied with the necessary software and equipment to implement the BankScan Project. Since its implementation, the FBI has benefited through an exponential increase in financial investigative efficiency and productivity.

Electronic Subpoena Production

The Electronic Subpoena Production initiative represents a joint undertaking of the FBI's CID, DOJ's Criminal Division Fraud Section, and the Internal Revenue Service. Electronic Subpoena Production requires financial institutions to digitally produce account data stored electronically by relying on existing Rule 17 of the Federal Rules of Criminal Procedure. When used in conjunction with BankScan, the introduction of this new process will substantially increase the efficiency and effectiveness of FBI forensic financial investigations.

Financial Analyst Conversion

In FY 2009, the FAU developed a selective conversion process to transition qualified FAs to the FAP to provide the FBI's investigative programs with the highest caliber of financial investigative work product and support. This effort will ensure that only those individuals who meet the FoA requirements are selectively converted to the FAP.

Significant Cases

The FAU has provided substantial support to major cases such as the Madoff, Stanford, and Bad Medicine (healthcare fraud) investigations.

Madoff Investigation: The FAU provided substantial support to the New York Field Office to address the Madoff investigation. The FAU coordinated with several field offices to provide three FoAs, equipment, and resources to support this investigation over a five-month period. The critical work performed by the FoAs significantly advanced the investigation and the respective statistical accomplishments.

Stanford Financial Group: The FAU supported the Houston Field Office by providing an FA to support the Stanford Financial Group investigation. This $7 billion Ponzi scheme has resulted in numerous indictments and guilty pleas. The financial investigation performed by the FA was a key contribution in furthering this investigation.

Bad Medicine: The FAU coordinated with multiple field offices to provide three FAs to expedite this financial investigation. By June 2012, 168 indictments charging 107 individuals have been returned. The forensic financial analysis performed by the FAs was critical to the investigation and the resulting indictments.

Scott Rothstein: The FAU augmented the Miami Field Office by providing FoAs and FAs in the ongoing Scott Rothstein financial investigation. The investigation into this $1 billion Ponzi scheme was advanced by the contributions of the FAs and FoAs and contributed to the five-count indictment and the subsequent guilty plea entered by the defendant.

National White Collar Crime Center (NW3C)

The mission of the NW3C is to provide training, investigative support, and research to agencies and entities involved in the prevention, investigation, and prosecution of economic and high-tech crime (http://www.nw3c.org).

The center is a nonprofit membership organization dedicated to supporting law enforcement in the prevention, investigation, and prosecution of economic and high-tech crime. NW3C has been continuously funded through competitive grants for over three decades. NW3C membership consists of law enforcement agencies from all 50 states and four continents.

While NW3C has no investigative authority itself, its job is to help law enforcement agencies better understand and utilize tools to combat economic and high-tech crime. Started in 1980, NW3C has been funded for over three decades by an annual congressional appropriation through the Bureau of Justice Assistance. NW3C is a nonprofit membership affiliated organization composed of state and local law enforcement, prosecutorial, and regulatory agencies. It provides a nationwide support system to state and local law enforcement for the prevention, investigation, and prosecution of economic and high-tech crime. NW3C membership expands across all 50 states, the U.S. Territories, and foreign countries. NW3C is a nonprofit membership organization that has been continuously funded through competitive grants for over three decades. Through a combination of training and critical support services, they equip state, local, tribal, and federal law enforcement agencies with skills and resources they need to tackle emerging economic and cyber crime problems.

For the general public, NW3C provides information and research so they too may become proactive in the prevention of economic and cyber crime. Victims of crimes can rely on NW3C to help them register Internet crime complaints through their Web site at www.ic3.gov and notify the appropriate authorities at local, state, and federal levels promptly, accurately, and securely. Membership is FREE; there are no application fees or yearly dues.

There are two types of membership, voting and associate. Voting member agencies have full rights and privileges to participate in NW3C activities and a right to vote for representation on NW3C's Board of Directors. Associate member agencies have limited access to NW3C services, full rights and privileges to literature and networking opportunities, and are charged a nominal fee for NW3C-sponsored training. NW3C does not offer membership to individuals nor private companies, only to eligible agencies.

To be eligible for membership, agencies must have a nexus to the prevention, investigation, or prosecution of economic crime, cyber crime, or terrorism and must meet the criteria of one of the following types:

Voting Membership

- State and local law enforcement agencies;
- State and local prosecutors; or
- State agencies with criminal investigative authority.

Associate Membership

- Any law enforcement agency or division of a federal or foreign government;
- State or local government agency with no statutory criminal investigative authority, or;
- Duly constituted permanent task force comprised of two or more of above agencies (voting or associate).

Frequently Asked Questions about NW3C

What support services does NW3C make available?

Specifically for a law enforcement audience, NW3C support services include training on financial investigations and cyber crime, investigative support, Internet crime complaint referrals, outreach programs, and research. Learn more about NW3C services and the benefits of membership from their Web site.

What kind of law enforcement training is available to an agency?

NW3C trainings have been delivered to enforcement officers nationwide. Find a list of their onsite classroom and computer-based trainings from their Web site.

How does a person file an Internet crime complaint?

The Internet Crime Complaint Center (IC3) is an alliance between NW3C and the Federal Bureau of Investigation. IC3's mission is to serve as a vehicle to receive, develop, and refer criminal complaints regarding the rapidly expanding arena of cyber crime. IC3 gives the victims of cybercrime a convenient and easy-to-use reporting mechanism that alerts authorities of suspected criminal or civil violations. For law enforcement and regulatory agencies at the federal, state, local, and international level, IC3 provides a central referral mechanism for complaints involving Internet-related crimes.

Readers can complete an online complaint form at www.ic3.gov. The analysts at the IC3 will determine which law enforcement agency should handle the complaint and will refer the complaint information on the reader's behalf.

Summary

- To reduce "white-collar" crime, the American public needs to recognize the need to prevent it and its seriousness.
- As noted on the FBI White-Collar Crime Web site, it is not a victimless crime. A single scam can destroy a company, devastate families by wiping out their life savings, or cost investors billions of dollars (or even all three, as in the Enron case).
- The concept that white-collar crime is not real crime needs to be discarded. The public needs to be aware of the damages that occur from this phenomenon.
- The Thompson Memorandum refers to a memorandum issued on January 20, 2003, by then U.S. Deputy Attorney General Larry D. Thompson. The subject of the memorandum was "Principles of Federal Prosecution of Business Organizations." The memo contained a set of principles to guide prosecutors as they make the decision whether to seek charges against a business organization.
- The main focus of the revisions was increased emphasis on and scrutiny of the authenticity of a corporation's cooperation. The memo notes that too often, business organizations, while purporting to cooperate with a department investigation, in fact take steps to

impede the quick and effective exposure of the complete scope of wrongdoing under investigation.

- Corporations should not be treated leniently because of their artificial nature nor should they be subject to harsher treatment. Vigorous enforcement of the criminal laws against corporate wrongdoers, where appropriate, results in great benefits for law enforcement and the public, particularly in the area of white-collar crime.
- The Thompson memo provides that, generally, prosecutors should apply the same factors in determining whether to charge a corporation as they do with respect to individuals.
- According to the memorandum, in determining whether to charge a corporation, that corporation's timely and voluntary disclosure of wrongdoing and its willingness to cooperate with the government's investigation may be relevant factors. In gauging the extent of the corporation's cooperation, the prosecutor may consider the corporation's willingness to identify the culprits within the corporation, including senior executives; to make witnesses available; to disclose the complete results of its internal investigation; and to waive attorney–client and work product protection.
- The mission of the AF/MLU is to promote the strategic use of the asset forfeiture and to ensure that field offices employ the money laundering violation in all investigations, where appropriate, to disrupt and/or dismantle criminal enterprises.
- The DOJ defines "money laundering" in the following manner: Money laundering is the process by which criminals conceal or disguise the proceeds of their crimes or convert those proceeds into goods and services. It allows criminals to infuse their illegal money into the stream of commerce, thus corrupting financial institutions and the money supply, thereby giving criminals unwarranted economic power.
- In March 2009, the FBI created the FAP and instituted the FAU within the CID, FCS. The FoA position was developed in an effort to attract and retain top-tier accounting professionals who possess the ability to conduct complex, thorough forensic financial investigations.

QUESTIONS IN REVIEW

1. What are some of the steps being taken to prevent money laundering?
2. What is the purpose and mission of NW3C?
3. Who are the voting members of the NW3C?
4. What is the BankScan initiative?
5. How does the felon propose to reduce white-collar crime?

Useful Links

Federal Bureau of Investigation: White-Collar Crime

http://www.fbi.gov/whitecollarcrime.htm

United States Secret Service: Financial Crimes Division

http://www.secretservice.gov/criminal.shtml

International Association of Financial Crimes Investigators

http://www.iafci.org/web/Home/AM/ContentManagerNet/HomePages/
IAFCI_1501_20080611T073612HomePage.aspx?Section = Home

National White Collar Crime Center (NW3C)

http://www.nw3c.org

Securities and Exchange Commission (SEC)

http://www.sec.gov

American Prosecutors Research Institute (APRI): White Collar Crime Unit

http://ndaa.org/elder_abuse_home.html

U.S. Department of Justice (DOJ): Tax Division

http://www.justice.gov/tax/

United States Department of Justice Criminal Division: Fraud Section

http://www.justice.gov/criminal/fraud/

Commodity Futures Trading Commission

http://www.cftc.gov

CyberAngels

http://www.cyberangels.org

FakeChecks.org

http://www.fakechecks.org/about.html

Federal Trade Commission: Identity Theft

http://www.ftc.gov/bcp/edu/microsites/idtheft/

Financial Crimes Enforcement Network (FinCEN)

http://www.fincen.gov

Financial Fraud Enforcement Task Force (FFETF)

http://www.stopfraud.gov

International Association of Financial Crimes Investigators

http://www.iafci.org/web/Home/AM/ContentManagerNet/HomePages/
IAFCI_1501_20080611T073612HomePage.aspx?Section = Home

Internet Crime Complaint Center (IC3)

http://www.ic3.gov

Appendix A

WHITE-COLLAR CRIMINALITY
REPRINTED FROM THE AMERICAN
SOCIOLOGICAL REVIEW
(VOLUME 5, FEBRUARY 1940, NUMBER 1)

EDWIN H. SUTHERLAND
Indiana University

THIS PAPER* is concerned with crime in relation to business. The economists are well acquainted with business methods but not accustomed to consider them from the point of view of crime; many sociologists are well acquainted with crime but not accustomed to consider it as expressed in business. This paper is an attempt to integrate these two bodies of knowledge. More accurately stated, it is a comparison of crime in the upper or white-collar class, composed of respectable or at least respected business and professional men, and crime in the lower class, composed of persons of low socioeconomic status. This comparison is made for the purpose of developing the theories of criminal behavior, not for the purpose of muckraking or of reforming anything except criminology.

The criminal statistics show unequivocally that crime, *as popularly conceived and officially measured*, has a high incidence in the lower class and a low incidence in the upper class; less than two percent of the persons committed to prisons in a year belong to the upper class. These statistics refer to criminals handled by the police, the criminal and juvenile courts, and the prisons, and to such crimes as murder, assault, burglary, robbery, larceny, sex offenses, and drunkenness, but exclude traffic violations.

The criminologists have used the case histories and criminal statistics derived from these agencies of criminal justice as their principal data. From them, they have derived general theories of criminal behavior. These theories are that, since crime is concentrated in the lower class, it is caused by poverty

---

* Perhaps it should be repeated that "white-collar" (upper) and "lower" classes merely designate persons of high and low socioeconomic status. Income and amount of money involved in the crime are not the sole criteria. Many persons of "low" socioeconomic status are "white-collar" criminals in the sense that they are well-dressed, well-educated, and have high incomes, but "white-collar" as used in this paper means "respected," "socially accepted and approved," "looked up to." Some people in this class may not be well-dressed or well-educated, nor have high incomes, although the "upper" usually exceed the "lower" classes in these respects as well as in social status.

or by personal and social characteristics believed to be associated statistically with poverty, including feeblemindedness, psychopathic deviations, slum neighborhoods, and "deteriorated" families. This statement, of course, does not do justice to the qualifications and variations in the conventional theories of criminal behavior, but it presents correctly their central tendency.

The thesis of this paper is that the conception and explanations of crime which have just been described are misleading and incorrect, that crime is in fact not closely correlated with poverty or with the psychopathic and sociopathic conditions associated with poverty, and that an adequate explanation of criminal behavior must proceed along quite different lines. The conventional explanations are invalid principally because they are derived from biased samples. The samples are biased in that they have not included vast areas of criminal behavior of persons not in the lower class. One of these neglected areas is the criminal behavior of business and professional men, which will be analyzed in this paper.

The "robber barons" of the last half of the nineteenth century were white-collar criminals, as practically everyone now agrees. Their attitudes are illustrated by these statements: Colonel Vanderbilt asked, "You don't suppose you can run a railroad in accordance with the statutes, do you?" A. B. Stickney, a railroad president, said to sixteen other railroad presidents in the home of J. P. Morgan in 1890, "I have the utmost respect for you gentlemen, individually, but as railroad presidents I wouldn't trust you with my watch out of my sight." Charles Francis Adams said, "The difficulty in railroad management... lies in the covetousness, want of good faith, and low moral tone of railway managers, in the complete absence of any high standard of commercial honesty."

The present-day white-collar criminals, who are more suave and deceptive than the "robber barons," are represented by Krueger, Stavisky, Whitney, Mitchell, Foshay, Insull, the Van Sweringens, Musica-Coster, Fall, Sinclair, and many other merchant princes and captains of finance and industry, and by a host of lesser followers. Their criminality has been demonstrated again and again in the investigations of land offices, railways, insurance, munitions, banking, public utilities, stock exchanges, the oil industry, real estate, reorganization committees, receiverships, bankruptcies, and politics. Individual cases of such criminality are reported frequently, and in many periods more important crime news may be found on the financial pages of newspapers than on the front pages. White-collar criminality is found in every occupation, as can be discovered readily in casual conversation with a representative of an occupation by asking him, "What crooked practices are found in your occupation?"

White-collar criminality in business is expressed most frequently in the form of misrepresentation in financial statements of corporations, manipulation in the stock exchange, commercial bribery, bribery of public officials directly or indirectly in order to secure favorable contracts and legislation, misrepresentation in advertising and salesmanship, embezzlement and misapplication of funds, short weights and measures and misgrading of commodities, tax frauds, misapplication of funds in receiverships and bankruptcies. These are what Al Capone called "the legitimate rackets." These and many others are found in abundance in the business world.

In the medical profession, which is here used as an example because it is probably less criminalistic than some other professions, are found illegal sale of alcohol and narcotics, abortion, illegal services to underworld criminals, fraudulent reports and testimony in accident cases, extreme cases of unnecessary treatment, fake specialists, restriction of competition, and fee-splitting. Fee-splitting is a violation of a specific law in many states and a violation of the conditions of admission to the practice of medicine in all. The physician who participates in fee-splitting tends to send his patients to the surgeon who will give him the largest fee rather than to the surgeon who will do the best work. It has been reported that two thirds of the surgeons in New York City split fees, and that more than one half of the physicians in a central western city who answered a questionnaire on this point favored fee-splitting.

These varied types of white-collar crimes in business and the professions consist principally of violation of delegated or implied trust, and many of them can be reduced to two categories: misrepresentation of asset values and duplicity in the manipulation of power. The first is approximately the same as fraud or swindling; the second is similar to the double-cross. The latter is illustrated by the corporation director who, acting on inside information, purchases land which the corporation will need and sells it at a fantastic profit to his corporation. The principle of this duplicity is that the offender holds two antagonistic positions, one of which is a position of trust, which is violated, generally by misapplication of funds, in the interest of the other position. A football coach, permitted to referee a game in which his own team was playing, would illustrate this antagonism of positions. Such situations cannot be completely avoided in a complicated business structure, but many concerns make a practice of assuming such antagonistic functions and regularly violating the trust thus delegated to them. When compelled by law to make a separation of their functions, they make a nominal separation and continue by subterfuge to maintain the two positions.

An accurate statistical comparison of the crimes of the two classes is not available. The most extensive evidence regarding the nature and prevalence of white-collar criminality is found in the reports of the larger investigations to which reference was made. Because of its scattered character, that evidence is assumed rather than summarized here. A few statements will be presented, as illustrations rather than as proof of the prevalence of this criminality.

The Federal Trade Commission in 1920 reported that commercial bribery was a prevalent and common practice in many industries. In certain chain stores, the net shortage in weights was sufficient to pay 3.4 percent on the investment in those commodities. Of the cans of ether sold to the Army between 1923 and 1925, 70 percent were rejected because of impurities. In Indiana, during the summer of 1934, 40 percent of the ice cream samples tested in a routine manner by the Division of Public Health were in violation of law. The Comptroller of the Currency in 1908 reported that violations of law were found in 75 percent of the banks examined in a three months' period. Lie detector tests of all employees in several Chicago banks, supported in almost all cases by confessions, showed that 20 percent of them had stolen bank property. A public accountant estimated, in the period prior to the Securities and Exchange Commission, that 80 percent of the financial statements of corporations were misleading. James M. Beck in 1916, said, "Diogenes would have been hard put to it to find an honest man in the Wall Street which I knew as a corporation lawyer."

White-collar criminality in politics, which is generally recognized as fairly prevalent, has been used by some as a rough gauge by which to measure white-collar criminality in business. James A. Farley said, "The standards of conduct are as high among officeholders and politicians as they are in commercial life," and Cermak, while mayor of Chicago, said, "There is less graft in politics than in business." John Flynn wrote, "The average politician is the merest amateur in the gentle art of graft, compared with his brother in the field of business." And Walter Lippmann wrote, "Poor as they are, the standards of public life are so much more social than those of business that financiers who enter politics regard themselves as philanthropists."

These statements obviously do not give a precise measurement of the relative criminality of the white-collar class, but they are adequate evidence that crime is not so highly concentrated in the lower class as the usual statistics indicate. Also, these statements obviously do not mean that every business and professional man is a criminal, just as the usual theories do not mean that every man in the lower class is a criminal. On the other hand, the preceding statements refer in many cases to the leading corporations in America and are not restricted to the disreputable business and professional men who are called quacks, ambulance chasers, bucket-shop operators, dead-beats, and fly-by-night swindlers.'

The financial cost of white-collar crime is probably several times as great as the financial cost of all the crimes which are customarily regarded as the "crime problem." An officer of a chain grocery store in one year embezzled $600,000, which was six times as much as the annual losses from five hundred burglaries and robberies of the stores in that chain. Public enemies numbered one to six secured $130,000 by burglary and robbery in 1938, while the sum stolen by Krueger is estimated at $250,000,000, or nearly two thousand times as much. *The New York Times* in 1931 reported four cases of embezzlement in the United States with a loss of more than a million dollars each and a combined loss of nine million dollars. Although a million-dollar burglar or robber is practically unheard of, these million-dollar embezzlers are small-fry among white-collar criminals. The estimated loss to investors in one investment trust from 1929 to 1935 was $580,000,000, due primarily to the fact that 75 percent of the values in the portfolio were in securities of affiliated companies, although it advertised the importance of diversification in investments and its expert services in selecting safe securities. In Chicago, the claim was made six years ago that householders had lost $54,000,000 in two years during the administration of a city sealer who granted immunity from inspection to stores which provided Christmas baskets for his constituents.

The financial loss from white-collar crime, great as it is, is less important than the damage to social relations. White-collar crimes violate trust and therefore create distrust, which lowers social morale and produces social disorganization on a large scale. Other crimes produce relatively little effect on social institutions or social organization.

White-collar crime is real crime. It is not ordinarily called crime, and calling it by this name does not make it worse, just as refraining from calling it crime does not make it better than it otherwise would be. It is called crime here in order to bring it within the scope of criminology, which is justified because it is in violation of the criminal law. The crucial question in this analysis is the criterion of violation of the criminal law. Conviction in the criminal court, which is sometimes suggested as the criterion, is not adequate because a large proportion of those who commit crimes are not convicted in criminal courts. This criterion, therefore, needs to be supplemented. When it is supplemented, the criterion of the crimes of one class must be kept consistent in general terms with the criterion of the crimes of the other class. The definition should not be the spirit of the law for white-collar crimes and the letter of the law for other crimes, or in other respects be more liberal for one class than for the other. Since this discussion is concerned with the conventional theories of the criminologists, the criterion of white-collar crime must be justified in terms of the procedures of those criminologists in dealing with other crimes. The criterion of white-collar crimes, as here proposed, supplements convictions in the criminal courts in four respects, in each of which the extension is justified because the criminologists who present the conventional theories of criminal behavior make the same extension in principle.

First, other agencies than the criminal court must be included, for the criminal court is not the only agency which makes official decisions regarding violations of the criminal law. The juvenile court, dealing largely with offenses of the children of the poor, in many states is not under the criminal jurisdiction. The criminologists have made much use of case histories and statistics of juvenile delinquents in constructing their theories of criminal behavior. This justifies the inclusion of agencies other than the criminal court which deal with white-collar offenses. The most important of these agencies are the administrative boards, bureaus, or commissions, and much of their work, although certainly not all, consists of cases which are in violation of the criminal law. The Federal Trade Commission recently ordered several automobile companies to stop advertising their interest rate on installment purchases as 6 percent, since it was actually 11 percent. Also it filed complaint against *Good Housekeeping*, one of the Hearst publications, charging that its seals led the public to believe that all products bearing those seals had been tested in their laboratories, which was contrary to fact. Each of these involves a charge of dishonesty, which might have been tried in a criminal court as fraud. A large proportion of the cases before these boards should be included in the data of the criminologists. Failure to do so is a principal reason for the bias in their samples and the errors in their generalizations.

Second, for both classes, behavior which would have a reasonable expectancy of conviction if tried in a criminal court or substitute agency should be defined as criminal. In this respect, convictability rather than actual conviction should be the criterion of criminality. The criminologists would not hesitate to accept as data a verified case history of a person who was a criminal but had never been convicted. Similarly, it is justifiable to include white-collar criminals who have not been convicted, provided reliable evidence is available. Evidence regarding such cases appears in many civil suits, such as stockholders' suits and patent-infringement suits. These cases might have been referred to the criminal court but they were referred to the civil court because the injured party was more interested in securing damages than in seeing punishment inflicted. This also happens in embezzlement cases, regarding which surety companies have much evidence. In a short consecutive series of embezzlements known to a surety company, 90 percent were not prosecuted because prosecution would interfere with restitution or salvage. The evidence in cases of embezzlement is generally conclusive, and would probably have been sufficient to justify conviction in all of the cases in this series.

Third, behavior should be defined as criminal if conviction is avoided merely because of pressure which is brought to bear on the court or substitute agency. Gangsters and racketeers have been relatively immune in many cities because of their pressure on prospective witnesses and public officials, and professional thieves, such as pickpockets and confidence men who do not use strong-arm methods, are even more frequently immune. The conventional criminologists do not hesitate to include the life histories of such criminals as data, because they understand the generic relation of the pressures to the failure to convict. Similarly, white-collar criminals are relatively immune because of the class bias of the courts and the power of their class to influence the implementation and administration of the law. This class bias affects not merely present-day courts but to a much greater degree affected the earlier courts which established the precedents and rules of procedure of the present-day courts. Consequently, it is justifiable to interpret the actual or potential failures of conviction in the light of known facts regarding the pressures brought to bear on the agencies which deal with offenders.

Fourth, persons who are accessory to a crime should be included among white-collar criminals as they are among other criminals. When the Federal Bureau of Investigation deals with a case of kidnapping, it is not content with catching the offenders who carried away the victim; they may catch and the court may convict twenty-five other persons who assisted by secreting the victim, negotiating the ransom, or putting the ransom money into circulation. On the other hand, the prosecution of white-collar criminals frequently stops with one offender. Political graft almost always involves collusion between politicians and business men but prosecutions are generally limited to the politicians. Judge Manton was found guilty of accepting $664,000 in bribes, but the six or eight important commercial concerns that paid the bribes have not been prosecuted. Pendergast, the late boss of Kansas City, was convicted for failure to report as a part of his income $315,000 received in bribes from insurance companies but the insurance companies which paid the bribes have not been prosecuted. In an investigation of an embezzlement by the president of a bank, at least a dozen other violations of law which were related to this embezzlement and involved most of the other officers of the bank and the officers of the clearing house, were discovered but none of the others was prosecuted.

This analysis of the criterion of white-collar criminality results in the conclusion that a description of white-collar criminality in general terms will be also a description of the criminality of the lower class. The respects in which the crimes of the two classes differ are the incidentals rather than the essentials of criminality. They differ principally in the implementation of the criminal laws which apply to them. The crimes of the lower class are handled by policemen, prosecutors, and judges, with penal sanctions in the form of fines, imprisonment, and death. The crimes of the upper class either result in no official action at all, or result in suits for damages in civil courts, or are handled by inspectors, and by administrative boards or commissions, with penal sanctions in the form of warnings, orders to cease and desist, occasionally the loss of a license, and only in extreme cases by fines or prison sentences. Thus, the white-collar criminals are segregated administratively from other criminals, and largely as a consequence of this, are not regarded as real criminals by themselves, the general public, or the criminologists.

This difference in the implementation of the criminal law is due principally to the difference in the social position of the two types of offenders. Judge Woodward, when imposing sentence upon the officials of the H. O. Stone and Company, bankrupt real estate firm in Chicago, who had been convicted in 1933 of the use of the mails to defraud, said to them, "You are men of affairs, of experience, of refinement and culture, of excellent reputation and standing in the business and social world." That statement might be used as a general characterization of white-collar criminals for they are oriented basically to legitimate and respectable careers. Because of their social status they have a loud voice in determining what goes into the statutes and how the criminal law as it affects themselves is implemented and administered. This may be illustrated from the Pure Food and Drug Law. Between 1879 and 1906, 140 pure food and drug bills were presented in Congress and all failed because of the importance of the persons who would be affected. It took a highly dramatic performance by Dr. Wiley in 1906 to induce Congress to enact the law. That law, however, did not create a new crime, just as the federal Lindbergh kidnapping law did not create a new crime; it merely provided a more efficient implementation of a principle which had been formulated previously in state laws. When an amendment to this law, which would bring within the scope of its agents fraudulent statements made over the radio or in the press, was presented to Congress, the publishers and advertisers organized support and sent a lobby to Washington which successfully fought the amendment principally under the slogans of "freedom of the press" and "dangers of bureaucracy." This proposed amendment, also, would not have created a new crime, for the state laws already prohibited fraudulent statements over the radio or in the press; it would have implemented the law so it could have been enforced. Finally, the Administration has not been able to enforce the law as it has desired because of the pressures by the offenders against the law, sometimes brought to bear through the head of the Department of Agriculture, sometimes through congressmen who threaten cuts in the appropriation, and sometimes by others. The statement of Daniel Drew, a pious old fraud, describes the criminal law with some accuracy, "Law is like a cobweb; it's made for flies and the smaller kinds of insects, so to speak, but lets the big bumblebees break through. When technicalities of the law stood in my way, I have always been able to brush them aside easy as anything."

The preceding analysis should be regarded neither as an assertion that all efforts to influence legislation and its administration are reprehensible nor as a particularistic interpretation of the criminal law. It means only that the upper class has greater influence in moulding the criminal law and its administration to its own interests than does the lower class. The privileged position of white-collar criminals before the law results to a slight extent from bribery and political pressures, principally from the respect in which they are held and without special effort on their part. The most powerful group in medieval society secured relative immunity by "benefit of clergy," and now our most powerful groups secure relative immunity by "benefit of business or profession."

In contrast with the power of the white-collar criminals is the weakness of their victims. Consumers, investors, and stockholders are unorganized, lack technical knowledge, and cannot protect themselves. Daniel Drew, after taking a large sum of money by sharp practice from Vanderbilt in the Erie deal, concluded that it was a mistake to take money from a powerful man on the same level as himself and declared that in the future he would confine his efforts to outsiders, scattered all over the country, who wouldn't be able to organize and fight back. White-collar criminality flourishes at points where powerful business and professional men come in contact with persons who are weak. In this respect, it is similar to stealing candy from a baby. Many of the crimes of the lower class, on the other hand, are committed against persons of wealth and power in the form of burglary and robbery. Because of this difference in the comparative power of the victims, the white-collar criminals enjoy relative immunity.

Embezzlement is an interesting exception to white-collar criminality in this respect. Embezzlement is usually theft from an employer by an employee, and the employee is less capable of manipulating social and legal forces in his own interest than is the employer. As might have been expected, the laws regarding embezzlement were formulated long before laws for the protection of investors and consumers.

The theory that criminal behavior in general is due either to poverty or to the psychopathic and sociopathic conditions associated with poverty can now be shown to be invalid for three reasons. First, the generalization is based on a biased sample which omits almost entirely the behavior of white-collar criminals. The criminologists have restricted their data, for reasons of convenience and ignorance rather than of principle, largely to cases dealt with in criminal courts and juvenile courts, and these agencies are used principally for criminals from the lower economic strata. Consequently, their data are grossly biased from the point of view of the economic status of criminals and their generalization that criminality is closely associated with poverty is not justified.

Second, the generalization that criminality is closely associated with poverty obviously does not apply to white-collar criminals. With a small number of exceptions, they are not in poverty, were not reared in slums or badly deteriorated families, and are not feebleminded or psychopathic. They were seldom problem children in their earlier years and did not appear in juvenile courts or child guidance clinics. The proposition, derived from the data used by the conventional criminologists, that "the criminal of today was the problem child of yesterday" is seldom true of white-collar criminals. The idea that the causes of criminality are to be found almost exclusively in childhood similarly is fallacious. Even if poverty is extended to include the economic stresses which afflict business in a period of depression, it is not closely correlated with white-collar criminality. Probably at no time within fifty years have white-collar crimes in the field of investments and of corporate management been so extensive as during the boom period of the twenties.

Third, the conventional theories do not even explain lower class criminality. The sociopathic and psychopathic factors which have been emphasized doubtless have something to do with crime causation, but these factors have not been related to a general process which is found both in white-collar criminality and lower class criminality and therefore they do not explain the criminality of either class. They may explain the manner or method of crime— why lower class criminals commit burglary or robbery rather than false pretenses.

In view of these defects in the conventional theories, an hypothesis that will explain both white-collar criminality and lower class criminality is needed. For reasons of economy, simplicity, and logic, the hypothesis should apply to both classes, for this will make possible the analysis of causal factors freed from the encumbrances of the administrative devices which have led criminologists astray. Shaw and McKay and others, working exclusively in the field of lower class crime, have found the conventional theories inadequate to account for variations within the data of lower class crime and from that point of view have been working toward an explanation of crime in terms of a more general social process. Such efforts will be greatly aided by the procedure which has been described.

The hypothesis which is here suggested as a substitute for the conventional theories is that white-collar criminality, just as other systematic criminality, is learned; that it is learned in direct or indirect association with those who already practice the behavior; and that those who learn this criminal behavior are segregated from frequent and intimate contacts with law-abiding behavior. Whether a person becomes a criminal or not is determined largely by the comparative frequency and intimacy of his contacts with the two types of behavior. This may be called the process of differential association. It is a genetic explanation both of white-collar criminality and lower class criminality. Those who become white-collar criminals generally start their careers in good neighborhoods and good homes, graduate from colleges with some idealism, and with little selection on their part, get into particular business situations in which criminality is practically a folkway and are inducted into that system of behavior just as into any other folkway. The lower class criminals generally start their careers in deteriorated neighborhoods and families, find delinquents at hand from whom they acquire the attitudes toward, and techniques of, crime through association with delinquents and in partial segregation from law-abiding people. The essentials of the process are the same for the two classes of criminals. This is not entirely a process of assimilation, for inventions are frequently made, perhaps more frequently in white-collar crime than in lower class crime. The inventive geniuses for the lower class criminals are generally professional criminals, while the inventive geniuses for many kinds of white-collar crime are generally lawyers.

A second general process is social disorganization in the community. Differential association culminates in crime because the community is not organized solidly against that behavior. The law is pressing in one direction, and other forces are pressing in the opposite direction. In business, the "rules of the game" conflict with the legal rules. A business man who wants to obey the law is driven by his competitors to adopt their methods. This is well illustrated by the persistence of commercial bribery in spite of the strenuous efforts of business organizations to eliminate it. Groups and individuals are individuated; they are more concerned with their specialized group or individual interests than with the larger welfare. Consequently, it is not possible for the community to present a solid front in opposition to crime. The Better Business Bureaus and Crime Commissions, composed of business and professional men, attack burglary, robbery, and cheap swindles, but overlook the crimes of their own members. The forces which impinge on the lower class are similarly in conflict. Social disorganization affects the two classes in similar ways.

I have presented a brief and general description of white-collar criminality on a framework of argument regarding theories of criminal behavior. That argument, stripped of the description, may be stated in the following propositions:

1. White-collar criminality is real criminality, being in all cases in violation of the criminal law.
2. White-collar criminality differs from lower class criminality principally in an implementation of the criminal law which segregates white-collar criminals administratively from other criminals.
3. The theories of the criminologists that crime is due to poverty or to psychopathic and sociopathic conditions statistically associated with poverty are invalid because, first, they are derived from samples which are grossly biased with respect to socioeconomic status; second, they do not apply to the white-collar criminals; and third, they do not even explain the criminality of the lower class, since the factors are not related to a general process characteristic of all criminality.
4. A theory of criminal behavior which will explain both white-collar criminality and lower class criminality is needed.
5. An hypothesis of this nature is suggested in terms of differential association and social disorganization.

Index

CPSIA information can be obtained
at www.ICGtesting.com
Printed in the USA
LVHW080417240222
711733LV00021B/106